■ ■ ■ ■ ■

A GUIDE TO SQL

featuring

ORACLE®

Philip J. Pratt

COURSE
TECHNOLOGY

ONE MAIN STREET, CAMBRIDGE, MA 02142

an International Thomson Publishing company I(T)P®

Cambridge • Albany • Bonn • Boston • Cincinnati • London • Madrid • Melbourne • Mexico City
New York • Paris • San Francisco • Singapore • Tokyo • Toronto • Washington

Credits:

Managing Editor	Kristen Duerr	**Composition House**	GEX, Inc.
Product Manager	Jennifer Normandin	**Cover Designers**	Dick Hannus/Hannus Design Associates; Efrat Reis
Production Editor	Roxanne Alexander		
Development Editor	Jessica Evans	**Interior Designer**	Efrat Reis
		Marketing Manager	Susanne Walker

For more information contact:

Course Technology
One Main Street
Cambridge, MA 02142

ITP Europe
Berkshire House 168-173
High Holborn
London WCIV 7AA
England

Nelson ITP, Australia
102 Dodds Street
South Melbourne, 3205
Victoria, Australia

ITP Nelson Canada
1120 Birchmount Road
Scarborough, Ontario
Canada M1K 5G4

International Thomson Editores
Seneca, 53
Colonia Polanco
11560 Mexico D.F. Mexico

ITP GmbH
Königswinterer Strasse 418
53227 Bonn
Germany

ITP Asia
60 Albert Street, #15-01
Albert Complex
Singapore 189969

ITP Japan
Hirakawacho Kyowa Building, 3F
2-2-1 Hirakawacho
Chiyoda-ku, Tokyo 102
Japan

ISBN: 0-7600-4923-8

Printed in the United States of America
4 5 6 7 8 9 CW 02 01 00 99

C O N T E N T S

P R E F A C E

Structured Query Language (or SQL, which is pronounced SE-QUEL) is a popular computer language that is used by diverse groups such as home computer owners, owners of small businesses, end users in large organizations, and programmers. Oracle is just one of the many database management systems that uses SQL. Although this book uses Oracle as a vehicle for teaching SQL, the chapter material, examples, and exercises in this book are designed to be completed using any implementation of SQL.

A Guide to SQL featuring Oracle is written for a wide range of teaching levels, from students taking introductory computer science classes to those students in advanced information systems classes. This textbook can be used for a stand-alone course on SQL or in conjunction with a database concepts textbook where students are required to learn SQL.

The chapters in this textbook should be covered in order. Students should complete the end-of-chapter exercises and the examples within the chapters for maximum learning. Because the content of Chapter 8 assumes that the reader has had at least one programming language, the instructor should determine whether students will understand the concepts. Students without a programming background will have difficulty understanding the topic of embedded SQL. Chapter 8 can be omitted from the textbook easily in situations where students are not comfortable with programming examples.

DISTINGUISHING FEATURES

Use of Examples

Each chapter contains multiple examples that use SQL to solve a problem. Following each example, students will read about the commands that are used to solve the stated problem, and then they will see the SQL commands used to arrive at the solution. For most students, learning though examples is the most effective way to master material. For this reason, instructors should encourage students to read the chapters at the computer and to input the commands shown in the figures.

Case Studies

One case study, the Premiere Products database, is presented in all of the examples within the chapters, and also in the first set of exercises at the end of each chapter. Although the database is small in order to be manageable, the examples and exercises for the Premiere Products database simulate what a real business can accomplish using SQL commands. Using the same case study as examples within the chapter and in the end-of-chapter exercises ensures a high level of continuity to reinforce learning.

A different case study—the Henry Books database—is used in a second set of exercises at the end of each chapter. This second case study gives students a chance to venture out "on their own" without the direct guidance of examples from the text.

Question and Answer Sections

A special type of exercise, called a Q&A, is used within each chapter. These exercises force students to consider special issues and understand important questions before continuing with their study. The answer to each Q&A appears after the question. Students are encouraged to formulate their own answer before reading the answer provided in the textbook to ensure that they understand new material before proceeding.

Exercises

Each chapter concludes with two sets of exercises in which students use SQL commands to solve realistic problems using the Premiere Products and Henry Books databases. Unless indicated otherwise in the exercise, students should complete the exercises at the computer using SQL commands.

Appendices

Two appendices are included in this textbook. Appendix A is an optional chapter that illustrates the creation and use of forms using the Oracle Forms Designer. Appendix B includes answers to the odd-numbered exercises in the book so students have a way of checking their progress while completing the end-of-chapter exercises.

Instructor Support

The Instructor's Manual to accompany *A Guide to SQL featuring Oracle* contains detailed teaching information including chapter objectives, key terms, technical notes, lecture notes, extra problems, teaching tips, and answers to end-of-chapter exercises. Transparency masters are included for most of the figures in the text.

Also provided with this text is Course Test Manager, a cutting-edge Windows-based testing software program, developed exclusively for Course Technology, that helps instructors design and administer examinations and practice tests. This full-featured program allows students to generate practice tests randomly that provide immediate on-screen feedback and detailed study guides for questions incorrectly answered. Instructors can also use Course Test Manager to create printed and online tests. You can create, preview, and administer a test on any or all chapters of this textbook entirely over a local area network. Course Test Manager can grade the tests students take automatically at the computer and can generate statistical information on individual as well as group performance. The Course Test Manager Test Bank to accompany your text comes along with the engine on the Instructor's CD-ROM. The test bank includes multiple-choice, true/false, short answer, and essay questions, many of which include graphics from the text.

ORGANIZATION OF THE TEXTBOOK

Chapter 1: Introduction to Database Management

Chapter 1 introduces the concept of databases and database management systems using the Premiere Products and Henry Books databases as examples. Many Q&A exercises are provided in the chapter to ensure that students understand how to manipulate the database on paper before they begin working at the computer.

Chapter 2: An Introduction to SQL

In Chapter 2, students will learn about important concepts and terminology associated with relational databases. They will create and run SQL commands to create tables, use data types, and add rows to tables. Chapter 2 also discusses the role and use of nulls.

Chapter 3: Single-Table Queries

Chapter 3 is the first of two chapters on using SQL commands to query a database. The queries in Chapter 3 all involve single tables. Included in this chapter are discussions of simple and compound conditions; computed columns; the SQL BETWEEN, LIKE, and IN operators; using SQL functions; nesting queries; grouping data; and retrieving columns with null values.

Chapter 4: Multiple-Table Queries

Chapter 4 completes the discussion of querying a database by demonstrating queries that join more than one table. Included in this chapter are discussions of the SQL IN and EXISTS operators, subqueries within subqueries, using aliases, joining a table to itself, SQL set operations, and the use of the ALL and ANY operators.

Chapter 5: Updating Data

In Chapter 5, students learn how to use the SQL COMMIT, ROLLBACK, UPDATE, INSERT, and DELETE commands to update table data. Students also learn how to create a new table from an existing table and how to change the structure of a table.

Chapter 6: Database Administration

Chapter 6 covers the database administration features of SQL, including the use of views; granting and revoking database privileges to users; creating, dropping, and using an index; using and obtaining information from the system catalog; and using integrity constraints to control data entry.

Chapter 7: Reports

Chapter 7 teaches students how to create basic and complex reports based on data in a table or view. Students will learn how to concatenate data, create a view for a report, change report column headings and formats, and add report titles. Students also will include totals and subtotals in a report and group data. The topics of scripts and spooling also are discussed.

Chapter 8: Embedded SQL

Chapter 8 is an optional chapter for those students who have completed at least one programming course. This chapter covers embedding SQL commands into a procedural language such as COBOL. Although COBOL is used as a vehicle to illustrate the concepts in this chapter, the material applies equally well to any language that supports embedding. Included in this chapter are discussions of the use of embedded SQL to insert new rows and change and delete existing rows. Also included is a discussion of how to retrieve single rows using embedded SQL commands and how to use cursors to retrieve multiple rows.

Appendix A: Introduction to the Oracle Forms Designer

Appendix A is an optional chapter for students using Oracle SQL. This appendix teaches students how to create and use a form to change, add, and delete data from a table. This presentation is not intended to be comprehensive, but rather, to show students an alternate method of adding, deleting, and changing data using a form.

Appendix B: Answers to Odd-Numbered Exercises

Answers to the odd-numbered exercises in all chapters appear in this appendix so students can make sure that they are completing the exercises correctly.

GENERAL NOTES TO THE STUDENT

Embedded Questions

At a number of places in the text, special questions have been inserted. Sometimes the purpose of these questions is to ensure that you understand some crucial material before you proceed. In other cases, the questions are designed to give you the chance to consider some special concept in advance of its actual presentation. In all cases, the answer to each question appears immediately after the question. You can simply read the question and its answer, but you will receive maximum benefit from the text if you take the time to determine the answer to the question and then check your answer against the one given in the text before you proceed with your reading.

End-of-Chapter Material

The end-of-chapter material consists of a summary and exercises. The summary briefly describes the material covered in the chapter. Scan the summary and make sure all the concepts are familiar to you. Following the summary are two sets of exercises. The first set uses the same Premiere Products database that is used in the examples in the chapter. First work the exercises in this set to make sure you understand how to use the commands presented in the chapter. Then complete the second set of exercises, using the Henry Books database, and apply what you learned in the chapter to a database that is not as familiar to you. (The answers to the odd-numbered exercises in both sets of exercises appear in Appendix B so you can check your work.)

ACKNOWLEDGMENTS

I would like to acknowledge several individuals for their contributions in the preparation of this book. I appreciate the efforts of the following individuals who reviewed the manuscript and made many helpful suggestions: Misty Vermaat, Purdue University Calumet; Lorna Bowen St. George, Old Dominion University, and George Federman, Santa Barbara Community College. The efforts of the following members of the staff at Course Technology have been invaluable and have made this book possible: Kristen Duerr, Managing Editor; Jennifer Normandin, Project Manager; Brian McCooey, Manuscript QA Project Leader; and Roxanne Alexander, Production Editor. It is always a pleasure to work with Jessica Evans, the Developmental Editor for this book. Thanks for all your efforts, Jess. You're still THE BEST!

CHAPTER 1

Introduction to Database Management

OBJECTIVES

- Understand the Premiere Products database, a database for a distributor of appliances, housewares, and sporting goods called Premiere Products
- Understand the Henry Books database, a database for a chain of bookstores called Henry Books

THE PREMIERE PRODUCTS DATABASE

The management of Premiere Products, a distributor of appliances, housewares, and sporting goods, determined that the company has grown to the point at which the maintenance of customer and order data, as well as inventory, no longer can be done manually. By placing the data on a computer, managed by a full-featured database management system, management will be able to ensure that the data is current and more accurate than in the present manual system. Management also will be able to produce a variety of useful reports. In addition, management wants to be able to ask questions concerning the data in the database and obtain answers to these questions easily and rapidly.

■   ■   ■   ■   ■

In deciding what data must be stored in the database, management has determined that Premiere Products must maintain the following information about its sales representatives, customers, and parts inventory:

1. Each sales rep's number, last name, first name, address, total commission, and commission rate

2. The customer number, last name, first name, address, current balance, and credit limit for each customer, as well as the number of the sales rep who represents the customer

3. The part number, part description, number of units on hand, item class, number of the warehouse where the item is stored, and unit price for each part in inventory

Premiere Products also must store information on orders. A sample order is shown in Figure 1.1. Note that there are three components to the order:

1. The **heading** (top) of the order contains the order number; order date; customer's number, name, and address; sales rep name and number.

2. The body of the order contains a number of **order lines**, sometimes called **line items**. Each order line contains a part number, a part description, the number of units of the ordered part, and the quoted price for the part. The order line also contains a total, usually called an **extension**, which is the product of the number ordered and the quoted price.

3. Finally, the **footing** (bottom) of the order contains the order total.

The additional items that Premiere Products must store for each order are as follows:

1. For each order: the order number, date the order was placed, and number of the customer who placed the order. Note that the customer's name and address and the number of the sales rep who represents the customer are stored with customer information. The name of the sales rep is stored with the sales rep information.

2. For each order line: the order number, part number, number of units ordered, and quoted price. Remember that the part description is stored with the information on parts. The product of the number of units ordered and the quoted price is not stored, because it can be computed easily when needed.

3. The overall order total is not stored as part of the database. Instead, the total will be computed whenever an order is printed or displayed on the screen.

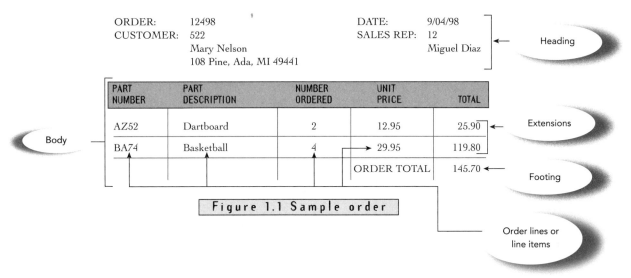

ORDER: 12498   DATE: 9/04/98
CUSTOMER: 522   SALES REP: 12
Mary Nelson   Miguel Diaz   ← Heading
108 Pine, Ada, MI 49441

Body →

PART NUMBER	PART DESCRIPTION	NUMBER ORDERED	UNIT PRICE	TOTAL
AZ52	Dartboard	2	12.95	25.90	← Extensions
BA74	Basketball	4	29.95	119.80
			ORDER TOTAL	145.70	← Footing

Order lines or line items

Figure 1.1 Sample order

Figure 1.2 shows sample data for Premiere Products. Notice that there are three sales representatives—numbered 03, 06, and 12. The name of sales rep number 03 is Mary Jones. Her street address is 123 Main. She lives in Grant, MI, and her ZIP code is 49219. Her total commission is $2,150.00 and her commission rate is 5 percent (.05).

You also see there are 10 customers—numbered 124, 256, 311, 315, 405, 412, 522, 567, 587, and 622. The name of customer number 124 is Sally Adams. Her street address is 481 Oak. She lives in Lansing, MI, and her ZIP code is 49224. Her current balance is $818.75 and her credit limit is $1,000. The number 03 in the column entitled SLSREP_NUMBER indicates that Sally is represented by sales rep number 03 (Mary Jones).

Skipping down to the table labeled PART, notice that there are 10 parts—part numbers AX12, AZ52, BA74, BH22, BT04, BZ66, CA14, CB03, CX11, and CZ81. Part AX12 is an iron and the company has 104 units of this part on hand. These parts are in item class HW (housewares) and are stored in warehouse 3. The price of an iron is $24.95. Other item classes are AP (appliances) and SG (sporting goods).

SALES_REP

SLSREP_NUMBER	LAST	FIRST	STREET	CITY	STATE	ZIP_CODE	TOTAL_COMMISSION	COMMISSION_RATE
03	Jones	Mary	123 Main	Grant	MI	49219	2150.00	.05
06	Smith	William	102 Raymond	Ada	MI	49441	4912.50	.07
12	Diaz	Miguel	419 Harper	Lansing	MI	49224	2150.00	.05

CUSTOMER

CUSTOMER_NUMBER	LAST	FIRST	STREET	CITY	STATE	ZIP_CODE	BALANCE	CREDIT_LIMIT	SLSREP_NUMBER
124	Adams	Sally	481 Oak	Lansing	MI	49224	$818.75	$1000	03
256	Samuels	Ann	215 Pete	Grant	MI	49219	$21.50	$1500	06
311	Charles	Don	48 College	Ira	MI	49034	$825.75	$1000	12
315	Daniels	Tom	914 Cherry	Kent	MI	48391	$770.75	$750	06
405	Williams	Al	519 Watson	Grant	MI	49219	$402.75	$1500	12
412	Adams	Sally	16 Elm	Lansing	MI	49224	$1817.50	$2000	03
522	Nelson	Mary	108 Pine	Ada	MI	49441	$98.75	$1500	12
567	Dinh	Tran	808 Ridge	Harper	MI	48421	$402.40	$750	06
587	Galvez	Mara	512 Pine	Ada	MI	49441	$114.60	$1000	06
622	Martin	Dan	419 Chip	Grant	MI	49219	$1045.75	$1000	03

ORDERS

ORDER_NUMBER	ORDER_DATE	CUSTOMER_NUMBER
12489	9/02/98	124
12491	9/02/98	311
12494	9/04/98	315
12495	9/04/98	256
12498	9/05/98	522
12500	9/05/98	124
12504	9/05/98	522

ORDER_LINE

ORDER_NUMBER	PART_NUMBER	NUMBER_ORDERED	QUOTED_PRICE
12489	AX12	11	$21.95
12491	BT04	1	$149.99
12491	BZ66	1	$399.99
12494	CB03	4	$279.99
12495	CX11	2	$22.95
12498	AZ52	2	$12.95
12498	BA74	4	$24.95
12500	BT04	1	$149.99
12504	CZ81	2	$325.99

PART

PART_NUMBER	PART_DESCRIPTION	UNITS_ON_HAND	ITEM_CLASS	WAREHOUSE_NUMBER	UNIT_PRICE
AX12	Iron	104	HW	3	$24.95
AZ52	Dartboard	20	SG	2	$12.95
BA74	Basketball	40	SG	1	$29.95
BH22	Cornpopper	95	HW	3	$24.95
BT04	Gas Grill	11	AP	2	$149.99
BZ66	Washer	52	AP	3	$399.99
CA14	Griddle	78	HW	3	$39.99
CB03	Bike	44	SG	1	$299.99
CX11	Blender	112	HW	3	$22.95
CZ81	Treadmill	68	SG	2	$349.95

Figure 1.2 Sample data for Premiere Products

Moving back up to the table labeled ORDERS, notice that there are seven orders—numbered 12489, 12491, 12494, 12495, 12498, 12500, and 12504. Order 12489 was placed on September 2, 1998, by customer 124 (Sally Adams).

The table labeled ORDER_LINE might seem strange at first glance. Why do you need a separate table for the order lines? Could they be included in the ORDERS table? The answer is yes. The table labeled ORDERS could be structured as shown in Figure 1.3. Notice that this table contains the same orders as shown in Figue 1.2, with the same dates and customer numbers. In addition, each table row in Figure 1.3 contains all the order lines for a given order. Examining the fifth row, for example, you see that order 12498 has two order lines. One of these order lines is for two AZ52s at $12.95 each and the other order line is for four BA74s at $24.95 each.

ORDERS

ORDER_ NUMBER	ORDER_ DATE	CUSTOMER_ NUMBER	PART_ NUMBER	NUMBER_ ORDERED	QUOTED_ PRICE
12489	9/02/98	124	AX12	11	$21.95
12491	9/02/98	311	BT04	1	$149.99
			BZ66	1	$399.99
12494	9/04/98	315	CB03	4	$279.99
12495	9/04/98	256	CX11	2	$22.95
12498	9/05/98	522	AZ52	2	$12.95
			BA74	4	$24.95
12500	9/05/98	124	BT04	1	$149.99
12504	9/05/98	522	CZ81	2	$325.99

Figure 1.3 Sample table structure

Question	How is the same information from Figure 1.3 represented in Figure 1.2?
Answer	Examine the ORDER_LINE table in Figure 1.2 and note the sixth and seventh rows. The sixth row indicates there is an order line on order 12498 for two AZ52s at $12.95 each. The seventh row indicates there is an order line on order 12498 for four BA74s at $24.95 each. Thus, the same information that you find in Figure 1.3 is represented in Figure 1.2 in two separate rows rather than in one row.

It might seem more effective not to use two rows to represent the same information that can be represented in one row. There is a problem, however, with the arrangement shown in Figure 1.3—the table is more complicated. In Figure 1.2, there is a single entry at each location in the table. In Figure 1.3, some of the individual positions within the table contain multiple entries, thus making it difficult to track the information between columns. In the row for order 12498, for example, it is crucial to know that the AZ52 corresponds to the 2 in the NUMBER_ORDERED column, not the 4, and to the $12.95 in the QUOTED_PRICE column, not the $24.95. There are practical issues to worry about, such as:

1. How much room do you allow for these multiple entries?

2. What if an order has more order lines than you have allowed room for?

3. Given a part, how do you determine which orders contain order lines for that part?

Certainly, none of these problems is unsolvable. They do add a level of complexity, however, that is not present in the arrangement shown in Figure 1.2. In the structure shown in that figure, there are no multiple entries to worry about; it doesn't matter how many order lines exist for any order; and finding all the orders that contain order lines for a given part is easy (just look for all order lines with the given part number in the PART_NUMBER column). In general, this simpler structure is preferable and that is why order lines have been placed in a separate table.

To test your understanding of the Premiere Products data, answer the following questions using the data in Figure 1.2.

Question	What are the numbers of all the customers represented by Mary Jones?
Answer	124, 412, and 622. (Look up the number of Mary Jones in the SALES_REP table and obtain the number 03. Then find all customers in the CUSTOMER table who have the number 03 in the SLSREP_NUMBER column.)

Question	What is the name of the customer who placed order 12491, and what is the name of the sales rep who represents this customer?
Answer	Don Charles is the customer, Miguel Diaz is the sales rep. (Look up the customer number in the ORDERS table and obtain the number 311. Then, find the customer in the CUSTOMER table who has number 311. Using this customer's sales rep number, which is 12, find the name of the sales rep in the SALES_REP table.)

Question	What are the parts that appear on order 12491? For each part, give the description, number ordered, and quoted price.
Answer	Part Number: BT04, Part Description: Gas Grill, Number Ordered: 1, Quoted Price: $149.99. Part Number: BZ66, Part Description: Washer, Number Ordered: 1, Quoted Price: $399.99. (Look up each ORDER_LINE table row in which the order number is 12491. Each of these rows contains a part number, the number ordered, and the quoted price. The only thing missing is the description of the part. Use the part number to look up the corresponding description in the PART table.)

Question	Why is the QUOTED_PRICE column part of the ORDER_LINE table? Can't you just take the part number and look up the price in the PART table?
Answer	If you don't have the QUOTED_PRICE column in the ORDER_LINE table, you must obtain the price for a part on an order line by looking up the price in the PART table. While this might not be bad, it does prevent Premiere Products from charging different prices to different customers for the same part. Because Premiere Products wants the flexibility to quote different prices to different customers, you include the QUOTED_PRICE column in the ORDER_LINE table. If you examine the ORDER_LINE table, you will see cases in which the quoted price matches the actual price in the PART table and cases in which it differs.

THE HENRY BOOKS DATABASE

Similar to the management of Premiere Products, Henry, the owner of a chain of bookstores called Henry Books, has decided it is time to computerize his operation. Like Premiere Products, he plans to store his data in a database and hopes to achieve the same benefits; that is, he wants to ensure that the data is current and accurate. He also hopes to produce several important reports. In addition, he wants to be able to ask questions concerning the data and to obtain answers to these questions easily and rapidly.

In running his chain of bookstores, Henry gathers and organizes information about publishers, authors, and books. Each book has a code that uniquely identifies the book. In addition, the bookstore records the title, publisher, type of book, price, and whether the book is paperback. The bookstore also records the author or authors of the books along with the number of units of the book that are in stock in each of the four branches that make up the Henry Books chain.

The information will be kept in a collection of tables. Figures 1.4, 1.5, and 1.6 show sample data for Henry Books.

BRANCH

BRANCH NUMBER	BRANCH_NAME	BRANCH LOCATION	NUMBER EMPLOYEES
1	Henry Downtown	16 Riverview	10
2	Henry On The Hill	1289 Bedford	06
3	Henry Brentwood	Brentwood Mall	15
4	Henry Eastshore	Eastshore Mall	09

PUBLISHER

PUBLISHER CODE	PUBLISHER_NAME	PUBLISHER_CITY	PUBLISHER STATE
AH	Arkham House Publ.	Sauk City	WI
AP	Arcade Publishing	New York	NY
AW	Addison Wesley	Reading	MA
BB	Bantam Books	New York	NY
BF	Best and Furrow	Boston	MA
JT	Jeremy P. Tarcher	Los Angeles	CA
MP	McPherson and Co.	Kingston	NY
PB	Pocket Books	New York	NY
RH	Random House	New York	NY
RZ	Rizzoli	New York	NY
SB	Schoken Books	New York	NY
SI	Signet	New York	NY
TH	Thames and Hudson	New York	NY
WN	W.W. Norton and Co.	New York	NY

AUTHOR

AUTHOR NUMBER	AUTHOR LAST	AUTHOR FIRST
01	Archer	Jeffrey
02	Christie	Agatha
03	Clarke	Arthur C.
04	Francis	Dick
05	Cussler	Clive
06	King	Stephen
07	Pratt	Philip
08	Adamski	Joseph
10	Harmon	Willis
11	Rheingold	Howard
12	Owen	Barbara
13	Williams	Peter
14	Kafka	Franz
15	Novalis	
16	Lovecraft	H. P.
17	Paz	Octavio
18	Camus	Albert
19	Castleman	Riva
20	Zinbardo	Philip
21	Gimferrer	Pere
22	Southworth	Rod
23	Wray	Robert

Figure 1.4 Collection of tables

Introduction to Database Management

BOOK

BOOK CODE	BOOK TITLE	PUBLISHER CODE	BOOK TYPE	BOOK PRICE	PAPERBACK
0180	Shyness	BB	PSY	7.65	Y
0189	Kane and Abel	PB	FIC	5.55	Y
0200	Stranger	BB	FIC	8.75	Y
0378	Dunwich Horror and Others	PB	HOR	19.75	N
079X	Smokescreen	PB	MYS	4.55	Y
0808	Knockdown	PB	MYS	4.75	Y
1351	Cujo	SI	HOR	6.65	Y
1382	Marcel Duchamp	PB	ART	11.25	Y
138X	Death on the Nile	BB	MYS	3.95	Y
2226	Ghost from the Grand Banks	BB	SFI	19.95	N
2281	Prints of the 20th Century	PB	ART	13.25	Y
2766	Prodigal Daughter	PB	FIC	5.45	Y
2908	Hymns to the Night	BB	POE	6.75	Y
3350	Higher Creativity	PB	PSY	9.75	Y
3743	First Among Equals	PB	FIC	3.95	Y
3906	Vortex	BB	SUS	5.45	Y
5163	Organ	SI	MUS	16.95	Y
5790	Database Systems	BF	CS	54.95	N
6128	Evil Under the Sun	PB	MYS	4.45	Y
6328	Vixen 07	BB	SUS	5.55	Y
669X	A Guide to SQL	BF	CS	23.95	Y
6908	DOS Essentials	BF	CS	20.50	Y
7405	Night Probe	BB	SUS	5.65	Y
7443	Carrie	SI	HOR	6.75	Y
7559	Risk	PB	MYS	3.95	Y
7947	dBASE Programming	BF	CS	39.90	Y
8092	Magritte	SI	ART	21.95	N
8720	Castle	BB	FIC	12.15	Y
9611	Amerika	BB	FIC	10.95	Y

Figure 1.5 The BOOK table

WROTE

BOOK_CODE	AUTHOR_NUMBER	SEQUENCE_NUMBER
0180	20	1
0189	01	1
0200	18	1
0378	16	1
079X	04	1
0808	04	1
1351	06	1
1382	17	1
138X	02	1
2226	03	1
2281	19	1
2766	01	1
2908	15	1
3350	10	1
3350	11	2
3743	01	1
3906	05	1
5163	12	2
5163	13	1
5790	07	1
5790	08	2
6128	02	1
6328	05	1
669X	07	1
6908	22	1
7405	05	1
7443	06	1
7559	04	1
7947	07	1
7947	23	2
8092	21	1
8720	14	1
9611	14	1

INVENT

BOOK_CODE	BRANCH_NUMBER	UNITS_ON_HAND
0180	1	2
0189	2	2
0200	1	1
0200	2	3
079X	2	1
079X	3	2
079X	4	3
1351	1	1
1351	2	4
1351	3	2
138X	2	3
2226	1	3
2226	3	2
2226	4	1
2281	4	3
2766	3	2
2908	1	3
2908	4	1
3350	1	2
3906	2	1
3906	3	2
5163	1	1
5790	4	2
6128	2	4
6128	3	3
6328	2	2
669X	1	1
6908	2	2
7405	3	2
7559	2	2
7947	2	2
8092	3	1
8720	1	3
9611	1	2

Figure 1.6 The WROTE and INVENT tables

Question	To check your understanding of the relationship between publishers and books, answer the following questions: Who published *Knockdown?* Which books did Signet publish?
Answer	Pocket Books; *Cujo, Organ, Carrie,* and *Magritte*. In the row in the BOOK table (see Figure 1.5), the publisher code for *Knockdown* is PB. Examining the PUBLISHER table (Figure 1.4), you see that PB is the code assigned to Pocket Books. To find the books published by Signet, look for its code in the PUBLISHER table and notice it is SI. Next, look for all records in the BOOK table for which the publisher code is SI and notice that Signet published *Cujo, Organ, Carrie,* and *Magritte*.

The table called WROTE (Figure 1.6) relates books and authors. The sequence number indicates the order in which the author of a particular text should be listed. The table called INVENT indicates the number of units of a particular book currently on hand at a particular branch. Row one, for example, indicates there are two units of the book whose code is 0180 currently on hand at Branch 1.

Question	To check your understanding of the relationship between authors and books, answer the following questions: Who wrote *Organ?* (Make sure to list the authors in the correct order.) Which books did Jeffrey Archer write?
Answer	Peter Williams and Barbara Owen; *Kane and Abel, Prodigal Daughter* and *First Among Equals*. To determine who wrote *Organ*, first you examine the BOOK table to find its book code (5163). Next, look for all rows in the WROTE table in which the book code (BOOK_CODE column) is 5163. There are two such rows. In one row the author number (AUTHOR_NUMBER column) is 12, and in the other, it is 13. All that is left to do is look in the AUTHOR table to find the authors who have been assigned the numbers 12 and 13. The answer is Barbara Owen (12) and Peter Williams (13). The sequence number for author 12 is 2, however, and the sequence number for author 13 is 1. Thus, listing the authors in the proper order results in Peter Williams and Barbara Owen. To find the books written by Jeffrey Archer, you look up his number in the AUTHOR table and find that it is 1. Then, look for all rows in the WROTE table for which the author number is 1. There are three such rows. The corresponding book codes are 0189, 2766, and 3743. Looking up these codes in the BOOK table, you find that Jeffrey Archer wrote *Kane and Abel, Prodigal Daughter,* and *First Among Equals*.

Question	A customer in Branch 1 wishes to purchase *Vortex*. Is it currently in stock in Branch 1?
Answer	No. Looking up the code for *Vortex* in the BOOK table, you find it is 3906. To find out how many copies are in stock in Branch 1, you look for a row in the INVENT table with 3906 in the BOOK_CODE column and 1 in the BRANCH_NUMBER column. Because there is no such row, Branch 1 doesn't have any copies of *Vortex*.

Question	You would like to obtain a copy of *Vortex* for this customer. Which other branches currently have it in stock and how many copies does each branch have?
Answer	Branch 2 has one copy; Branch 3 has two. You already know that the code for *Vortex* is 3906. (If you didn't, you would look it up in the BOOK table.) To find out the branches that currently have copies, look for rows in the INVENT table with 3906 in the BOOK_CODE column. There are two such rows. The first one indicates that Branch 2 currently has one copy. The second one indicates that Branch 3 currently has two copies.

SUMMARY

1. Premiere Products is an organization whose requirements include the following:
   a. sales representatives
   b. customers
   c. orders
   d. parts
   e. order lines

2. The database for Henry Books contains information about the following:
   a. branches
   b. publishers
   c. books
   d. authors
   e. inventory

EXERCISES (Premiere Products)

Answer each of the following questions using the Premiere Products data as shown in Figure 1.2. No computer work is involved. In later chapters, you will use a database management system to answer questions.

1. Find the names of all the customers who have a credit limit of at least $1500.

2. Give the order numbers of those orders placed by customer 124 on September 5, 1998.

3. Give the part number, description, and on-hand value (units on hand ∗ price) for each part in item class AP.

4. Find the number and name of each customer whose last name is Nelson.

5. How many customers have a credit limit of $1000?

6. Find the total balance for all the customers represented by sales rep 12.

7. For each order, list the order number, order date, customer number, and customer name.

8. For each order placed on September 5, 1998, list the order number, order date, customer number, and customer name.

9. Find the number and name of each sales rep who represents any customer with a credit limit of $1000.

10. For each order, list the order number, order date, customer number, customer name, along with the number and name of the sales rep who represents the customer.

EXERCISES (Henry Books)

Answer each of the following questions using the database as shown in Figures 1.4, 1.5, and 1.6. No computer work is involved. In later chapters, you will use a database management system to answer questions.

1. List the name of each publisher located in New York state.

2. List the name of each branch that has at least 10 employees.

3. List the code and title of each book whose type is HOR.

4. List the code and title of each book whose type is HOR and is in paperback.

5. List the code and title of each book whose type is HOR or whose publisher code is PB.

6. List the code and title of each paperback book whose type is ART and whose price is less than $12.00.

7. Customers who are part of a special program get a 10 percent discount. To see what the discounted prices would be, list the book code, title, and discounted price of all books. (Use the BOOK_PRICE field to calculate this.)

8. Find the code and name of each publisher for which the word "and" is contained somewhere within the publisher name.

9. List the code and title of each book whose type is FIC, MYS, or ART.

10. How many books are of type MYS?

11. Find the average price for books of type HOR.

12. For each book, list the book code, title, publisher code, and publisher name.

13. For each branch, list the branch number as well as the book code, book title, and number of units on hand of each book currently in stock at the branch.

CHAPTER 2

An Introduction to SQL

OBJECTIVES

- Understand the concepts and terminology associated with relational databases
- Create and run SQL commands
- Create tables using SQL
- Identify and use data types to define the columns in SQL tables
- Understand and use nulls
- Add rows to tables

INTRODUCTION

You already might be an experienced user of a database management system (DBMS). You can find a DBMS at your school's library, at a site on the Internet, or any other place where data is retrieved using a computer. In this chapter, you will learn about the concepts and terminology associated with the relational model for database management. Then you will learn how to create a database by describing and defining the tables and columns that make up the database. In this text, you will study a language called **SQL (Structured Query Language)**. You use SQL to manipulate data in relational databases. In SQL, you type commands to obtain the desired results.

In the mid 1970s SQL was developed under the name SEQUEL at the IBM San Jose research facilities to be the data manipulation language for IBM's prototype relational model DBMS, System R. In 1980, the language was renamed SQL to avoid confusion with an unrelated hardware product called SEQUEL. SQL is used as the data manipulation language for IBM's current production offering in the relational DBMS arena, DB2. Most relational DBMSs, including Oracle, use a version of SQL as a data manipulation language.

In this chapter you also will learn how to assign data types for columns in the database; learn about a special type of value, called a null value; and see how such values are handled during database creation. Finally, you will learn how to load a database by adding data to the tables that are created.

■ ■ ■ ■ ■

RELATIONAL DATABASES

A **relational database** is essentially a collection of tables like the ones you saw for Premiere Products in Chapter 1 (see also Figure 2.1). A relational database is perceived by the user as being just such a collection. (The phrase "perceived by the user" simply indicates that this is how things *appear* to the user, not what the DBMS is actually doing behind the scenes.) You might wonder why this model is not called the "table" model, or something similar if a database is a collection of tables. Formally, these tables are called **relations**, and this is where the model gets its name.

SALES_REP

SLSREP_ NUMBER	LAST	FIRST	STREET	CITY	STATE	ZIP_CODE	TOTAL_ COMMISSION	COMMISSION_ RATE
03	Jones	Mary	123 Main	Grant	MI	49219	2150.00	.05
06	Smith	William	102 Raymond	Ada	MI	49441	4912.50	.07
12	Diaz	Miguel	419 Harper	Lansing	MI	49224	2150.00	.05

CUSTOMER

CUSTOMER_ NUMBER	LAST	FIRST	STREET	CITY	STATE	ZIP_CODE	BALANCE	CREDIT_ LIMIT	SLSREP_ NUMBER
124	Adams	Sally	481 Oak	Lansing	MI	49224	$818.75	$1000	03
256	Samuels	Ann	215 Pete	Grant	MI	49219	$21.50	$1500	06
311	Charles	Don	48 College	Ira	MI	49034	$825.75	$1000	12
315	Daniels	Tom	914 Cherry	Kent	MI	48391	$770.75	$750	06
405	Williams	Al	519 Watson	Grant	MI	49219	$402.75	$1500	12
412	Adams	Sally	16 Elm	Lansing	MI	49224	$1817.50	$2000	03
522	Nelson	Mary	108 Pine	Ada	MI	49441	$98.75	$1500	12
567	Dinh	Tran	808 Ridge	Harper	MI	48421	$402.40	$750	06
587	Galvez	Mara	512 Pine	Ada	MI	49441	$114.60	$1000	06
622	Martin	Dan	419 Chip	Grant	MI	49219	$1045.75	$1000	03

ORDERS

ORDER_ NUMBER	ORDER_ DATE	CUSTOMER_ NUMBER
12489	9/02/98	124
12491	9/02/98	311
12494	9/04/98	315
12495	9/04/98	256
12498	9/05/98	522
12500	9/05/98	124
12504	9/05/98	522

ORDER_LINE

ORDER_ NUMBER	PART_ NUMBER	NUMBER_ ORDERED	QUOTED_ PRICE
12489	AX12	11	$21.95
12491	BT04	1	$149.99
12491	BZ66	1	$399.99
12494	CB03	4	$279.99
12495	CX11	2	$22.95
12498	AZ52	2	$12.95
12498	BA74	4	$24.95
12500	BT04	1	$149.99
12504	CZ81	2	$325.99

PART

PART_ NUMBER	PART_ DESCRIPTION	UNITS_ ON_HAND	ITEM_ CLASS	WAREHOUSE_ NUMBER	UNIT_ PRICE
AX12	Iron	104	HW	3	$24.95
AZ52	Dartboard	20	SG	2	$12.95
BA74	Basketball	40	SG	1	$29.95
BH22	Cornpopper	95	HW	3	$24.95
BT04	Gas Grill	11	AP	2	$149.99
BZ66	Washer	52	AP	3	$399.99
CA14	Griddle	78	HW	3	$39.99
CB03	Bike	44	SG	1	$299.99
CX11	Blender	112	HW	3	$22.95
CZ81	Treadmill	68	SG	2	$349.95

Figure 2.1 Sample data for Premiere Products

Entities, Attributes, and Relationships

There are some terms and concepts that are very important for you to know in the database environment. The terms *entity*, *attribute*, and *relationship* are fundamental when discussing databases. An **entity** is like a noun; it is a person, place, thing, or event. The entities of interest to Premiere Products, for example, are such things as customers, orders, and sales reps. The entities that are of interest to a school include students, faculty, and classes; a real estate agency is interested in clients, houses, and agents; and a used car dealer is interested in vehicles, customers, and manufacturers.

An **attribute** is a property of an entity. The term is used here exactly as it is used in everyday English. For the entity person, for example, the list of attributes might include such things as eye color and height. For Premiere Products, the attributes of interest for the entity customer are such things as first name, last name, address, city, and so on.

The final key term is relationship. A **relationship** is the association between entities. There is an association between customers and sales reps, for example, at Premiere Products. A sales rep is associated with all of his or her customers, and a customer is associated with his or her sales rep. Technically, you say that a sales rep is related to all of his or her customers, and a customer is related to his or her sales rep.

This particular relationship is called a **one-to-many relationship** because one sales rep is associated with many customers, but each customer is associated with only one sales rep. (In this type of relationship, the word *many* is used in a way that is different from everyday English; it might not always mean a large number. In this context, for example, the term *many* means that a sales rep may be associated with *any* number of customers. That is, one sales rep can be associated with zero, one, or more customers.)

How does a DBMS that follows the relational model handle entities, attributes of entities, and relationships between entities? Entities and attributes are fairly simple. Each entity has its own table. In the Premiere Products database, there is one table for sales reps, a separate table for customers, and so on. The attributes of an entity become the columns in the table. In the table for sales reps, for example, there is a column for the sales rep number, columns for the sales reps' names, and so on.

What about relationships? At Premiere Products there is a one-to-many relationship between sales reps and customers (each sales rep is related to the *many* customers he or she represents, and each customer is related to the *one* sales rep who represents the customer). How is this relationship implemented in a relational model database? The answer is by using common columns in two or more tables. Consider Figure 2.1 again. The SLSREP_NUMBER column of the SALES_REP table and the SLSREP_NUMBER column of the CUSTOMER table are used to implement the relationship between sales reps and customers. Given a sales rep, you can use these columns to determine all the customers he or she represents; and, given a customer, you can use these columns to find the sales rep who represents the customer.

With this background, a relation is essentially a two-dimensional table. If you consider the tables in Figure 2.1, however, you can see that there are certain restrictions that should be placed on relations. Each column should have a unique name, and entries within each column should "match" this column name. For example, if the column name is CREDIT_LIMIT, all entries in that column must be credit limits. Also, each row should be unique. After all, if two rows are identical, the second row doesn't provide any new information. For maximum flexibility, the order of the columns and rows should be immaterial. Finally, the table should be as simple as possible. To do this you can restrict each position to a single entry by not allowing multiple entries (or **repeating groups**) in an individual location in the table (see Figure 2.2).

ORDERS

ORDER_ NUMBER	ORDER_ DATE	CUSTOMER_ NUMBER	PART_ NUMBER	NUMBER_ ORDERED	QUOTED_ PRICE
12489	9/02/98	124	AX12	11	$21.95
12491	9/02/98	311	BT04	1	$149.99
			BZ66	1	$399.99
12494	9/04/98	315	CB03	4	$279.99
12495	9/04/98	256	CX11	2	$22.95
12498	9/05/98	522	AZ52	2	$12.95
			BA74	4	$24.95
12500	9/05/98	124	BT04	1	$149.99
12504	9/05/98	522	CZ81	2	$325.99

Repeating groups

Figure 2.2 Poor table structure

These ideas lead to the following definitions:

Definition: A **relation** is a two-dimensional table in which the entries in the table are single-valued (each location in the table contains a single entry); each column has a distinct name (or attribute name); all values in a column are values of the same attribute; the order of the rows and columns is immaterial; and each row contains unique values.

From that definition, you can say that a **relational database** is a collection of relations.

> **Note** Rows in a table (relation) often are called **records** and columns often are called **fields**. Rows also are called **tuples** and columns are called **attributes**.

There is a commonly accepted shorthand representation of the structure of a relational database. You can write the name of the table and then, within parentheses, list all the columns (fields) in the table. For example, the database for Premiere Products can be written as follows:

SALES_REP (SLSREP_NUMBER, LAST, FIRST, STREET, CITY, STATE, ZIP_CODE, TOTAL_COMMISSION, COMMISSION_RATE)
CUSTOMER (CUSTOMER_NUMBER, LAST, FIRST, STREET, CITY, STATE, ZIP_CODE, BALANCE, CREDIT_LIMIT, SLSREP_NUMBER)
ORDERS (ORDER_NUMBER, ORDER_DATE, CUSTOMER_NUMBER)
ORDER_LINE (ORDER_NUMBER, PART_NUMBER, NUMBER_ORDERED, QUOTED_PRICE)
PART (PART_NUMBER, PART_DESCRIPTION, UNITS_ON_HAND, ITEM_CLASS, WAREHOUSE_NUMBER, UNIT_PRICE)

Note In general, SQL is not case sensitive. You can type commands using uppercase or lowercase letters. There is one exception to this rule, however. When you are inserting character values into a table, you must use the correct case.

Notice that there is some duplication of names—the SLSREP_NUMBER column appears in both the SALES_REP table and in the CUSTOMER table. If you write SLSREP_NUMBER, how would a user of the DBMS or the DBMS itself know which SLSREP_NUMBER column you are referring to? You need a way to associate the correct table with the column name. One common approach to this problem is to write both the table name and the column name, separated by a period. Thus, the SLSREP_NUMBER column in the CUSTOMER table is written as CUSTOMER.SLSREP_NUMBER; the SLSREP_NUMBER column in the SALES_REP table is written as SALES_REP.SLSREP_NUMBER. This technique of including the table name with the column name is known as **qualifying** the names. It is always acceptable to qualify data names, even if there is no possibility of confusion. If confusion can arise, however, it is essential to qualify the names.

The **primary key** of a table (or relation) is the column, or collection of columns, that uniquely identifies a given row. In the SALES_REP table, for example, the sales rep's number uniquely identifies a given row. (Sales rep 06 occurs in only one row of the table, for instance.) Thus, the SLSREP_NUMBER column is the table's primary key. Primary keys usually are indicated by underlining the column (or collection of columns) that contains the primary key. The complete shorthand representation for the Premiere Products database is as follows, where the underlined column name indicates the table's primary key:

SALES_REP (SLSREP_NUMBER, LAST, FIRST, STREET, CITY, STATE, ZIP_CODE, TOTAL_COMMISSION, COMMISSION_RATE)
CUSTOMER (CUSTOMER_NUMBER, LAST, FIRST, STREET, CITY, STATE, ZIP_CODE, BALANCE, CREDIT_LIMIT, SLSREP_NUMBER)
ORDERS (ORDER_NUMBER, ORDER_DATE, CUSTOMER_NUMBER)
ORDER_LINE (ORDER_NUMBER, PART_NUMBER, NUMBER_ORDERED, QUOTED_PRICE)
PART (PART_NUMBER, PART_DESCRIPTION, UNITS_ON_HAND, ITEM_CLASS, WAREHOUSE_NUMBER, UNIT_PRICE)

Question	Why does the primary key for the ORDER_LINE table consist of two columns, instead of one?
Answer	No single column in the ORDER_LINE table uniquely identifies a given row. Two columns, ORDER_NUMBER and PART_NUMBER, are required to create a unique row.

DATABASE CREATION

Before you begin loading and accessing data in a table, you must describe the layout of each table to be contained in the database.

Example 1:	Describe the layout of the SALES_REP table to the DBMS.

The SQL command used to describe the layout of a table is CREATE TABLE. The CREATE TABLE command is followed by the name of the table to be created, and then in parentheses by the names and data types of the columns that comprise the table. The **data type** indicates the type of data that can be contained in the column (for example, characters, numbers, or dates) as well as the maximum number of characters or digits. The rules for naming tables and columns vary slightly from one version of SQL to another. If you have any questions about naming tables or columns, consult your system's manual or your DBMS's online Help system. Some typical naming conventions are as follows:

1. The name cannot be longer than 18 characters. (In Oracle, names can be up to 30 characters in length.)

2. The name must start with a letter.

3. The name can contain letters, numbers, and underscores (_).

4. The name cannot contain spaces.

The names used in this text should work for any SQL implementation.

The appropriate SQL command for Example 1 is shown in Figure 2.3. In this SQL CREATE TABLE command, which uses the data definition features of SQL, you are describing a table that will be named SALES_REP. The table will contain nine columns: SLSREP_NUMBER, LAST, FIRST, STREET, CITY, STATE, ZIP_CODE, TOTAL_COMMISSION, and COMMISSION_RATE. The SLSREP_NUMBER column will contain two characters, the LAST column will contain ten characters, and the STATE column will contain two characters. The TOTAL_COMMISSION column will contain numbers only and those numbers are limited to seven digits, including two decimal places. Similarly, the COMMISSION_RATE column is three digits long, including two decimal places. You can visualize the SQL commands in Figure 2.3 as setting up a blank table with column headings for each column name.

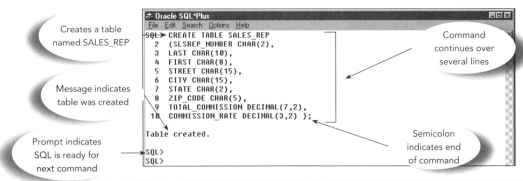

Figure 2.3 CREATE TABLE command for SALES_REP table

SQL COMMANDS

In SQL, commands are **free format**; that is, no rule says that a particular word must begin in a particular position on the line. The previous SQL command could have been written as follows:

CREATE TABLE SALES_REP (SLSREP_NUMBER CHAR(2), LAST CHAR(10), FIRST CHAR(8), STREET CHAR(15), CITY CHAR(15), STATE CHAR(2), ZIP_CODE CHAR(5), TOTAL_COMMISSION DECIMAL(7,2), COMMISSION_RATE DECIMAL(3,2));

The manner in which the command is written simply makes the command more readable. Throughout the text, we will strive for such readability when writing SQL commands.

You can press the Enter key to end a line and then continue typing the command on the next line. You indicate the end of a command line by typing a semicolon.

Note	Ending the command with a semi-colon is a requirement in Oracle, as well as in many other systems, but it is not universal.

The most recent command you type is stored in the **command buffer**. You can edit the command in the buffer by using the special editing commands shown in Table 2.1.

execute command w/out displaying it /

Table 2.1 Editing commands

ACTIVITY	COMMAND	ABBREVIATION
Add text at end of current line	APPEND text	A text
Change current line	Type the line number	
Change text in current line	CHANGE /old/new	C /old/new
Delete all lines from buffer	CLEAR BUFFER	CL BUFF
Delete current line	DEL	
Edit the entire command currently in the buffer using an editor such as Notepad	EDIT	
Insert line following current line	INPUT	I
List the command currently in the buffer	LIST	L
Run the command currently in the buffer	RUN	R

Consider the SQL command shown in Figure 2.4.

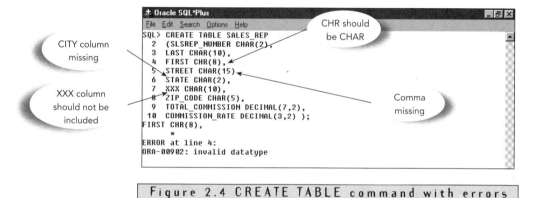

Figure 2.4 CREATE TABLE command with errors

There are several mistakes in this command. In line 4, CHAR is misspelled. Line 5 is missing a comma. The CITY column is missing and line 7 should be deleted.

Figure 2.5 illustrates how you can use Oracle editing commands to make the necessary corrections. The first command, L, lists the entire SQL command in the buffer. The second command, 4, moves the current position to line 4 in the buffer. The C /CHR/CHAR command changes CHR to CHAR. The next two commands move the current position to line 5 and add a comma to the end of the line. The 7 and DEL commands move the current position to line 7 and then delete the line. Finally the 5 and INPUT commands move the current position to record 5 and then insert a new line following the current line 5. After inserting this line, you also can insert additional lines. To indicate there are no other lines to be added, press the Enter key.

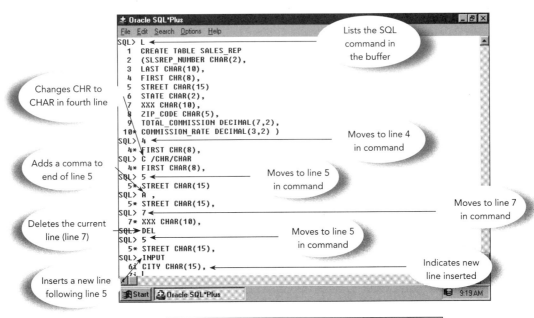

Figure 2.5 Correcting a command

After making changes, it's a good idea to use the L command to list the modified SQL command so you can verify that your changes are correct. If you type a semicolon after a command, the command will run (or execute) immediately. To run the command you have just edited, type RUN. Typing RUN displays the command again before it is executed. If you simply want to execute the command without first displaying it, type a slash (/).

DROPPING A TABLE

Sometimes you find that a table in the database is no longer needed. In this case, you can use the DROP TABLE command to delete it. The command DROP TABLE is followed by the name of the table you want to delete. To delete the SALES_REP table, for example, the command would be written as follows:

DROP TABLE SALES_REP;

Suppose in your CREATE TABLE command you inadvertently type LST instead of LAST or you type CHAR(5) instead of CHAR(15). Let's say that you didn't discover the error until the command was executed. In this case, you can delete the entire table using the DROP TABLE command and then create the correct table using the CREATE TABLE command. Later in this text, you will learn how to change a table's structure without having to delete the entire table.

You should note that when you drop a table, you also drop any data that you have entered into the table. It's a good idea to check your CREATE TABLE commands carefully and correct any problems before adding data.

CHAPTER 2

DATA TYPES

There are other data types besides DECIMAL (numeric) and CHAR (text). While the actual data types vary somewhat from one implementation of SQL to another, Table 2.2 shows the commonly used data types.

Table 2.2 Common Data Types

DATA TYPE	DESCRIPTION
CHAR(n)	Character string n characters long. Columns that contain numbers but will not be used for arithmetic operations usually are assigned a data type of CHAR. The CUSTOMER_NUMBER column, for example, is a CHAR column because the customer numbers will not be used in any calculations.
DATE	Dates in the form DD-MON-YY or MM/DD/YYYY. For example, May 12, 1998 could be stored as 12-MAY-98 or as 5/12/1998. (Note: The specific format in which the dates are stored varies from one implementation of SQL to another.)
DECIMAL (p,q)	Decimal number p digits long with q of these being decimal places to the right of the decimal point. The data type DECIMAL(5,2) represents a number with three places to the left of the decimal and two places to the right (for example, 100.00). (Note: The specific meaning of DECIMAL varies from one implementation of SQL to another. In some implementations, the decimal point counts as one of the places and in other implementations it does not. Likewise, in some implementations a minus sign counts as one of the places, but in others it does not.)
INTEGER	Integers (numbers without a decimal part); the acceptable range is -2147483648 to 2147483647.
SMALLINT	Like INTEGER but does not occupy as much space; range is -32768 to 32767. This data type is a better choice than INTEGER if you are certain that numbers will be within the indicated range.

SIMILAR

NULLS

Occasionally, when a new row is entered into a table or an existing row is modified, the values for one or more columns are unknown or unavailable. For example, a customer's name and address can be added even though he or she does not have an assigned sales rep or a credit limit established. In other cases, some values might never be known; perhaps there is a customer who does not have a sales rep.

In SQL you handle this problem by using a special value to represent the situation in which an actual value is unknown or not applicable. This special value is called a **null data value**, or simply a **null**. For each column in the table, you can choose whether to allow nulls.

Question	Should a user be allowed to enter null values for the primary key?
Answer	No; it doesn't make sense to allow a user to enter null values for the primary key. For example, the wisdom of storing a record for a customer whose customer number is unknown is questionable at best. If you store two customer records without values in the primary key column, you will have no way to tell them apart.

Implementation of Nulls

You must have a mechanism to indicate which columns cannot contain null values. You do this by using the NOT NULL clause within the CREATE TABLE command. Those columns whose description includes NOT NULL cannot accept null values. Other columns might accept null values.

For example, suppose that the SLSREP_NUMBER, LAST, and FIRST columns in the SALES_REP table cannot accept null values, but all other columns in the SALES_REP table can. The corresponding CREATE TABLE command is as follows:

```
CREATE TABLE SALES_REP
(SLSREP_NUMBER CHAR(2) NOT NULL,
LAST CHAR(10) NOT NULL,
FIRST CHAR(8) NOT NULL,
STREET CHAR(15),
CITY CHAR(15),
STATE CHAR(2),
ZIP_CODE CHAR(5),
TOTAL_COMMISSION DECIMAL(7,2),
COMMISSION_RATE DECIMAL(3,2) );
```

Any attempt to store a null value in either the SLSREP_NUMBER, LAST, or FIRST columns will be rejected by the system. An attempt to store a null value in the STREET column, however, will be accepted.

LOADING A TABLE WITH DATA

Once the tables have been created, you can load data into them. To load a table, you add the necessary rows to each table using the INSERT command.

The INSERT Command

When adding rows to character columns, make sure you enclose the values in single quotation marks (for example, 'Jones').

Note	Values must be enclosed in single quotation marks for any column whose type is character (CHAR) even if the data contain numbers. Because the ZIP_CODE column has a CHAR data type, for example, ZIP codes must be enclosed in single quotation marks even though they are numbers.

Example 2:	Add sales rep 03 from Figure 2.1 to the database.

The command to add records is the INSERT command. You type INSERT INTO followed by the name of the table into which you are adding data. Then you type the VALUES command followed by the specific values to be inserted. The command for this example and its results are shown in Figure 2.6. Note that the character strings ('03', 'Jones', 'Mary', and so on) are enclosed in single quotation marks because they are values for character columns.

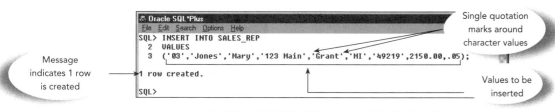

Message indicates 1 row is created

Single quotation marks around character values

Values to be inserted

Figure 2.6 INSERT command

Note	Remember to type the values in the same case as those shown in the text to avoid problems later when retrieving data from the database.

Example 3:	Add the second and third sales reps to the table.

```
SQL> INSERT INTO ___ ↵
        VALUES ↵
        ( . . . 
        ); ↵
```

You could use the INSERT command to add the rows to the table. However, an easier, faster way to add rows is to modify the previous INSERT command to add the record for the second sales rep. In Figure 2.7, the L command lists the command currently in the buffer, in this case, the previous INSERT command.

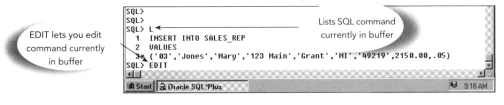

Figure 2.7 Modifying the INSERT command

The EDIT command lets you use an editor, such as Notepad, to update the command in the buffer (see Figure 2.8). You make the necessary changes (see Figure 2.9), save them, and then exit the editor. Type RUN to run the modified command.

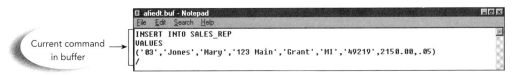

Figure 2.8 Using an editor to modify the INSERT commmand

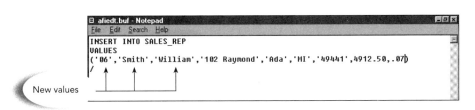

Figure 2.9 Modified INSERT command

Figure 2.10 shows how to use the EDIT command to add the second and third records to the SALES_REP table.

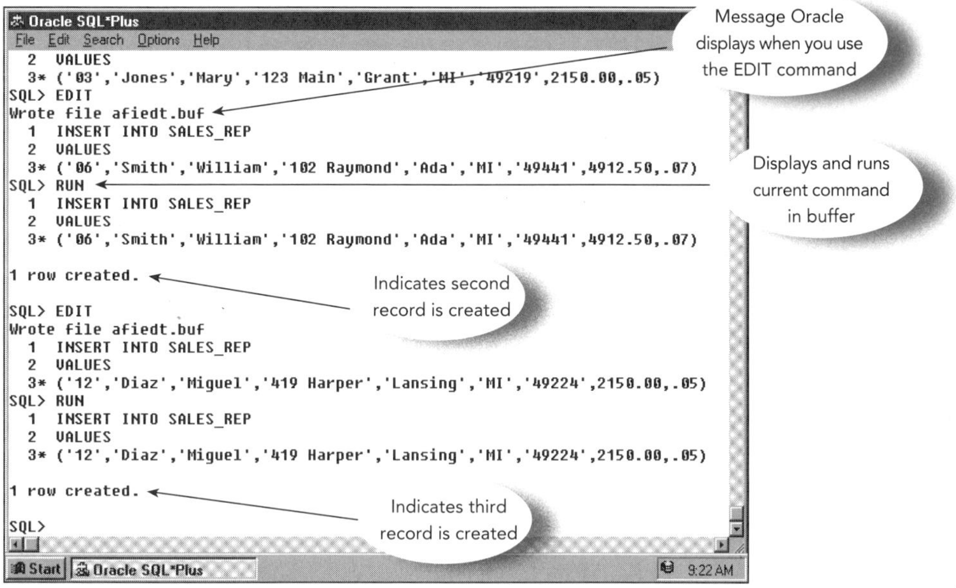

Figure 2.10 Inserting additional rows

The INSERT Command with Nulls

To enter a null value into a table, you use a special format of the INSERT command. In this special format, you identify the names of the columns into which non-null values can be entered, and then list only these non-null values after the VALUES command. See Example 4.

Example 4: Add sales rep 18 to the table. Her name is Elyse Martin. All fields except SLSREP_NUMBER, LAST, and FIRST are null.

In this case you do not enter a value of null; you enter only the non-null values. To do so, you must indicate precisely which values you are entering by listing the corresponding columns as shown in Figure 2.11. The command shown in the figure indicates that you are entering data in only the SLSREP_NUMBER, LAST, and FIRST columns, and that you *will not* enter a value into any other field.

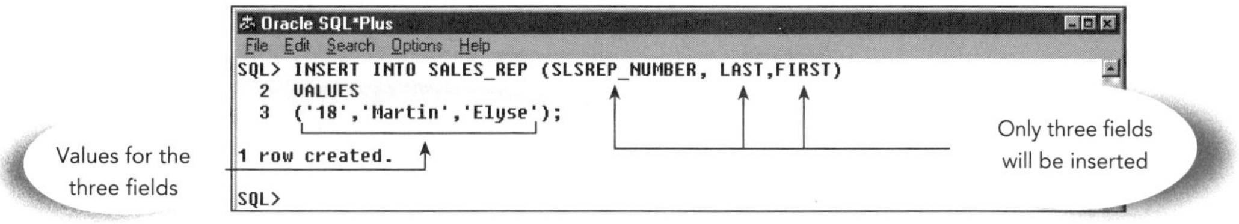

Figure 2.11 Inserting a row containing null values

VIEWING DATA IN A TABLE

You can view data in the table to make sure that it is entered correctly by using the SQL SELECT command as shown in Figure 2.12. You might notice that some of the data in Figure 2.12 scrolls off the right side of the screen. You can use the horizontal scroll bar to see the data. In some implementations of SQL, the extra data will wrap to a second line for improved readability.

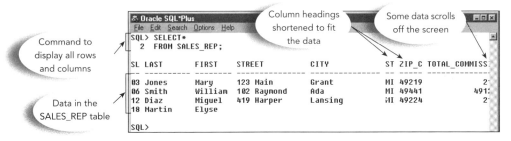

Figure 2.12 Viewing the data

CORRECTING ERRORS IN THE DATABASE

After reviewing the data in the table, you might find that you need to change the value in a field. You can use the UPDATE command, as shown in Figure 2.13, to correct errors. The command shown in the figure changes to Marlin the last name in the row in which the sales rep number is 18.

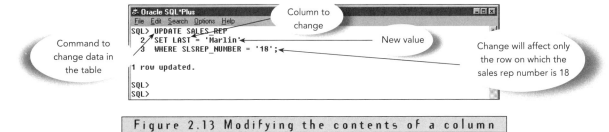

Figure 2.13 Modifying the contents of a column

If you need to delete a record, you can use the DELETE command. The command in Figure 2.14 deletes the row on which the sales rep number is 18.

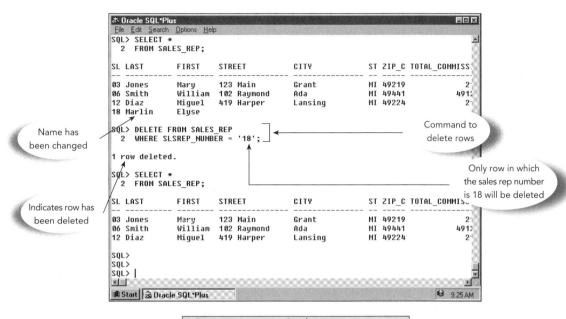

Figure 2.14 Deleting a row

ADDITIONAL TABLES

When you are creating tables and adding rows to them, you can use an editor to create a file containing the CREATE TABLE and INSERT commands. Such a file is called a script. Scripts are covered in Chapter 7. Doing this saves you from having to type the commands over and over. To create a file in Oracle, type EDIT followed by the name of the file you want to create. Oracle will ask if you want to create a new file; you should respond "Yes." Oracle assigns the file extension SQL automatically.

Figure 2.15 illustrates the process. The file being created is named cre_cust.SQL, and it contains a CREATE TABLE command for the CUSTOMER table. Notice that two fields, LAST and FIRST, are specified as NOT NULL. Additionally, the CUSTOMER_NUMBER field is the table's primary key, indicating that the CUSTOMER_NUMBER column will be the unique identifier of rows within the table. With this column designated as the primary key, the DBMS will reject any attempt to store a customer number if that number already exists in the table. (No primary key was specified for the SALES_REP table. You will see how to add a primary key later in the text.)

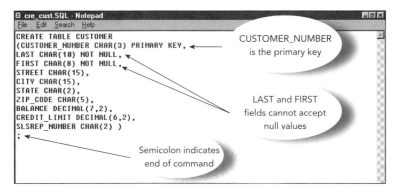

*under
Notepad.*

Figure 2.15 CREATE TABLE command for CUSTOMER table

To run this command in Oracle, save the file then exit the editor. Then type @ (the "at" symbol) followed by the name of the file. In this case, you would type @cre_cust. Once you press the Enter key, Oracle executes the command and creates the table.

After creating the table, you could create another file containing all the necessary INSERT commands to add the necessary records to the table. Each command must end with a semi-colon. Figure 2.16 shows a portion of such a file for the CUSTOMER table.

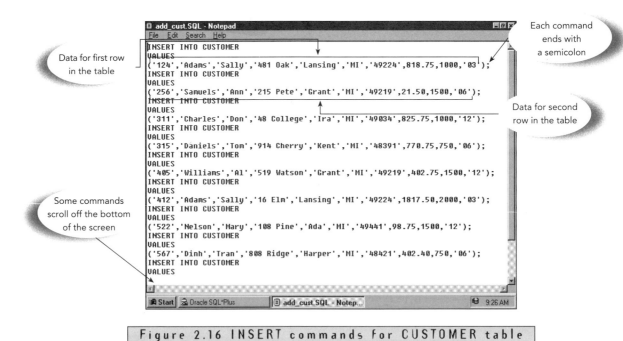

Figure 2.16 INSERT commands for CUSTOMER table

Figures 2.17 through 2.22 show files containing the necessary CREATE TABLE and INSERT commands for the other tables in the Premiere Products database. Figure 2.17 contains a CREATE TABLE command for the ORDERS table and Figure 2.18 contains INSERT TABLE commands for the rows in the ORDERS table. Notice the way dates are entered.

```
☐ cre_ord.SQL - Notepad                                    _ ☐ ✕
File   Edit   Search   Help
CREATE TABLE ORDERS
(ORDER_NUMBER CHAR(5) PRIMARY KEY,◄──────  ORDER_NUMBER is
ORDER_DATE DATE,                              the primary key
CUSTOMER_NUMBER CHAR(3) )
;
```

Figure 2.17 CREATE TABLE command for ORDERS table

```
☐ Add_ord.sql - Notepad                                    _ ☐ ✕
File   Edit   Search   Help
INSERT INTO ORDERS
VALUES
('12489','2-SEP-98','124');
INSERT INTO ORDERS ◄──────────  Format used to
VALUES                            enter dates
('12491','2-SEP-98','311');
INSERT INTO ORDERS
VALUES
('12494','4-SEP-98','315');
INSERT INTO ORDERS
VALUES
('12495','4-SEP-98','256');
INSERT INTO ORDERS
VALUES
('12498','5-SEP-98','522');
INSERT INTO ORDERS
VALUES
('12500','5-SEP-98','124');
INSERT INTO ORDERS
VALUES
('12504','5-SEP-98','522');
```

Figure 2.18 INSERT commands for ORDERS table

Figure 2.19 contains a CREATE TABLE command for the PART table, and Figure 2.20 contains the appropriate INSERT TABLE commands, although some lines scroll off the screen.

```
☐ cre_part.SQL - Notepad                                   _ ☐ ✕
File   Edit   Search   Help
CREATE TABLE PART
(PART_NUMBER CHAR(4) PRIMARY KEY, ◄──────  PART_NUMBER is
PART_DESCRIPTION CHAR(12),                   the primary key
UNITS_ON_HAND DECIMAL(4,0),
ITEM_CLASS CHAR(2),
WAREHOUSE_NUMBER CHAR(1),
UNIT_PRICE DECIMAL(6,2) )
;
```

Figure 2.19 CREATE TABLE command for PART table

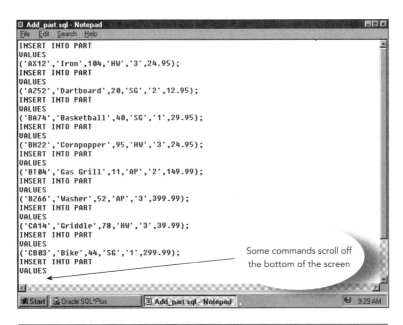

Figure 2.20 INSERT commands for PART table

Figure 2.21 contains a CREATE TABLE command for the ORDER_LINE table. Notice the way the primary key is defined when the primary key consists of more than one field. Figure 2.22 contains the appropriate INSERT TABLE commands.

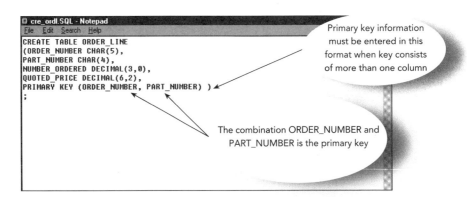

Figure 2.21 CREATE TABLE command for ORDER_LINE table

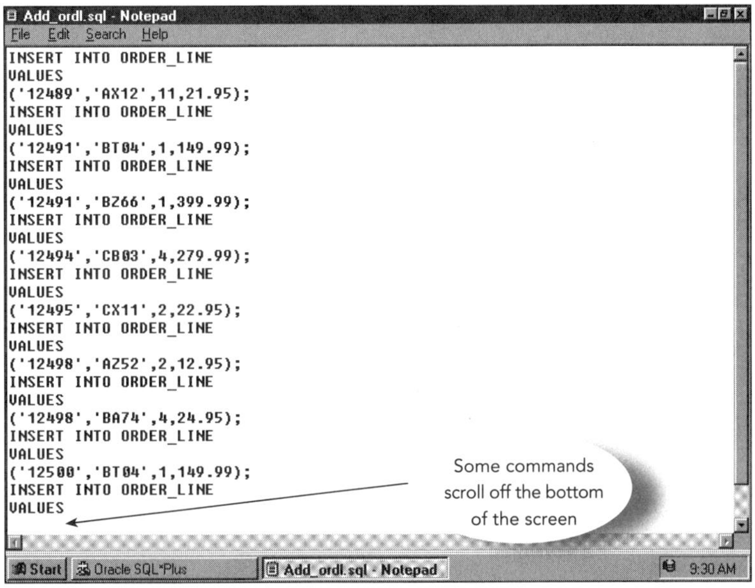

Figure 2.22 INSERT commands for rows in ORDER_LINE table

DESCRIBING A TABLE

The CREATE TABLE command clearly shows the structure of the table. The command indicates all the fields, data types, and lengths of the fields. The CREATE TABLE command also indicates which fields cannot accept nulls.

When you work with a table, you might not have access to the CREATE TABLE command that was originally used to create the table. For example, someone other than you might have created the table; or perhaps you created the table several months ago but did not save the command. You still might want to examine the table's structure, however, to see details concerning the columns in the table. Each DBMS gives you a way of examining these details. In Oracle, you can use the DESCRIBE command as shown in Figure 2.23. The display contains all the columns in the SALES_REP table and their corresponding data types.

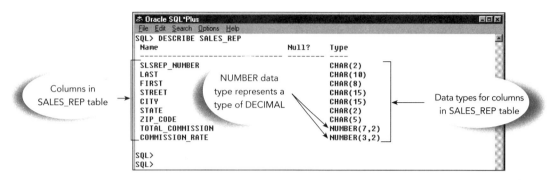

Figure 2.23 DESCRIBE command for SALES_REP table

Note	In Figure 2.23, Oracle uses the word NUMBER instead of DECIMAL. Also, no semicolon is necessary at the end of the command because this is not a standard SQL command.

In this chapter you learned how to create and run SQL commands, create tables, and add rows to these tables. In the next chapter, you will learn to use SQL commands to create and run queries that retrieve data from the tables. In Chapter 3, you will create queries that involve data from a single table. In Chapter 4, you will learn how to create queries that involve multiple tables.

SUMMARY

1. A relational database is a collection of related tables. An entity is a person, place, thing, or event. Tables in the database are entities. An attribute is a property of an entity. Attributes are the columns in the tables. A relationship is the association between tables in the database. Relationships are defined by how the data is related in columns in the tables.

2. Use the CREATE TABLE command to create a table by typing the table name and then listing, in parentheses, the columns in the table.

3. The primary key of a table is the column, or collection of columns, that uniquely identifies a given row in the table. Primary keys are usually identified by underlining the column name(s).

4. You can use the editing commands listed in Table 2.1 to edit the current SQL command in the command buffer.

5. Use the DROP TABLE command to delete a table and all its data from the database.

6. The possible data types are INTEGER, SMALLINT, DECIMAL, CHAR, and DATE.

7. A null data value (or null) is a special value that is used when the actual value for a column is unknown or unavailable. The NOT NULL command is used to identify columns that cannot accept null values, such as the table's primary key.

8. Use the INSERT command to load data into a table.

9. Use the SELECT command to view the data in a table.

10. Use the UPDATE command to change the value in a column.

11. Use the DELETE command to delete a row in a table.

12. You can use an editor, such as Notepad, to create commands that create tables and add rows to them. To run a saved command, type @ followed by the name of the file.

13. You can use the CREATE TABLE or the DESCRIBE command to describe the layout of a table.

EXERCISES (PREMIERE PRODUCTS)

If you are using Oracle for these exercises and wish to print a copy of your commands and results, you need to save the commands in a file. To do this, type SPOOL followed by the name of the file you are creating, and then press the Enter key. All the commands you enter from that point will be saved in the file that you named. For example, to save the commands and results to a file named CHAPTER2.SQL on the A drive, the command is as follows:

SPOOL A:CHAPTER2.SQL

When you have finished entering and running your commands, type SPOOL OFF, and press the Enter key to stop saving commands to the file. Then start any program that can open *.txt files, open the file that you saved, and print it using the Print command on the File menu.

1. Use the CREATE TABLE command to create all the tables in the Premiere Products database. The CREATE TABLE commands you need are shown in Figures 2.3, 2.15, 2.17, 2.19, and 2.21.

2. Add all the sales reps shown in Figure 2.1 to the SALES_REP table using the INSERT command.

3. Add the customers shown in Figure 2.1 to the CUSTOMER table.

4. Add the orders shown in Figure 2.1 to the ORDERS table.

5. Add the order line data shown in Figure 2.1 to the ORDER_LINE table.

6. Add the part information shown in Figure 2.1 to the PART table.

EXERCISES (HENRY BOOKS)

1. Use the CREATE TABLE command to create all the tables in the Henry Books database. The information you need is shown in Figure 2.24.

BRANCH

COLUMN	TYPE	LENGTH	DECIMAL PLACES	NULLS ALLOWED?	DESCRIPTION
BRANCH_NUMBER	Char	1		No	Branch number (key)
BRANCH_NAME	Char	20			Branch name
BRANCH_LOCATION	Char	20			Branch location
NUMBER_EMPLOYEES	Decimal	2	0		Number of employees

PUBLISHER

COLUMN	TYPE	LENGTH	DECIMAL PLACES	NULLS ALLOWED?	DESCRIPTION
PUBLISHER_CODE	Char	2		No	Publisher code (key)
PUBLISHER_NAME	Char	20			Publisher name
PUBLISHER_CITY	Char	20			Publisher city
PUBLISHER_STATE	Char	2			Publisher state

AUTHOR

COLUMN	TYPE	LENGTH	DECIMAL PLACES	PUBLISHER STATE	DESCRIPTION
AUTHOR_NUMBER	Char	2		No	Author number (key)
AUTHOR_NAME	Char	20			Author last name
AUTHOR_FIRST	Char	20			Author first name

BOOK

COLUMN	TYPE	LENGTH	DECIMAL PLACES	NULLS ALLOWED?	DESCRIPTION
BOOK_CODE	Decimal	4	0	No	Book code (key)
BOOK_TITLE	Char	30			Book title
PUBLISHER_CODE	Char	2			Publisher code
BOOK_TYPE	Char	3			Book type
BOOK_PRICE	Decimal	4	2		Book price
PAPERBACK	Char	1			Paperback (Y, N)

WROTE

COLUMN	TYPE	LENGTH	DECIMAL PLACES	NULLS ALLOWED?	DESCRIPTION
BOOK_CODE	Char	4		No	Book code (key)
AUTHOR_NUMBER	Char	2			Author number (key)
SEQUENCE_NUMBER	Decimal	1	0		Sequence number

INVENT

COLUMN	TYPE	LENGTH	DECIMAL PLACES	NULLS ALLOWED?	DESCRIPTION
BOOK_CODE	Char	4		No	Book code (key)
BRANCH_NUMBER	Char	1			Branch number (key)
UNITS_ON_HAND	Decimal	2	0		Units on hand

Figure 2.24 Table layouts for Henry Books database

2. Add the branch information shown in Figure 1.4 (in Chapter 1) to the BRANCH table using the INSERT command.

3. Add the publisher information shown in Figure 1.4 to the PUBLISHER table.

4. Add the author information shown in Figure 1.4 to the AUTHOR table.

5. Add the book information shown in Figure 1.5 to the BOOK table.

6. Add the author and book information shown in Figure 1.6 to the WROTE table.

7. Add the inventory information shown in Figure 1.6 to the INVENT table.

8. Why is the BOOK_CODE column a character column instead of a decimal column?

CHAPTER 3

Single-Table Queries

OBJECTIVES

- Retrieve data from a database using SQL commands
- Use compound conditions
- Use computed columns
- Use the SQL LIKE operator
- Use the SQL IN operator
- Sort data using the ORDER BY command
- Sort data using multiple keys and in ascending and descending order
- Use SQL functions
- Use nested subqueries
- Group data using the GROUP BY command
- Select individual groups using the HAVING clause
- Retrieve columns with null values

INTRODUCTION

In this chapter you will learn about the SQL SELECT command that is used to retrieve data in a database. You will examine the manner in which data can be sorted and use SQL functions to count rows and calculate totals. You also will learn a special feature of SQL that allows SELECT commands to be nested; that is, one SELECT command placed inside another. Finally, you will learn how to group rows that have matching values in some column.

■   ■   ■   ■   ■

SIMPLE QUERIES

One of the most important features of a database management system is its capability to answer a wide variety of questions concerning the data in the database. When you need to find data that answers a specific question, the question is called a query. A **query** is simply a question represented in a way that the DBMS can understand.

In SQL, the command used to create a query is the SELECT command. The basic form of a SQL SELECT command is simple: it appears as SELECT-FROM. First you type the word SELECT, and then list the columns that you wish to include in the query. This portion of the command is called the **SELECT clause**. Next you type the word FROM, followed by the name of the table that contains the data you need to query. This portion of the command is called the **FROM clause**. Finally, when needed, you include the word WHERE followed by any conditions (restrictions) that apply to the data you want to retrieve. This portion of the command is optional and is called the **WHERE clause**. For example, if you need to retrieve the records for only those customers having a $1,000 credit limit, the WHERE clause would include a condition specifying that the value in the CREDIT_LIMIT column must be 1000 (CREDIT_LIMIT = 1000).

Remember, there are no special format rules for constructing SQL commands. In this text, we place the FROM command and the WHERE command (when it is used) on separate lines only to make the commands more readable and understandable.

Note	The various implementations of SQL differ on exactly how the query output is displayed. The column headings and number formats may differ. For example, the implementation used in this text truncates (shortens) the column headings to fit the width of the column data. Although your output should contain the same data that appears in the text, its format could differ slightly.

Retrieve Certain Columns and All Rows

You can write a command to retrieve specified columns and all rows from the table, as shown in Example 1.

Example 1:	List the customer number, last name, first name, and balance of every customer.

Because you need to list *all* customers, you do not need to include a WHERE clause (in other words, there are no restrictions). The query is shown in Figure 3.1.

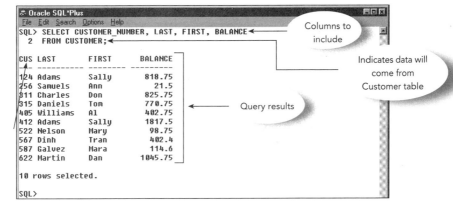

Figure 3.1 SELECT command to select certain columns

Retrieve All Columns and All Rows

You can use the same command as shown in Example 1 to retrieve all columns and all rows from the table. However, as Example 2 illustrates, you can use a shortcut to do this.

Example 2: List the complete PART table.

Instead of listing all the column names after the SELECT command, you can use an asterisk (*) to indicate that you want all columns listed. The result will list all columns in the order in which you described them to the system during data definition. If you want all the columns listed, but in a different order, you would type the column names in the order in which you want them to appear. In this case, assuming that the default order is appropriate, you can use the query shown in Figure 3.2.

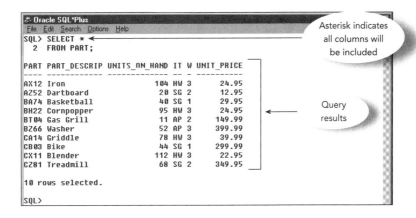

Figure 3.2 SELECT command to select all columns

Use of the WHERE Clause – Simple Conditions

You can use the WHERE clause to retrieve records that satisfy some condition, as shown in Example 3.

Example 3:	What is the name of customer number 124?

You can use the WHERE clause to restrict the query output to customer number 124 as shown in Figure 3.3. Recall that data for character columns, such as the CUSTOMER_NUMBER column, must be enclosed in single quotation marks.

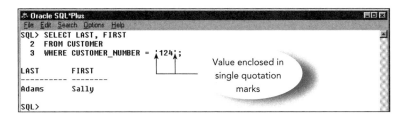

Figure 3.3 SELECT command with a condition

The condition in the preceding WHERE clause is called a simple condition. A **simple condition** has the form: column name, comparison operator, and then either another column name or a value. The available comparison operators are shown in Table 3.1. Note that there are two different operators for not equal to (< > and !=). You must use the one that is right for your implementation of SQL. (If you use the wrong operator, your system will not accept it.)

Table 3.1 Comparison operators

COMPARISON OPERATOR	DESCRIPTION
=	Equal to
<	Less than
>	Greater than
<=	Less than or equal to
>=	Greater than or equal to
< >	Not equal to (used by most implementations of SQL)
!=	Not equal to (used by some implementations of SQL)

Example 4:	Find the customer number for every customer whose last name is Adams.

The only difference between this example and the previous one is that in Example 3, there could not be more than one row in the answer. (Because the CUSTOMER_NUMBER column is the primary key of the CUSTOMER table, there can be only one customer whose number matches the given number.) In Example 4, the results can, and do, contain more than one row as shown in Figure 3.4.

```
Oracle SQL*Plus                                                    _ □ ×
File  Edit  Search  Options  Help
SQL> SELECT CUSTOMER_NUMBER
  2   FROM CUSTOMER
  3   WHERE LAST = 'Adams';

CUS
---
124
412

SQL>
```

Figure 3.4 SELECT command with a condition that
retrieves multiple rows

Note	In general, SQL is not case sensitive. You can use uppercase or lowercase letters in any way you choose. The one important exception, however, is when you include values within quotation marks as you do when entering conditions. Make sure to use correct case for these values.

Example 5:	Find the customer number, last name, first name, and current balance for every customer whose balance exceeds the credit limit.

A simple condition also can involve a comparison of two columns as shown in Figure 3.5. The WHERE clause uses a comparison operator to find those rows in which the credit limit is greater than the balance.

```
Oracle SQL*Plus                                                    _ □ ×
File  Edit  Search  Options  Help
SQL> SELECT CUSTOMER_NUMBER, LAST, FIRST, BALANCE
  2   FROM CUSTOMER
  3   WHERE BALANCE > CREDIT_LIMIT;

CUS LAST       FIRST      BALANCE
--- ---------- -------- ---------
315 Daniels    Tom        770.75
622 Martin     Dan       1045.75

SQL>
```

Figure 3.5 SELECT command involving a comparison

Compound Conditions

The conditions you have seen so far are called simple conditions. The next examples require compound conditions. **Compound conditions** are formed by connecting two or more simple conditions using the AND, OR, and NOT operators. When simple conditions are connected by the AND operator, all the simple conditions must be true in order for the compound condition to be true. When simple conditions are connected by the OR operator, the compound condition will be true whenever any one of the simple conditions is true. Preceding a condition by the NOT operator reverses the truth of the original condition. For example, if the original condition is true, the new condition will be false; if the original condition is false, the new one will be true.

| Example 6: | List the description of every part that is in warehouse number 3 and that has more than 100 units on hand. |

In this example, you need to retrieve those parts that meet *both* conditions—the warehouse number is equal to 3 *and* the number of units on hand is greater than 100. To find the answer, you must form a compound condition using the AND operator as shown in Figure 3.6. The query examines the data in the PART table in the Premiere Products database, and lists the parts that are located in warehouse number 3 and for which there are more than 100 units on hand.

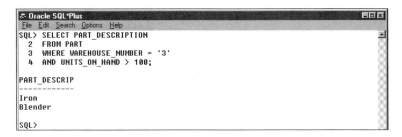

Figure 3.6 SELECT command involving an AND condition

For readability, we placed each of the simple conditions on a separate line. Some people prefer to put the conditions on the same line with parentheses around each simple condition, as shown in Figure 3.7. Either way, these two methods accomplish the same thing. In this text, we usually will place simple conditions on separate lines, without parentheses.

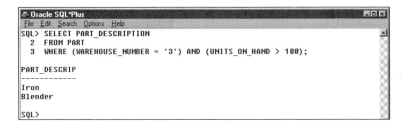

Figure 3.7 SELECT command with WHERE clause and AND condition on a single line

| Example 7: | List the description of every part that is in warehouse number 3 or that has more than 100 units on hand. |

In this example, you want those parts for which the warehouse number is equal to 3 *or* the number of units on hand is greater than 100 *or* both. To do this you form a compound condition using the OR operator as shown in Figure 3.8.

```
* Oracle SQL*Plus                                            _ □ X
File  Edit  Search  Options  Help
SQL> SELECT PART_DESCRIPTION
  2  FROM PART
  3  WHERE WAREHOUSE_NUMBER = '3'
  4  OR UNITS_ON_HAND > 100;

PART_DESCRIP
------------
Iron
Cornpopper
Washer
Griddle
Blender

SQL>
```

Figure 3.8 SELECT command involving an OR condition

Example 8:   List the description of every part that is not in warehouse 3.

For this example, you could use a simple condition with the conditional operator for *not equal to* (WHERE WAREHOUSE_NUMBER != '3'). As an alternative, you could use the EQUAL operator (=) in the condition, and precede the entire condition with the NOT operator as shown in Figure 3.9.

```
* Oracle SQL*Plus                                            _ □ X
File  Edit  Search  Options  Help
SQL> SELECT PART_DESCRIPTION
  2  FROM PART
  3  WHERE NOT (WAREHOUSE_NUMBER = '3');

PART_DESCRIP
------------
Dartboard
Basketball
Gas Grill
Bike
Treadmill

SQL>
```

Figure 3.9 SELECT command involving NOT condition

The condition WAREHOUSE_NUMBER = '3' does not need to be enclosed in parentheses but doing so makes the command more readable. Note that by phrasing the condition in this form, we have avoided the problem of determining whether our implementation of SQL uses the < > or != not equal to operator.

Use of BETWEEN

Example 9 requires a compound condition to determine the answer.

Example 9:   List the customer number, last name, first name, and balance for every customer whose balance is between $500 and $1,000.

You can use the SELECT command and the AND operator as shown in Figure 3.10 to retrieve the data.

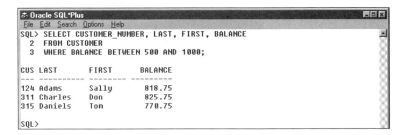

Figure 3.10 SELECT command involving AND condition on single column

An alternative to this approach uses the BETWEEN operator as shown in Figure 3.11.

Figure 3.11 SELECT command involving BETWEEN condition

The BETWEEN operator is not an essential feature of SQL. You have just seen that you can arrive at the same answer without it. Using the BETWEEN operator, however, does make certain SELECT commands simpler.

Use of Computed Columns

You can use computed columns in SQL queries. A **computed column** is a column that does not exist in the database but can be computed using data in the existing columns. Computations can involve any arithmetic operator shown in Table 3.2.

Table 3.2 Arithmetic operators

ARITHMETIC OPERATOR	DESCRIPTION
+	Addition
–	Subtraction
*	Multiplication
/	Division

Example 10: Find the customer number, last name, first name, and available credit for every customer who has a credit limit of at least $1,500.

There is no column for available credit in our database. The available credit, however, can be computed from two columns that are present—CREDIT_LIMIT and BALANCE. To do this, you use the expression

AVAILABLE_CREDIT=CREDIT_LIMIT-BALANCE. See the command shown in Figure 3.12.

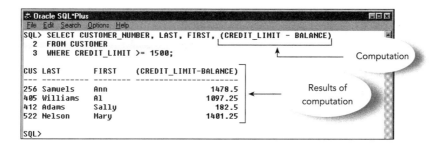

Figure 3.12 SELECT command involving computed column

The parentheses around the calculation (CREDIT_LIMIT - BALANCE) are not essential but improve readability.

Note Some implementations of SQL use special headings for computed columns, such as SUM1 or COUNT2, or allow you to assign computed columns a name of your choice.

Example 11: Find the customer number, last name, first name, and available credit for every customer who has at least $1,000 of available credit.

You can use computed columns in comparisons as shown in Figure 3.13. Again the parentheses around the calculation (CREDIT_LIMIT - BALANCE) are used to improve readability.

```
 Oracle SQL*Plus
File  Edit  Search  Options  Help
SQL> SELECT CUSTOMER_NUMBER, LAST, FIRST, (CREDIT_LIMIT - BALANCE)
  2   FROM CUSTOMER
  3   WHERE (CREDIT_LIMIT - BALANCE) >= 1000;

CUS LAST        FIRST     (CREDIT_LIMIT-BALANCE)
--- ---------- --------- ----------------------
256 Samuels     Ann                       1478.5
405 Williams    Al                       1097.25
522 Nelson      Mary                     1401.25

SQL>
```

Figure 3.13 SELECT command with computation in the condition

Use of LIKE

In most cases, your conditions will involve exact matches. For example, you want to retrieve records for every customer whose last name is Adams. In some cases, however, exact matches will not work. For example, you might know that the desired value contains only a certain collection of characters. In such cases, you use the LIKE operator with a wildcard symbol. This operator is illustrated in the next example.

Example 12: List the customer number, last name, first name, and complete address of every customer who lives on Pine; that is, whose address contains the letters "Pine."

All you know is that the addresses that you want contain a certain collection of characters ("Pine") somewhere within them, but you don't know where.

Fortunately, SQL has a facility that you can use in this situation. The percent sign (%) is used as a **wildcard** to represent any collection of characters. The condition LIKE '%Pine%', as shown in Figure 3.14, will retrieve information for every customer whose street contains some collection of characters, followed by the letters "Pine," followed by some other characters. Note that this query also would retrieve information for a customer whose address was "123 Pinell."

Wildcard symbols

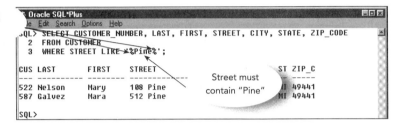

Figure 3.14 SELECT command with wildcards

Note	Another wildcard symbol is the underscore (_), which represents any individual character. For example, "T_m" represents the letter "T" followed by any single character followed by the letter "m" and would retrieve records that include the words Tim, Tom, or T3m, for example.

Note	In a large database, you should use wildcards only when absolutely necessary. Searches involving wildcards can be extremely slow. Also, make sure to use wildcards effectively to retrieve the correct records.

Use of IN

An IN clause provides a concise way of phrasing certain conditions, as Example 13 illustrates. You will see another use for the IN clause in more complex examples later in this chapter.

Example 13:	List the customer number, last name, first name, and credit limit for every customer with a credit limit of $1,000, $1,500, or $2,000.

In this query you will use the SQL IN operator to determine whether a credit limit is $1,000, $1,500, or $2,000. You also could obtain the same answer by using the condition WHERE CREDIT_LIMIT = 1000 OR CREDIT_LIMIT = 1500 OR CREDIT_LIMIT = 2000. The new approach, as shown in Figure 3.15, is simpler. Here the IN clause contains a collection of values: 1000, 1500, and 2000. The condition is true for those rows in which the value in the CREDIT_LIMIT column is in this collection.

```
Oracle SQL*Plus                                           _ □ X
File  Edit  Search  Options  Help
SQL> SELECT CUSTOMER_NUMBER, LAST, FIRST, CREDIT_LIMIT
  2  FROM CUSTOMER
  3  WHERE CREDIT_LIMIT IN (1000, 1500, 2000);

CUS LAST        FIRST     CREDIT_LIMIT
--- ---------- --------- ------------
124 Adams       Sally            1000
256 Samuels     Ann              1500
311 Charles     Don              1000
405 Williams    Al               1500
412 Adams       Sally            2000
522 Nelson      Mary             1500
587 Galvez      Mara             1000
622 Martin      Dan              1000

8 rows selected.

SQL>
```

Figure 3.15 SELECT command involving IN condition

SORTING

Recall that the order of rows in a table is immaterial to the DBMS. From a practical standpoint, when you are querying a relational database, there is no defined order in which the results are displayed. Rows can be displayed in the order in which the data was originally entered, but even this is not certain. If the order in which the data is displayed is important, you can *specifically* request that the results display in a desired order. In SQL, you do this by using the ORDER BY command.

Use of ORDER BY

The ORDER BY command is used to list data in a specific order, as shown in Example 14.

Example 14:   List the customer number, last name, first name, and balance of every customer. Order the output in ascending (increasing) order by balance.

The column on which data is to be sorted is called a **sort key** or simply a **key**. In this case, because the output is to be ordered (sorted) by balance, the sort key is the BALANCE column. To sort the output, use the ORDER BY clause, followed by the sort key. The query is shown in Figure 3.16.

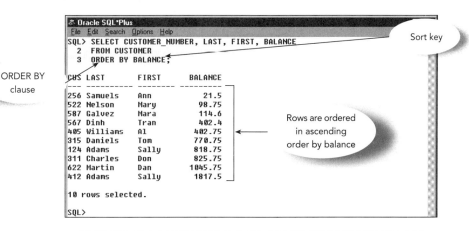

ORDER BY clause

Sort key

Rows are ordered in ascending order by balance

```
Oracle SQL*Plus
File  Edit  Search  Options  Help
SQL> SELECT CUSTOMER_NUMBER, LAST, FIRST, BALANCE
  2  FROM CUSTOMER
  3  ORDER BY BALANCE;

CUS LAST        FIRST     BALANCE
--- ---------- --------- ----------
256 Samuels     Ann           21.5
522 Nelson      Mary         98.75
587 Galvez      Mara         114.6
567 Dinh        Tran         402.4
405 Williams    Al          402.75
315 Daniels     Tom         770.75
124 Adams       Sally       818.75
311 Charles     Don         825.75
622 Martin      Dan        1045.75
412 Adams       Sally       1817.5

10 rows selected.

SQL>
```

Figure 3.16 SELECT command to order rows

Sorting with Multiple Keys in Descending Order

Sometimes you might need to sort data by more than one key, as shown in Example 15.

Example 15: List the customer number, last name, first name, and credit limit of every customer, ordered by credit limit in descending order and by last name within credit limit. The output should be sorted by credit limit in descending order. Sort the output by last name within each group of customers with the same credit limit.

This example involves two new ideas: sorting on multiple keys—CREDIT_LIMIT and LAST—and using descending order for one of the keys. If you are sorting on more than one field (such as sorting by LAST and then by CREDIT_LIMIT), the more important column (CREDIT_LIMIT) is called the **major key** (or the **primary sort key**) and the less important column (LAST) is called the **minor key** (or the **secondary sort key**). To sort on multiple keys, you list the keys in order of importance in the ORDER BY clause. To sort in descending order, you follow the name of the sort key with the DESC operator. The query is shown in Figure 3.17.

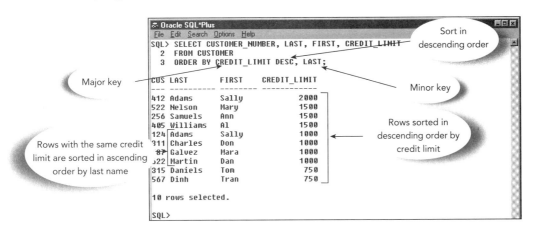

Figure 3.17 SELECT command with multiple sort keys

USING FUNCTIONS

SQL has functions to calculate sums, averages, counts, maximum values, and minimum values. These functions and their descriptions are shown in Table 3.3.

Table 3.3 SQL Functions

FUNCTION	DESCRIPTION
AVG	Calculates the average value in a data series
COUNT	Determines the number of rows in a data series
MAX	Determines the maximum value in a data series
MIN	Determines the minimum value in a data series
SUM	Calculates a total of the values

Use of the COUNT Function

The COUNT function, as you will see in Example 16, calculates a count of the number of rows in a table.

Example 16: How many parts are in item class HW?

For this query you need to determine the total number of rows in the PART table with the value HW in the ITEM_CLASS column. You could count the part numbers in such rows or the total number of part descriptions or the number of entries in any other column. It doesn't make any difference, because each count should provide the same answer. Rather than picking one column, most implementations of SQL allow you to use the asterisk (*) to represent any column. In this case, the query is shown in Figure 3.18.

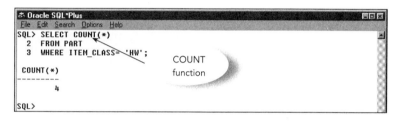

Figure 3.18 SELECT command to count rows

If your implementation of SQL does not allow the use of the asterisk, the query would be written as follows:

```
SELECT COUNT (PART_NUMBER)
FROM PART
WHERE ITEM_CLASS = 'HW';
```

Use of the SUM Function

If you want to calculate the total of all customers' balances, you can use the SUM function as illustrated in the next example.

Example 17: Find the number of customers and the total of their balances.

When you use SUM, you must specify the column to total, and the column data type must be numeric. (How could you calculate a sum of names or addresses?) The query is shown in Figure 3.19.

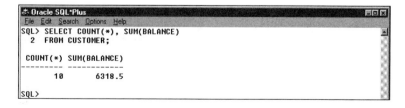

Figure 3.19 SELECT command to calculate a count and a sum

Using the AVG, MAX, and MIN functions is similar to using SUM, except a different statistic is calculated. Figure 3.20 shows the use of these three functions.

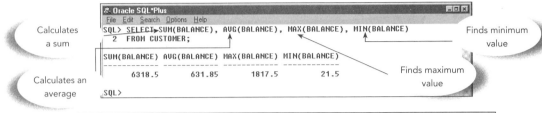

Calculates a sum

Calculates an average

Finds minimum value

Finds maximum value

Figure 3.20 SELECT command with several functions

Note	When you use SUM, AVG, MAX, or MIN, any null value in the column is ignored; that is, it is eliminated from the computation.

Note	Null values in numeric fields can cause strange results when statistics are computed. Suppose that the BALANCE column accepts null values, there are currently four customers with records in the CUSTOMER table, and their respective balances are $100, $200, $300, and null (unknown). When you calculate the average balance, most implementations will ignore the null value and obtain $200 (($100 + $200 + $300)/3). Similarly, if you calculate the total of the balances, the null value is ignored and you get a total of $600. If you count the number of customers in the table, however, the row containing the null is included; you get a result of 4. Thus the total of the balances ($600) divided by the number of customers (4) is not equal to the average balance ($200).

Use of DISTINCT

The DISTINCT operator is not a function. In some situations, however, this operator is useful when used in conjunction with the COUNT function. Before examining such a situation, you need to understand how to use the DISTINCT operator. Example 18 illustrates the most common use of DISTINCT.

Example 18:	Find the customer number of every customer who currently has an open order.

The command seems fairly simple. If a customer currently has an open order, there must be at least one row in the ORDERS table in which that customer's number appears. Thus you could use the query shown in Figure 3.21 to find the customer numbers with open orders. Note that customer numbers 124 and 522 each appear more than once in the output. The reason for this is that each customer currently has more than one open order in the ORDERS table and thus each customer number appears more than once. Suppose you want to list each customer only once, as in Example 19.

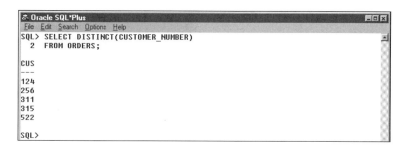

Figure 3.21 Results with repeated customer numbers

Example 19:   Find the customer number of every customer who currently has an open order.
List each customer only once.

To ensure uniqueness, you can use the DISTINCT operator as shown in Figure 3.22.

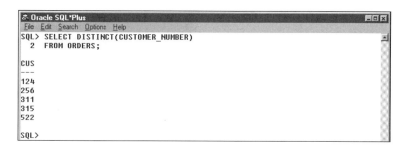

Figure 3.22 Results without repeated customer numbers

Now let's examine the relationship between COUNT and DISTINCT.

Example 20:   Count the number of customers who currently have open orders.

The query shown in Figure 3.23 shows the number of customers with records in the CUSTOMER_NUMBER column.

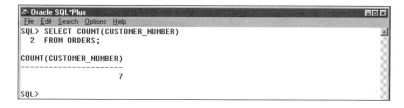

Figure 3.23 Count including repeated customer numbers

Question	What's wrong with the query results shown in Figure 3.23?
Answer	The answer, 7, is the result of counting the customers who have open orders multiple times—once for each separate order they currently have on file. The result counts each customer number, and does not eliminate redundant customer numbers to provide an accurate count of the number of customers.

To solve this problem, you can use the DISTINCT operator as shown in Figure 3.24.

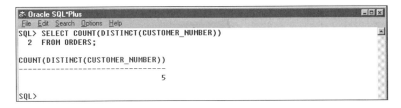

Figure 3.24 Count without repeated customer numbers

NESTING QUERIES

Sometimes obtaining the results you need is a two-step process (or more). This process is illustrated in the next two examples.

Subqueries

You can use subqueries to obtain query results in a single command by placing one query inside another. The inner query is called a **subquery** and it is evaluated first. Then the outer query can use the results of the subquery to find its results, as shown in Example 21.

Example 21:	What is the largest credit limit awarded to any customer of sales rep 06?

Use the MAX function as shown in Figure 3.25.

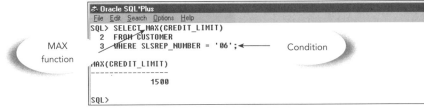

Figure 3.25 Selecting maximum credit limit

Example 22:	Display the customer number, last name, and first name of every customer in the Premiere Products database who has the credit limit found in Example 21.

You need to find all customers with this credit limit, not just customers of sales rep 06. After viewing the answer to the previous example (1500), you could use the command shown in Figure 3.26.

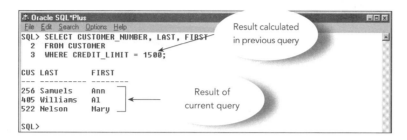

```
Oracle SQL*Plus
File  Edit  Search  Options  Help
SQL> SELECT CUSTOMER_NUMBER, LAST, FIRST        Result calculated
  2   FROM CUSTOMER                             in previous query
  3   WHERE CREDIT_LIMIT = 1500;

CUS LAST       FIRST

256 Samuels    Ann
405 Williams   Al       ◄──────  Result of
522 Nelson     Mary              current query

SQL>
```

Figure 3.26 Query using previous result

Example 23: Find the answer to Examples 21 and 22 in one step.

Now you need to achieve the same result as in the previous two examples, but in a single step. You can use a **subquery** to find the answer. The form for subqueries is shown in Figure 3.27. The portion in parentheses is the subquery. This subquery is evaluated first, producing a temporary table. The table is used strictly in evaluating the query and is not available to the user or displayed. This temporary table is deleted after the evaluation of the query is complete. In this case the temporary table has only a single column MAX(CREDIT_LIMIT), and a single row containing the number 1500.

```
Oracle SQL*Plus
File  Edit  Search  Options  Help
SQL> SELECT CUSTOMER_NUMBER, LAST, FIRST        IN operator
  2   FROM CUSTOMER
  3   WHERE CREDIT_LIMIT IN ◄
  4   (SELECT MAX(CREDIT_LIMIT)
  5   FROM CUSTOMER
  6   WHERE SLSREP_NUMBER = '06');
                                                 Subquery to find
CUS LAST       FIRST                             maximum credit limit
                                                 is evaluated first
256 Samuels    Ann
405 Williams   Al
522 Nelson     Mary

SQL>
```
Outer query uses results of subquery

Figure 3.27 Using IN and a subquery

The outer query is evaluated next. The outer query will retrieve the customer number, last name, and first name of every customer whose credit limit is in the temporary table result produced by the subquery. Because that table contains only the maximum credit limit for the customers of sales rep number 06, you obtain the desired list of customers. Incidentally, because the subquery in this case produces a table containing only a single value (the maximum credit limit), this query also could have been formulated as shown in Figure 3.28. In this command you are asking for those customers whose credit limit is *equal to* the one unique credit limit obtained by the subquery. In general, unless you know that the subquery *must* produce a single value, the prior command using IN is the correct one to use.

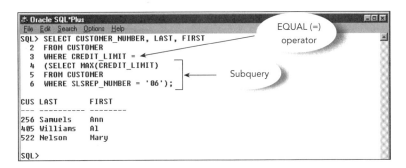

Figure 3.28 Query using EQUAL condition and a subquery

In Example 24, the subquery again produces a single value, but you use the > operator rather than the = operator in the condition.

Example 24: List the customer number, first name, last name, and balance for every customer whose balance is greater than the average balance.

In this case, you use a subquery to obtain the average balance. Because this subquery produces a single number, you can compare each customer's balance with this number as shown in Figure 3.29.

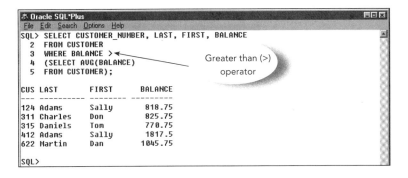

Figure 3.29 Query using greater than operator and a subquery

Note   SQL will not allow you to use the condition BALANCE > AVG(BALANCE) in the WHERE clause. You must use a subquery to obtain the average balance. Then you can use the results of the subquery in your condition as illustrated in the figure.

GROUPING

Grouping creates groups of rows that share some common characteristic. If customers are grouped by credit limit, for example, the first group would contain customers with a $750 credit limit, the second group would contain customers with a $1,000 credit limit, and so on. If order lines are grouped by order number, those order lines for order 12489 would form one group, those for order 12491 would form a second group, and so on.

When you group records, any calculations indicated in the SELECT command are performed for the entire group. For example, if customers are grouped by credit limit and the query requests the average balance, the results include the average balance for the group of customers with a $750 credit limit, the average balance for the group with a $1,000 credit limit, and so on. The following examples illustrate this process.

Using GROUP BY

The GROUP BY command allows you to group data in a particular order, and then calculate statistics if desired, as shown in Example 25.

Example 25:	List the total for each order.

To obtain the total for a particular order, first you multiply the number of units ordered by the quoted price for each order line in the order. Then you add these results. You repeat this process for each order. To do so, you cannot simply include SUM(NUMBER_ORDERED * QUOTED_PRICE) in the query. This expression would calculate the grand total for all order lines; the grand total would not be broken down by order. To calculate individual totals you can use the GROUP BY command. In this case, the command GROUP BY ORDER_NUMBER causes the order lines for each order to be grouped; that is, all order lines with the same order number form a group. Any statistics, such as totals, requested in the SELECT command are calculated for each group. It is important to note that the GROUP BY command does not sort the data in a particular order. You must use the ORDER BY command to sort data. Assuming that the report is to be ordered by order number, you can use the command shown in Figure 3.30.

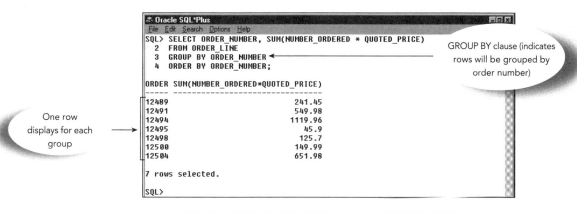

Figure 3.30 Grouping by a column

When rows are grouped, one line of output is produced for each group. The only data that can be displayed are statistics calculated for the group or columns whose values are the same for all rows in a group.

Question	Would it be appropriate to display the order number?
Answer	Yes, because the output is grouped by order number; the order number in one row in a group must be the same as the order number in any other row in the group.

Question	Would it be appropriate to display a part number?
Answer	No, because the part number varies from one row in a group to another. (The same order can contain many parts.) Thus, SQL would not be able to determine which part number to display for the group. The system displays an error message if you attempt to display a part number.

SAME AS
WHERE

Using HAVING

The HAVING command is used for groups, as shown in Example 26.

Example 26:	List the total for those orders over $200.

This example is like the previous one; the only difference is the restriction to display totals for orders that are greater than $200. This restriction does not apply to individual rows but rather to *groups*. Because the WHERE command applies only to rows, it is not the appropriate command to accomplish the kind of selection that is required. Fortunately, the HAVING clause does for groups what the WHERE does for rows. In Figure 3.31, the row created for a group will display only if the sum calculated for the group is larger than $200; additionally all groups will be ordered by order number.

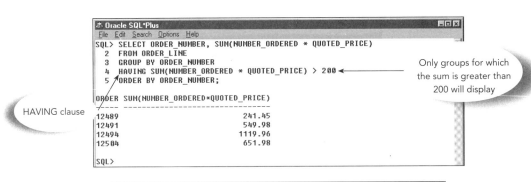

Figure 3.31 Query using a HAVING clause

HAVING vs. WHERE

Just as the WHERE clause can be used to limit the *rows* that are included in the result of a SQL command, the HAVING clause can be used to limit the *groups* that are included. The following examples illustrate the difference between these two clauses.

Example 27:	List each credit limit and the number of customers having each limit.

In order to count the number of customers who have a given credit limit, the data must by grouped by credit limit. The command is shown in Figure 3.32.

```
Oracle SQL*Plus                                              _ □ ×
File  Edit  Search  Options  Help
SQL> SELECT CREDIT_LIMIT, COUNT(*)
  2   FROM CUSTOMER
  3   GROUP BY CREDIT_LIMIT;

CREDIT_LIMIT  COUNT(*)
------------  --------
         750         2
        1000         4
        1500         3
        2000         1

SQL>
```

Figure 3.32 Counting the rows in a group

Example 28: Repeat Example 27, but list only those credit limits held by more than one customer.

Because this condition involves a group total, a HAVING clause is used as shown in Figure 3.33.

```
Oracle SQL*Plus                                              _ □ ×
File  Edit  Search  Options  Help
SQL> SELECT CREDIT_LIMIT, COUNT(*)
  2   FROM CUSTOMER
  3   GROUP BY CREDIT_LIMIT
  4   HAVING COUNT(*) > 1;

CREDIT_LIMIT  COUNT(*)
------------  --------
         750         2
        1000         4
        1500         3

SQL>
```

Figure 3.33 Displaying groups that contain more than one row

Example 29: List each credit limit and the total number of customers of sales rep 03 who have this limit.

The condition involves only rows, so the WHERE clause is appropriate as shown in Figure 3.34.

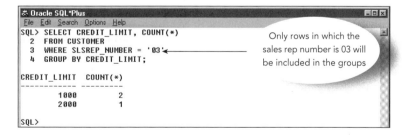

```
Oracle SQL*Plus                                              _ □ ×
File  Edit  Search  Options  Help
SQL> SELECT CREDIT_LIMIT, COUNT(*)              Only rows in which the
  2   FROM CUSTOMER                             sales rep number is 03 will
  3   WHERE SLSREP_NUMBER = '03'                be included in the groups
  4   GROUP BY CREDIT_LIMIT;

CREDIT_LIMIT  COUNT(*)
------------  --------
        1000         2
        2000         1

SQL>
```

Figure 3.34 Restricting the rows to be grouped

Example 30: Repeat Example 29, but list only those credit limits held by more than one customer.

Because the conditions involve rows and groups, both a WHERE clause and a HAVING clause are required. The command is shown in Figure 3.35.

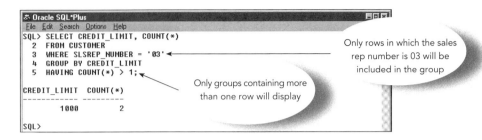

Figure 3.35 Restricting the rows and the groups

In Example 30, rows from the original table are considered only if the sales rep number is 03. These rows are then grouped by credit limit and the count is calculated. Only groups for which the calculated count is greater than 1 are displayed.

NULLS

Sometimes a condition involves a column that can be null, as illustrated in Example 31.

Example 31:   List the customer number, last name, and first name of every customer whose street value is null (unknown).

You might expect the condition to be something like STREET = NULL. The correct format is actually STREET IS NULL. (To select a customer whose street is not null, you use the condition STREET IS NOT NULL.) The command is shown in Figure 3.36. In the current Premiere Products database, no customer has a null street value; therefore no rows are retrieved in the query results.

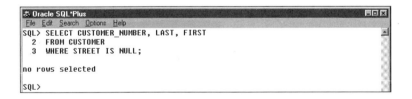

Figure 3.36 Selecting rows containing null values

In this chapter you learned how to create queries to retrieve data from a single table by constructing an appropriate SELECT command. In the next chapter you will learn how to create queries that involve multiple tables. The queries you created in this chapter used the clauses and operators shown in Table 3.4.

Table 3.4 SQL query clauses and operators

CLAUSE OR OPERATOR	DESCRIPTION
AND operator	All simple conditions must be true in order for the compound condition to be true
BETWEEN operator	Specifies a range of values in a condition
DESC operator	Sorts the query results in descending order based on the column name
DISTINCT operator	Ensures uniqueness in the condition by eliminating redundant values
FROM clause	Indicates the table from which to retrieve the specified columns
GROUP BY clause	Groups rows based on the specified column
HAVING clause	Limits a condition to the groups that are included
IN operator	Finds a value in a group of values specified in the condition
IS NOT NULL operator	Finds rows that do not contain a null value in the specified column
IS NULL operator	Finds rows that contain a null value in the specified column
LIKE operator	Indicates a pattern of characters to find in a condition
NOT operator	Reverses the truth or falsity of the original condition
OR operator	The compound condition is true whenever any of the simple conditions is true
ORDER BY clause	Lists the query results in the specified order based on the column name
SELECT clause	Specifies the columns to retrieve in the query
WHERE clause	Specifies any conditions for the query

SUMMARY

1. The basic form of a SQL command is SELECT-FROM. Specify the columns to be listed after the word SELECT (or use * for all columns), then specify the table name that contains these columns after the word FROM. Optionally, you can include conditions after the word WHERE.

2. Simple conditions are written in the form: column name, comparison operator, column name or value. Simple conditions can involve any of the comparison operators =, >, >=, <, <=, or < > or != (not equal to).

3. Compound conditions are formed by combining simple conditions using the operators AND, OR, or NOT.

4. You can use the BETWEEN operator to indicate a range of values in a condition.

5. Computed columns can be used in SQL commands by using arithmetic operators and writing the computation in place of a column name.

6. To check for a value in a character column that is similar to a particular string of characters, use the LIKE clause. The % wildcard represents any collection of characters. The _ wildcard represents any single character.

7. To check whether a column contains one of a particular set of values, use the IN clause.

8. Use the ORDER BY clause to sort data. List sort keys in order of importance. To sort in descending order, follow the sort key with DESC.

9. SQL contains the functions COUNT, SUM, AVG, MAX, and MIN.

10. To avoid duplicates, either when listing or counting values, precede the column name with the DISTINCT operator.

11. When one SQL query is placed inside another, it is called a nested query. The inner query, called a subquery, is evaluated first.

12. Use the GROUP BY clause to group data.

13. Use the HAVING clause to restrict the output to certain groups.

14. Use the phrase IS NULL in the WHERE clause to find rows containing a null value in some column.

EXERCISES (PREMIERE PRODUCTS)

Use SQL and Figure 1.2 in Chapter 1 to complete the following exercises.

If you are using Oracle for these exercises and wish to print a copy of your commands and results, type SPOOL followed by the name of a file and then press the Enter key. All the commands from that point on are saved in the file that you named. For example, to save the commands and results to a file named CHAPTER3.SQL on the A: drive, the command is as follows:

SPOOL A:CHAPTER3.SQL

When you have finished, type SPOOL OFF, and then press the Enter key to stop saving commands to the file. Then start any program that opens *.txt files, open the file that you saved, and print it using the Print command on the File menu.

1. List the part number and part description for all parts.

2. List all rows and columns for the complete SALES_REP table.

3. Find the last name and first name for every customer who has a credit limit of at least $800.

4. Give the order number for every order placed by customer number 124 on 9/05/98.

5. List the customer number, last name, and first name for every customer represented by sales rep 03 or sales rep 12.

6. List the part number and part description for every part that is not in item class HW.

7. List the part number and part description for every part that has between 100 and 200 units on hand. Do this two ways.

8. Give the part number, part description, and on-hand value (units on hand * unit price) for each part in item class AP. (On-hand value is really units on hand * cost, but we do not have a cost column in the PART table.)

9. List the part number, part description, and on-hand value for each part whose on-hand value is at least 1,000.

10. List the part number and part description for every part whose item class is HW or SG. Use the IN operator in your command.

11. Find the customer number, last name, and first name for every customer whose first name begins with the letter "D."

12. List all details about all parts. Order the output by part description.

13. List all details about all parts. Order the output by part number within item class.

14. Find out how many customers have a balance that is less than their credit limit.

15. Find the total of the balances for all customers represented by sales rep 12 and having a balance that is less than their credit limit.

16. List the part number, part description, and units on hand of all parts whose number of units on hand is more than average.

17. What is the command to determine the least expensive part in the database?

18. What is the command to determine the most expensive part in the database?

19. What is the command to determine how many customers are in the database?

20. List the sum of the balances for all customers for every sales rep. Order and group the results using the sales rep number.

21. List the item class and the sum of the value of parts on hand. Group the results by item class.

22. Find any parts with an unknown part description.

EXERCISES (HENRY BOOKS)

Use SQL and Figures 1.4 through 1.6 in Chapter 1 to complete the following exercises.

1. List the book code and book title for every book.

2. List the complete PUBLISHER table.

3. List the name of every publisher located in New York state.

4. List the name of every publisher not located in New York state.

5. List the name of every branch that has at least 10 employees.

6. List the code and title of every book whose type is HOR.

7. List the code and title of every book whose type is HOR and that is paperback.

8. List the code and title of every book whose type is HOR or whose publisher code is PB.

9. List the code, title, and price for each book with a price that is greater than $10 but less than $20.

10. List the book code and title of every book whose type is MYS and whose price is less than $20.

11. Customers who are part of a special program get a 15 percent discount on regular book prices. To determine the discounted prices, list the book code, title, and discounted price of every book. (Your calculated field should determine 85 percent of the current price; that is, 100 percent less a 15 percent discount.)

12. Find the name of every publisher containing the word "and."

13. List the book code and title of every book whose type is FIC, MYS, or ART. Use the IN operator in your command.

14. Repeat Exercise 13 and list the books in alphabetical order by title.

15. Repeat Exercise 13 and list the books in descending order by book code.

16. List the last and first name of every author. Order the output by last name.

17. Find out how many book types are available. (Do not include duplicates.)

18. Find out how many books are of type MYS.

19. Calculate the average price for each type of book.

20. Repeat Exercise 19, but consider only paperback books.

21. What is the command to determine the name of the most expensive book?

22. What is the command to determine how many employees Henry has?

23. What is the command to determine the branch name that employs the least people?

24. What is the command to determine the title of the most expensive book published by Pocket Books?

CHAPTER 4

Multiple-Table Queries

OBJECTIVES

- Retrieve data from more than one table by joining tables
- Use the IN and EXISTS operators to query multiple tables
- Use a subquery within a subquery
- Use an alias
- Join a table to itself
- Perform set operations (union, intersection, and difference)
- Use the ALL and ANY operators in a query

INTRODUCTION

In this chapter you will learn how to retrieve data from two or more tables using one SQL statement. You will see how tables can be joined together and how similar results are obtained using the IN and EXISTS operators. Then you will use aliases to simplify queries and join a table to itself. You also will see how the set operations of union, intersection, and difference can be implemented using SQL commands. Finally, you will examine two other SQL operators: ALL and ANY.

■　■　■　■　■

QUERYING MULTIPLE TABLES

In Chapter 3 you learned how to retrieve data from a single table. Sometimes, however, you might need to retrieve data from two or more tables. To do this, you must join the tables. Then you formulate a query using the same commands that you use for single tables.

Joining Two Tables

One common way to retrieve data from more than one table is to **join** the tables together by finding rows in the two tables that have identical values in matching columns. You can join tables by using the appropriate conditions in the WHERE clause, as you will see in Example 1.

Example 1:	List the customer number, last name, and first name for every customer together with the sales rep number, last name, and first name for the sales rep who represents each customer.

Because the customers' numbers and names are in the CUSTOMER table and the sales reps' numbers and names are in the SALES_REP table, you need to join the tables in the same SQL command so you can retrieve data from each table. To join tables you must:

1. Indicate in the SELECT clause all columns to display.

2. List in the FROM clause all tables involved in the query.

3. Give condition(s) in the WHERE clause to restrict the data to be retrieved. Indicate that the conditions affect only those rows from the two tables that match (rows that have common values in matching columns).

There can be a problem, however, when matching columns. The matching columns in this example are both named SLSREP_NUMBER: there is a column in the SALES_REP table named SLSREP_NUMBER, and a column in the CUSTOMER table that also is named SLSREP_NUMBER. If you reference the SLSREP_NUMBER column, it is not clear which table the column is from. In this case it is necessary to **qualify** the SLSREP_NUMBER column by specifying which column you are referencing. You can do this by separating the table name and the column name with a period. The SLSREP_NUMBER column in the SALES_REP table is written as SALES_REP.SLSREP_NUMBER, and the SLSREP_NUMBER column in the CUSTOMER table is written as CUSTOMER.SLSREP_NUMBER. The query format and results are shown in Figure 4.1. Notice that because both the SALES_REP and the CUSTOMER tables contain columns named LAST and FIRST, you must qualify these column names as well.

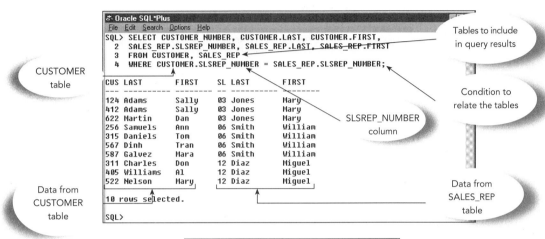

Figure 4.1 Joining tables

Question	In the first row of output in Figure 4.1, the customer number is 124, the last name is Adams, and the first name is Sally. These values represent the first row of the CUSTOMER table. Why is the sales rep number 03, the last name of the sales rep Jones, and the first name Mary?
Answer	In the CUSTOMER table, the sales rep number for customer number 124 is 03. (This indicates that customer number 124 is *related* to sales rep 03.) In the SALES_REP table, the last name of sales rep number 03 is Jones and the first name is Mary.

Whenever there is potential ambiguity among column names, you *must* qualify the columns involved in the query. It is permissible to qualify other columns as well, even if there is no possibility of confusion. Some people prefer to qualify all column names; in this text, however, we will qualify column names only when it is necessary to avoid confusion.

Example 2: List the customer number, last name, and first name of every customer whose credit limit is $1,000 together with the sales rep number, last name, and first name of the sales rep who represents each customer.

In Example 1, the condition in the WHERE clause was used only to relate a customer with a sales rep and join the tables. Whereas relating a customer to a sales rep is essential in this example as well, you also need to restrict the output to rows for those customers having a credit limit of $1,000. You can do this by using a compound condition, as shown in Figure 4.2.

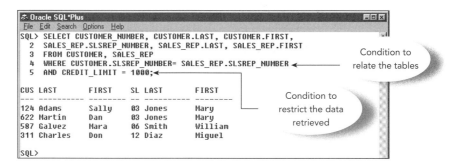

Figure 4.2 Restricting the rows in a join

Example 3:   For every part on order, list the order number, part number, part description, number of units ordered, quoted price, and the unit price.

A part is considered to be on order if there is a row in the ORDER_LINE table in which the part appears. You can find the order number, number of units ordered, and the quoted price in the ORDER_LINE table. To find the part description and the unit price, however, you need to look in the PART table. Then you need to find rows in the ORDER_LINE table and rows in the PART table that match (rows containing the same part number). The query format and results are shown in Figure 4.3.

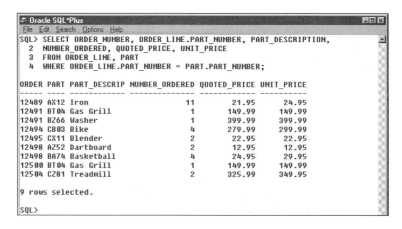

Figure 4.3 Joining the ORDER_LINE and PART tables

Question	Can PART.PART_NUMBER be used in place of ORDER_LINE.PART_NUMBER in the SELECT clause?
Answer	Yes, because the values for these two columns must match to satisfy the condition ORDER_LINE.PART_NUMBER = PART.PART_NUMBER.

Comparison of JOIN, IN, and EXISTS

You join tables in SQL by including a condition in the WHERE clause to ensure that matching columns have equal values in them for example, ORDER_LINE.PART_NUMBER = PART.PART_NUMBER.
You can obtain similar results by using either the IN operator (used in Chapter 3) or the EXISTS operator with a subquery. The choice is a matter of personal preference because either approach obtains the same results. The following examples illustrate the use of each operator.

Example 4:	Find the description for every part included in order number 12491.

Because this query also involves retrieving data from the ORDER_LINE and PART tables as illustrated in Example 3, you could approach it in a similar fashion. There are two basic differences, however, between Example 3 and Example 4. First, this query does not require as many columns; and second, it involves only order number 12491. The fact that there are fewer columns means there will be fewer attributes listed in the SELECT clause. Restricting the query to a single order is accomplished by adding the condition ORDER_NUMBER = '12491' to the WHERE clause. The query format and results are shown in Figure 4.4.

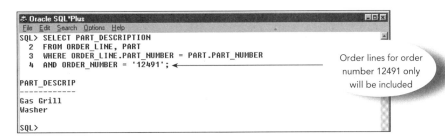

Figure 4.4 Restricting rows when joining the ORDER_LINE and PART tables

Notice that the ORDER_LINE table is listed in the FROM clause even though you don't need to display any columns from the ORDER_LINE table. The WHERE clause contains columns from the ORDER_LINE table, so it is necessary to include the table name in the FROM clause.

Using IN

Another way to join tables in a query is to use the IN operator with a subquery. In Example 4, you can use a subquery first to find all part numbers in the ORDER_LINE table that appear in any row in which the order number is 12491. Then you can find the part description for any part whose number is in this list. The query format and results are shown in Figure 4.5.

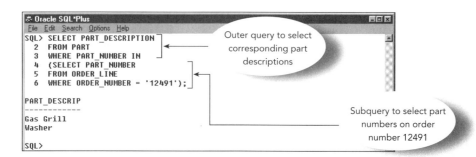

Figure 4.5 Using IN instead of a join to query two tables

Here, evaluating the subquery produces a temporary table consisting of those part numbers (BT04 and BZ66) that are present in order number 12491. Executing the remaining portion of the query produces part descriptions for each part whose number is in this temporary table; in this case, gas grill (BT04) and washer (BZ66).

Using EXISTS

You also can use the EXISTS operator to retrieve data from more than one table, as shown in Example 5.

Example 5:   Find the order number and order date for every order that contains part number BT04.

This query is similar to the one in Example 4 but this time the query involves the ORDERS table and not the PART table. Here the query can be handled in either of the ways just demonstrated. Using the formulation involving IN produces the command shown in Figure 4.6.

```
Oracle SQL*Plus
File  Edit  Search  Options  Help
SQL> SELECT ORDER_NUMBER, ORDER_DATE
  2  FROM ORDERS
  3  WHERE ORDER_NUMBER IN
  4  (SELECT ORDER_NUMBER
  5  FROM ORDER_LINE
  6  WHERE PART_NUMBER = 'BT04');

ORDER ORDER_DAT
----- ---------
12491 02-SEP-98
12500 05-SEP-98

SQL>
```

Figure 4.6 Using IN to select order information

Using the EXISTS operator provides another approach to the problem, as shown in Figure 4.7.

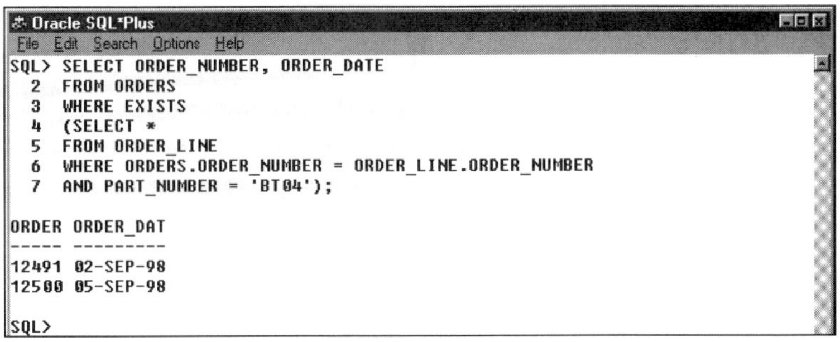

```
Oracle SQL*Plus
File  Edit  Search  Options  Help
SQL> SELECT ORDER_NUMBER, ORDER_DATE
  2  FROM ORDERS
  3  WHERE EXISTS
  4  (SELECT *
  5  FROM ORDER_LINE
  6  WHERE ORDERS.ORDER_NUMBER = ORDER_LINE.ORDER_NUMBER
  7  AND PART_NUMBER = 'BT04');

ORDER ORDER_DAT
----- ---------
12491 02-SEP-98
12500 05-SEP-98

SQL>
```

Figure 4.7 Using EXISTS to select order information

The subquery in Figure 4.7 is the first you have seen that involves a table mentioned in the outer query; the subquery is called a **correlated subquery**. In this case, the ORDERS table, which is listed in the FROM clause of the outer query, is used in the subquery (ORDERS.ORDER_NUMBER). For this reason you need to qualify the ORDER_NUMBER column in the subquery. You did not need to qualify the columns in the previous queries involving IN.

This query works as follows. For each row in the ORDERS table, the subquery is executed using the value of ORDERS.ORDER_NUMBER that occurs in that row. The inner query produces a list of all rows in the ORDER_LINE table in which ORDER_LINE.ORDER_NUMBER matches this value and in which the PART_NUMBER is equal to BT04. You can use the EXISTS operator in front of a subquery to create a condition that is true if one or more rows are obtained when the subquery is executed; otherwise, the condition is false.

To illustrate the process, consider order numbers 12491 and 12494 in the ORDERS table. Order number 12491 is included because a row exists in the ORDER_LINE table with this order number and part number BT04. When the subquery executes, there will be at least one row in the results, which, in turn, makes the EXISTS condition true. Order number 12494, however, will not be included because no row exists in the ORDER_LINE table with this order number and part number BT04. There will be no rows contained in the results of the subquery, which, in turn, makes the EXISTS condition false.

Using a Subquery within a Subquery

You can use a **nested query**, or a subquery within a subquery, to find data using one SQL statement.

Example 6: Find the order number and order date for every order that includes a part located in warehouse number 3.

One way to approach this problem is first to determine the list of part numbers in the PART table for every part located in warehouse number 3. Then you obtain a list of order numbers in the ORDER_LINE table with a corresponding part number in the part number list. Finally, you retrieve those order numbers and order dates in the ORDERS table for which the order number is in the list of order numbers obtained during the second step. The query format and results are shown in Figure 4.8.

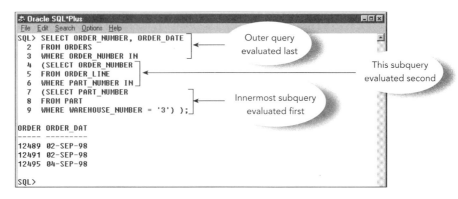

As you would expect, the queries are evaluated from the innermost query to the outermost query. The query in this example is evaluated in three steps:

1. The innermost query is evaluated first, producing a temporary table of part numbers for those parts located in warehouse number 3.

2. The next subquery is evaluated, producing a second temporary table with a list of order numbers. Each order number in this collection has a row in the ORDER_LINE table for which the part number is in the temporary table produced in Step 1.

3. The outer query is evaluated last, producing the desired list of order numbers and order dates. Only those orders whose numbers are in the temporary table produced in Step 2 are included in the result.

An alternative formulation involves joining the ORDERS, ORDER_LINE, and PART tables. The query format and results are shown in Figure 4.9.

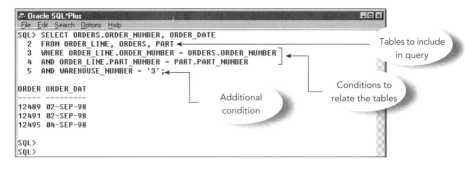

Figure 4.9 Joining three tables

In this formulation, the conditions ORDER_LINE.ORDER_NUMBER = ORDERS.ORDER_NUMBER and ORDER_LINE.PART_NUMBER = PART.PART_NUMBER join the tables. The condition WAREHOUSE_NUMBER = 3 restricts the output to only those parts located in warehouse number 3.

The query results are correct regardless of which formulation is used. You can use whichever approach you prefer.

You might wonder whether one approach is more efficient than the other. Good mainframe systems have built-in optimizers that analyze queries to determine the best way to satisfy them. Given a good optimizer, it should not make any difference how you formulate the query. If you are using a system without such an optimizer, the formulation of a query *can* make a difference in the speed with which the query is executed. If you are working with very large databases and efficiency is a prime concern, you can consult your system's manual or try some timings yourself. Try running the same query both ways to see if you notice a difference in the speed of execution. In small databases, there should not be a significant time difference between the two approaches.

A Comprehensive Example

The following query involves several of the features already discussed. It illustrates all the major clauses that you can use in the SELECT command. It also illustrates the order in which these clauses must appear.

Example 7: List the customer number, order number, order date, and order total for every order with a total of over $100.

The query format and results are shown in Figure 4.10.

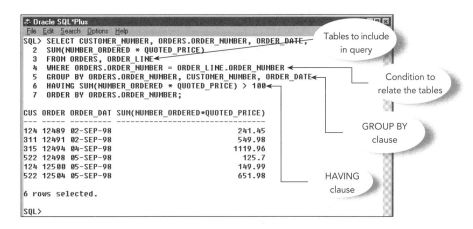

Figure 4.10 Comprehensive example

In this example, the ORDERS and ORDER_LINE tables are joined by listing both tables in the FROM clause and relating them in the WHERE clause. Selected data is sorted by ORDER_NUMBER, using the ORDER BY clause. The GROUP BY clause indicates that the data is to be grouped by order number, customer number, and order date. For each group, the SELECT statement indicates that the customer number, order number, order date, and order total (SUM(NUMBER_ORDERED * QUOTED_PRICE)) will display. Not all groups will display, however. The HAVING clause indicates that only those groups will display whose SUM(NUMBER_ORDERED * QUOTED_PRICE) is greater than 100.

Note that for each order, the order number, customer number, and order date are the same. Thus, it would seem that merely grouping by order number would be sufficient. Most implementations of SQL, including Oracle, still require that both customer number and order date be listed in the GROUP BY clause. Recall that the SELECT statement can include statistics calculated for only the groups or columns whose values are known to be the same for each row in a group. By stating that the data is to be grouped by order number, customer number, and order date, you tell the system that the values in these columns must be the same for each row in a group. A more sophisticated implementation would realize that given the structure of this database, grouping by order number alone is sufficient to ensure the uniqueness of both customer number and order date.

USING AN ALIAS

When tables are listed in the FROM clause, you can give each table an **alias,** or an alternate name, that you can use in the rest of the statement. You do this by typing the name of the table, pressing the Spacebar, and then typing the name of the alias. No commas or periods separate the two names.

You use an alias for two basic reasons. The first use is for simplicity. In Example 8, you will assign the SALES_REP table the alias S and the CUSTOMER table the alias C. By doing this, you can type "S" instead of SALES_REP and "C" instead of CUSTOMER in the remainder of the query. The query in this example is relatively simple, so you might not see the full benefit of this feature. If the query is complex and requires you to qualify the names, this feature can simplify the process greatly.

Example 8:   List the sales rep number, last name, and first name for every sales rep together with the customer number, last name, and first name for each customer the sales rep represents.

The query format and results using aliases are shown in Figure 4.11.

Alias for SALES_REP table

Alias for CUSTOMER table

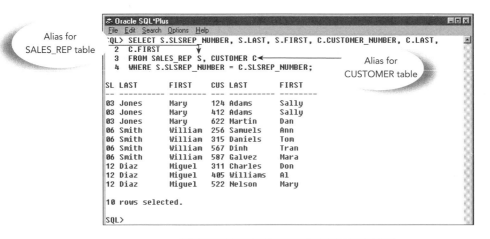

Figure 4.11 Using aliases

In addition to their role in simplifying queries, aliases are essential in certain situations, as illustrated in Example 9.

MORE COMPLEX JOINS

The joins you have seen so far have been simple. Sometimes, however, you need to join a table to itself, or join more than one table in a query.

Joining a Table to Itself

Sometimes it is necessary to join a table to itself, as illustrated in Example 9.

| Example 9: | Find every pair of customers who have the same first and last name. |

If you had two separate tables for customers and the query requested customers in the first table having the same name as customers in the second table, you could use a regular join operation to find the answer. Here, however, there is only one table, CUSTOMER, that stores all the customer names. You actually can treat the CUSTOMER table as two tables in the query by creating an alias as illustrated in Example 8. The FROM clause would be as follows:

FROM CUSTOMER F, CUSTOMER S

SQL treats this clause as a query of two tables: one that has the alias F, and another that has the alias S. The fact that both tables are really the single CUSTOMER table is not a problem. The query format and results are shown in Figure 4.12.

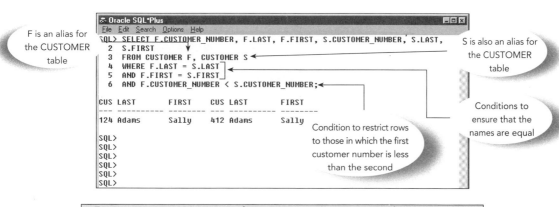

F is an alias for the CUSTOMER table

S is also an alias for the CUSTOMER table

Condition to restrict rows to those in which the first customer number is less than the second

Conditions to ensure that the names are equal

Figure 4.12 Using aliases to join a table to itself

You are requesting a customer number, last name, and first name from the F table, followed by a customer number, last name, and first name from the S table. The query is subject to three conditions: the last names must match, the first names must match, and the customer number from the first table must be less than the customer number from the second table.

| Question | Why is the condition F.CUSTOMER_NUMBER <S.CUSTOMER_NUMBER important in the query formulation? |
| Answer | If you did not include this condition, the query result would be as shown in Figure 4.13. The first row is included because it is true that customer number 124 (Sally Adams) has the same name as customer number 124 (Sally Adams). |

Answer (cont)

The second row indicates that customer number 124 (Sally Adams) has the same name as customer number 412 (Sally Adams). This important information should be included. The next row, however, repeats the same information because customer number 412 (Sally Adams) has the same name as customer number 124 (Sally Adams). Of these three rows, the only row that should be included in the query results is the second row. The second row also is the only one of the three rows in which the first customer number (124) is less than the second customer number (412). This is why the actual query includes the condition F.CUSTOMER_NUMBER < S.CUSTOMER_NUMBER.

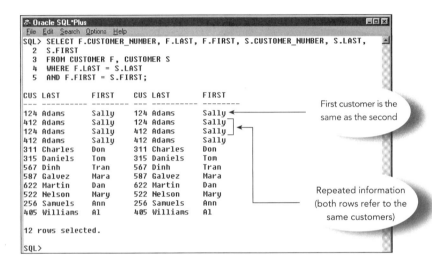

Figure 4.13 Incorrect joining of a table to itself

Joining Four Tables

It is possible to join several tables as illustrated in Example 10. For each pair of tables you join, you include a condition indicating how the columns are related.

Example 10: For every part on order, list the part number, number ordered, order number, order date, the customer number, last name, and first name of the customer who placed the order, and the last name and first name of the sales rep who represents each customer.

A part is on order if it occurs in any row in the ORDER_LINE table. The part number, number ordered, and order number are all found in the ORDER_LINE table. If these requirements were the only requirements of the query, the formulation would be as follows:

```
SELECT PART_NUMBER, NUMBER_ORDERED, ORDER_NUMBER
FROM ORDER_LINE
```

This formulation is not sufficient, however. You also need the order date and customer number, which are in the ORDERS table; the customer last name and first name, which are in the CUSTOMER table; and the sales rep last name and first name, which are in the SALES_REP table. Thus, you need to join *four* tables: ORDER_LINE, ORDERS, CUSTOMER, and SALES_REP. The procedure for doing this is essentially the same as the one for joining two tables. The difference is that the condition in the WHERE clause will be a compound condition. The WHERE clause in this case is written as follows:

WHERE ORDERS.ORDER_NUMBER = ORDER_LINE.ORDER_NUMBER
AND CUSTOMER.CUSTOMER_NUMBER = ORDERS.CUSTOMER_NUMBER
AND SALES_REP.SLSREP_NUMBER = CUSTOMER.SLSREP_NUMBER

The first condition relates an order line to an order with a matching order number. The second condition relates the order to the customer with a matching customer number. The final condition relates the customer to a sales rep based on a matching sales rep number.

For the complete query, you list all the desired columns in the SELECT clause and qualify any names that appear in more than one table. In the FROM clause, you list all four tables that are involved in the query. The query format and results are shown in Figure 4.14.

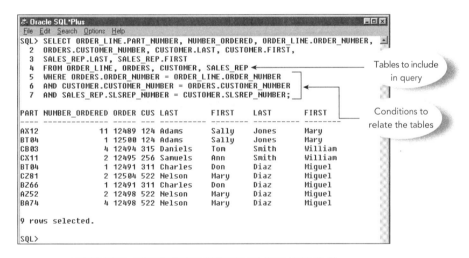

Figure 4.14 Joining four tables

Question	Is it necessary to qualify the PART_NUMBER column, which also appears as a column in the PART table?
Answer	No, if the PART table were used as one of the tables in the query, you would have to qualify PART_NUMBER; because this is not the case, the qualification is unnecessary. Among the tables listed in the query, only one column is labeled PART_NUMBER.

Certainly this last query is more involved than many of the previous ones. You might think that SQL is not such an easy language to use after all. If you take it one step at a time, however, the query in Example 10 really isn't that difficult. To construct a detailed query in a step-by-step fashion, do the following:

1. List in the SELECT clause all the columns that you want to display. If the name of any column appears in more than one table, precede the column name with the table name (that is, qualify the column name).

2. List in the FROM clause all the table names involved in the query. Usually you include the table names that contain the columns listed in the SELECT clause. Occasionally, however, there might be a table that does not contain any columns used in the SELECT clause but does contain columns used in the WHERE clause. In this case the table name also must be listed. For example, if you do not need to list a customer number or name, but you need to list the sales rep name, no columns from the CUSTOMER table would be listed in the SELECT clause. The CUSTOMER table is still required, however, because columns from it must be used in the WHERE clause.

3. Take one pair of tables at a time, and indicate in the WHERE clause the condition that relates the tables. Join these conditions with the AND operator. If there are any other conditions, include them in the WHERE clause and connect them to the others with the AND operator. For example, if you wanted parts present on orders placed by only those customers having a $1,000 credit limit, you would add one more condition to the WHERE clause as shown in Figure 4.15.

Figure 4.15 Restricting the rows when joining four tables

SET OPERATIONS

In SQL, you can use the normal set operations: union, intersection, and difference. The **union** of two tables is a table containing every row that is in either the first table or in the second table or both. The **intersection (intersect)** of two tables is a table containing every row that is in both tables. The **difference (minus)** of two tables is the set of every row that is in the first table but not in the second table.

For example, suppose that TEMP1 is a table containing the customer number, last name, and first name of every customer represented by sales rep 12. Further suppose that TEMP2 is a table containing the customer number, last name, and first name of those customers who currently have orders on file (see Figure 4.16a).

The union of TEMP1 and TEMP2 (TEMP1 UNION TEMP2) would consist of the customer number, last name, and first name of those customers who are represented by sales rep number 12 *or* who currently have orders on file *or* both. The intersection of these two tables (TEMP1 INTERSECT TEMP2) would contain those customers who are represented by sales rep number 12 *and* who have orders on file. The difference of these two tables (TEMP1 MINUS TEMP2) would contain those customers who are represented by sales rep number 12 but *who do not* have orders on file. The results of these set operations are shown in Figure 4.16b.

TEMP1

CUSTOMER_NUMBER	LAST	FIRST
311	Charles	Don
405	Williams	Al
522	Nelson	Mary

TEMP2

CUSTOMER_NUMBER	LAST	FIRST
124	Adams	Sally
256	Samuels	Ann
311	Charles	Don
315	Daniels	Tom
522	Nelson	Mary

Figure 4.16a Tables of customers of sales rep 12 (TEMP1) and customers who have orders (TEMP2)

TEMP1 UNION TEMP2

CUSTOMER_NUMBER	LAST	FIRST
124	Adams	Sally
256	Samuels	Ann
311	Charles	Don
315	Daniels	Tom
405	Williams	Al
522	Nelson	Mary

TEMP1 INTERSECT TEMP2

CUSTOMER_NUMBER	LAST	FIRST
311	Charles	Don
522	Nelson	Mary

TEMP1 MINUS TEMP2

CUSTOMER_NUMBER	LAST	FIRST
405	Williams	Al

Figure 4.16b Union, intersect, and minus of the TEMP1 and TEMP2 tables

There is an obvious restriction on the set operations. It does not make sense, for example, to talk about the union of the CUSTOMER table and the ORDERS table. What might rows in this union look like? The two tables in the union *must* have the same structure; that is, they must be union-compatible. Two tables are **union-compatible** if they have the same number of columns and if their corresponding columns have identical data types and lengths.

Note that the definition of union-compatible does not state that the columns of the two tables must be identical but rather that the columns must be of the same type. Thus, if one column is CHAR(20), the matching column also must be CHAR(20).

Example 11: List the customer number, last name, and first name for every customer who is either represented by sales rep number 12 or who currently has orders on file, or both.

You can create a table containing the customer number, last name, and first name for every customer who is represented by sales rep number 12. You do this by selecting the customer numbers and names from the CUSTOMER table for which the sales rep number is 12. Then you can create another table containing the customer number, last name, and first name for every customer who currently has orders on file. You do this by creating a join of the CUSTOMER table and the ORDERS table. The two tables created by this process have the same structure; that is, the following three columns: CUSTOMER_NUMBER, LAST, and FIRST. Because the tables are union-compatible, it is possible to take the union of these two tables. The union format and results are shown in Figure 4.17.

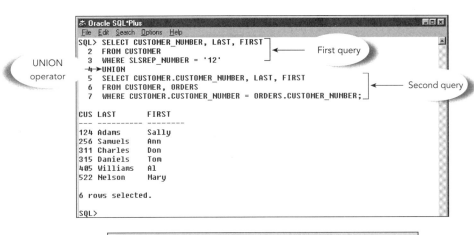

Figure 4.17 Using the UNION operator

If the SQL implementation truly supports the union operation, any duplicate rows will be removed automatically. For example, any customer who is represented by sales rep number 12 *and* who currently has orders on file will not be listed twice. Oracle correctly removes duplicates. Some implementations of SQL, however, support a union operation but do not remove such duplicates.

Example 12: List the customer number, last name, and first name for every customer who is either represented by sales rep number 12 or who currently has orders on file.

The only difference between this query and the one in Example 11 is that here the appropriate operation is INTERSECT. The query and its results are shown in Figure 4.18.

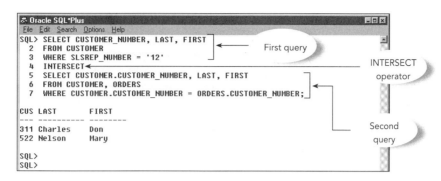

Figure 4.18 Using the INTERSECT operator

Example 13: List the customer number, last name, and first name for every customer who is either represented by sales rep number 12 or who does not have orders currently on file.

The only difference between this query and the ones in Examples 11 and 12 is that here the appropriate operation is MINUS. The query and its results are shown in Figure 4.19.

```
Oracle SQL*Plus
File  Edit  Search  Options  Help
SQL> SELECT CUSTOMER_NUMBER, LAST, FIRST
  2  FROM CUSTOMER                              First query
  3  WHERE SLSREP_NUMBER = '12'
  4  MINUS
  5  SELECT CUSTOMER.CUSTOMER_NUMBER, LAST, FIRST
  6  FROM CUSTOMER, ORDERS                       Second query
  7  WHERE CUSTOMER.CUSTOMER_NUMBER = ORDERS.CUSTOMER_NUMBER;

CUS LAST       FIRST
--- ---------- --------
405 Williams   Al

SQL>
SQL>
```
MINUS operator

Figure 4.19 Using the MINUS operator

ALL AND ANY

The ALL and ANY operators can be used with subqueries to produce a single column of numbers. If the subquery is preceded by the ALL operator, the condition is true only if it satisfies *all* values produced by the subquery. If the subquery is preceded by the ANY operator, the condition is true if it satisfies *any* value (one or more) produced by the subquery. The next examples illustrate the use of these operators.

Example 14: Find the customer number, last name, first name, current balance, and sales rep number for every customer whose balance is larger than the individual balances of every customer of sales rep 12.

Whereas this query can be satisfied by finding the maximum balance of the customers represented by sales rep number 12 in a subquery and then finding all customers whose balance is greater than this number, there is an alternative. You can use the ALL operator, as shown in Figure 4.20, to simplify the process.

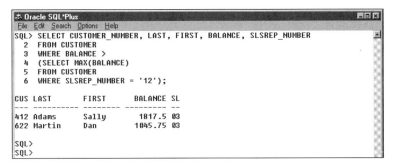

Figure 4.20 SELECT command with ALL condition

To some users, this formulation might seem more natural than finding the maximum balance in the subquery. For other users, the opposite might be true. You can employ whichever approach you prefer.

Question	How would you get the same result for Example 14 without using the ALL operator?
Answer	You could query for every customer whose balance is greater than the maximum balance of any customer of sales rep number 12, as shown in Figure 4.21.

Figure 4.21 Alternative to ALL condition

Example 15: Find the customer number, last name, first name, current balance, and sales rep number of every customer whose balance is larger than the balance of at least one customer of sales rep number 12.

This query can be satisfied by finding the minimum balance of the customers represented by sales rep number 12 in a subquery and then finding all customers whose balance is greater than this number. Again there is an alternative. You can use the ANY operator, as shown in Figure 4.22, to simplify the process.

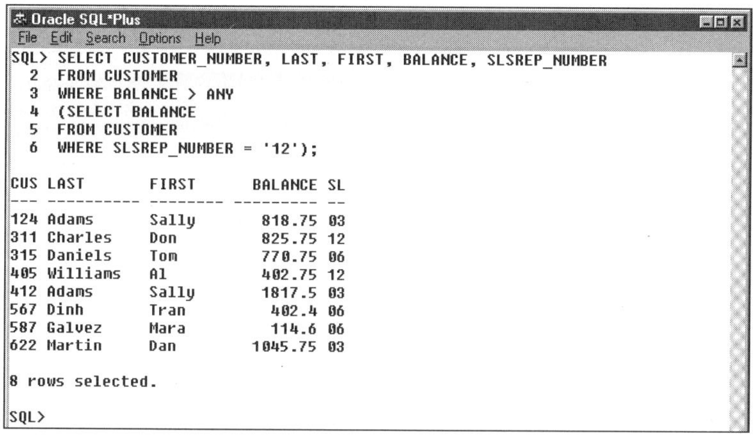

```
Oracle SQL*Plus                                                    _ □ ×
File  Edit  Search  Options  Help
SQL> SELECT CUSTOMER_NUMBER, LAST, FIRST, BALANCE, SLSREP_NUMBER
  2    FROM CUSTOMER
  3    WHERE BALANCE > ANY
  4    (SELECT BALANCE
  5    FROM CUSTOMER
  6    WHERE SLSREP_NUMBER = '12');

CUS LAST        FIRST      BALANCE SL
--- ---------- -------- --------- --
124 Adams       Sally      818.75 03
311 Charles     Don        825.75 12
315 Daniels     Tom        770.75 06
405 Williams    Al         402.75 12
412 Adams       Sally      1817.5 03
567 Dinh        Tran        402.4 06
587 Galvez      Mara        114.6 06
622 Martin      Dan       1045.75 03

8 rows selected.

SQL>
```

Figure 4.22 SELECT command with ANY condition

Question How would you get the same results without using the ALL operator?

Answer You could query for the customers whose balance is greater than the minimum balance of any customers of sales rep number 12, as shown in Figure 4.23.

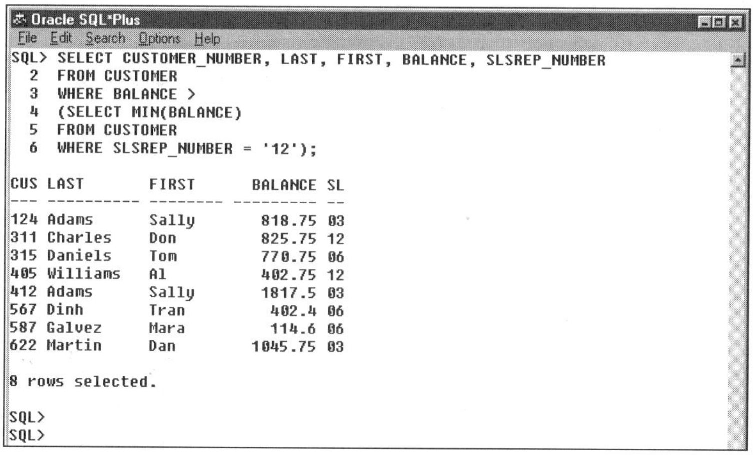

```
Oracle SQL*Plus                                                    _ □ ×
File  Edit  Search  Options  Help
SQL> SELECT CUSTOMER_NUMBER, LAST, FIRST, BALANCE, SLSREP_NUMBER
  2    FROM CUSTOMER
  3    WHERE BALANCE >
  4    (SELECT MIN(BALANCE)
  5    FROM CUSTOMER
  6    WHERE SLSREP_NUMBER = '12');

CUS LAST        FIRST      BALANCE SL
--- ---------- -------- --------- --
124 Adams       Sally      818.75 03
311 Charles     Don        825.75 12
315 Daniels     Tom        770.75 06
405 Williams    Al         402.75 12
412 Adams       Sally      1817.5 03
567 Dinh        Tran        402.4 06
587 Galvez      Mara        114.6 06
622 Martin      Dan       1045.75 03

8 rows selected.

SQL>
SQL>
```

Figure 4.23 Alternative to ANY condition

In this chapter you learned how to use SQL commands to join tables. You learned about situations in which it is necessary to qualify column names, and you saw how to do so. You learned to use subqueries to query multiple tables and to use the IN and EXISTS operators in the process. You learned how to use an alias and saw situations where using aliases is beneficial. You used the SQL set operations UNION, INTERSECT, and MINUS to find rows in one, two, or both tables. Finally, you used the ALL and ANY operators to simplify certain SQL queries. In the next chapter you will use SQL commands to update the data in your tables.

SUMMARY

1. To join tables together, indicate in the SELECT clause all columns to display, list in the FROM clause all tables to join, and then include in the WHERE clause any conditions requiring values in matching columns to be equal.

2. When referring to matching columns in different tables, you must qualify the column names to avoid confusion. You do this using the following format: table name.column name.

3. You can use the IN operator or the EXISTS command with an appropriate subquery as an alternative way of performing a join.

4. A subquery can contain another subquery. The innermost subquery is executed first.

5. The name of a table in a FROM clause can be followed by an alias, which is an alternate name for the table. The alias can be used in place of the table name throughout the SQL command.

6. By using two different aliases for the same table in a single SQL command, a table can be joined to itself.

7. The UNION command creates a union of two tables; that is, the collection of rows that are in either or both of the tables. The INTERSECT command creates the intersection of two tables; that is, the collection of rows that are in both tables. The MINUS command creates the difference of two tables; that is, the collection of rows that are in the first table but not in the second table. To perform any of these operations, the tables must be union-compatible.

8. Two tables are union-compatible if they have the same number of columns and if their corresponding columns have identical data types and lengths.

9. If a subquery is preceded by the ALL command, the condition is true only if it is satisfied by *all* values produced by the subquery.

10. If a subquery is preceded by the ANY command, the condition is true if it is satisfied by *any* value (one or more) produced by the subquery.

EXERCISES (PREMIERE PRODUCTS)

Use SQL to complete the following exercises.

If you are using Oracle for these exercises and wish to print a copy of your commands and results, type SPOOL followed by the name of a file and then press the Enter key. All the commands from that point on will be saved in the file that you named. For example, to save the commands and results to a file called CHAPTER4.SQL on drive A, the command is as follows:

SPOOL A:CHAPTER4.SQL

When you have finished entering and running your commands, type SPOOL OFF, and then press the Enter key to stop saving commands to the file. Then start any program that can open *.txt files, open the file that you saved, and print it using the Print command on the File menu.

1. For every order, list the order number and order date along with the customer number, last name, and first name of the customer who placed the order.

2. For every order placed on September 5, 1998, list the order number and order date along with the customer number, last name, and first name of the customer who placed the order.

3. For every order, list the order number, order date, part number, number of units ordered, and quoted price for each order line that makes up the order.

4. Use the IN operator to find the customer number, last name, and first name for every customer who placed an order on September 5, 1998.

5. Repeat Exercise 4, but this time use the EXISTS operator in your answer.

6. Find the customer number, last name, and first name for every customer who did not place an order on September 5, 1998.

7. For every order, list the order number, order date, part number, part description, and item class for each part that makes up the order.

8. Repeat Exercise 7, but this time order the rows by item class and then by order number.

9. Use a subquery to find the sales rep number, last name, and first name for every sales rep who represents at least one customer with a credit limit of $2000.

10. Repeat Exercise 9, but this time do not use a subquery.

11. Find the customer number, last name, and first name for every customer who currently has an order on file for an iron.

12. List the part number, part description, and item class for every pair of parts that are in the same item class and have the same warehouse number.

13. List the part description, part number, order number, and order date for every order placed by Mary Nelson that contains an order line for a treadmill.

14. List the part description, part number, order number, and order date for every order placed by Mary Nelson that does not contain an order line for a treadmill.

15. List the order number and order date for every order that was either placed by Mary Nelson or that contains an order line for an iron.

16. List the order number and order date for every order that was placed by Mary Nelson and that contains an order line for an iron.

17. List the order number and order date for every order that was placed by Mary Nelson and that does not contain an order line for an iron.

18. List the part number, part description, unit price, and item class for every part that has a unit price greater than the unit price of any part in item class HW. Use either the ALL or ANY operator in your query. (*Hint:* Be careful about which operator you use.)

19. If you used ALL in Exercise 18, repeat the exercise using ANY. If you used ANY, repeat the exercise using ALL. Then run the new command. What question does this command answer?

EXERCISES (HENRY BOOKS)

Use SQL to complete the following exercises.

1. For every book, list the book code, book title, publisher code, and publisher name.

2. For every book published by Signet, list the book title and book price.

3. List the book title and book code for every book published by Bantam Books that has a book price greater than $10.

4. List the book code, book title, and units on hand for every book in branch number 3.

5. List the book title for every book of type ART that is published by Best and Furrow.

6. Find the book title for every book written by author number 01. Use the IN operator in your formulation.

7. Repeat Exercise 6, but this time use the EXISTS operator in your formulation.

8. Find the book title and book code for every book located in branch number 2.

9. Find the publisher code and name for every pair of publishers that are located in the same city.

10. Find the units on hand, book title, and author's last name for every book in branch number 4.

11. Repeat Exercise 10, but this time list only paperback books.

12. Find the book code and title for every book whose price is over $5.00 or was published in New York.

13. Find the book code and title for every book whose price is over $5.00 and was published in New York state.

14. Find the book code and title for every book whose price is over $5.00 but was not published in New York.

15. Find the book title and publisher code for every book whose price is greater than the book price of any book of type CS.

16. Find the book title and publisher code for every book whose price is greater than at least one book of type HOR.

CHAPTER 5

Updating Data

OBJECTIVES

- Use the COMMIT and ROLLBACK commands to make permanent data updates or to cancel updates
- Change data using the UPDATE command
- Add new data using the INSERT command
- Delete data using the DELETE command
- Create a new table from an existing table
- Use nulls in UPDATE commands
- Alter the rows in an existing table
- Change the structure of a table

INTRODUCTION

In this chapter you will learn how to make changes to the data in a table. You will use the UPDATE command to change data in one or more rows in a table, use the INSERT command to add new rows, and use the DELETE command to delete rows. You also will create a new table from an existing table and use nulls in update operations. Finally, you will learn how to change the structure of a table in a variety of ways.

■   ■   ■   ■   ■

COMMIT AND ROLLBACK

When you update the data in a table, your updates are only temporary and can be cancelled at anytime during your current work session. Updates become permanent automatically when you exit from the DBMS. During your current work session, however, you can make permanent changes immediately by running the COMMIT command. To do this, execute the update and make sure it is correct and then type the COMMIT command, followed by a semicolon.

To cancel updates, use the ROLLBACK command. Any updates made since you ran the most recent COMMIT command will be reversed when you run the ROLLBACK command. If you have not run the COMMIT command, all updates made during the current session will be reversed. You should note that the ROLLBACK command reverses changes only to the data and not changes to the structure of a table, such as adding or deleting a column. For example, if you change the length of a character column, you cannot use the ROLLBACK command to return the column length to its original state.

CHANGING EXISTING DATA IN A TABLE

The data stored in your tables is subject to constant change. Prices change, addresses change, commission amounts change, and so on. To keep the data current, you must be able to make these changes to the data in your tables. You can use the UPDATE command to change rows in which a specific condition is true.

| Example 1: | Change the last name of customer number 256 in the Premiere Products database to Jones. |

Use the SQL UPDATE command to make changes to existing data in the table. The format for using the UPDATE command is UPDATE <table name> SET <column name> = <new value>. When necessary, include a WHERE clause to indicate the row(s) in which the change is to take place. The command shown in Figure 5.1 changes the last name of customer number 256 to Jones. You know that the data is updated when you see the confirmation message that one row is updated. The SELECT command that follows the UPDATE command is an optional part of the UPDATE. The SELECT command is included here to show the data in the table after the change has been made. In general, it is recommended that you use a SELECT command to display the data you changed so you can verify that the change was made as you intended.

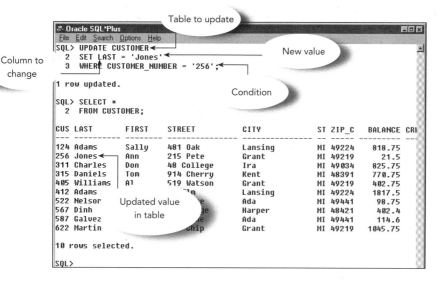

```
Oracle SQL*Plus                                          _ □ ×
File  Edit  Search  Options  Help
SQL> UPDATE CUSTOMER ◄
  2    SET LAST = 'Jones' ◄
  3    WHERE CUSTOMER_NUMBER = '256';

1 row updated.

SQL> SELECT *
  2  FROM CUSTOMER;

CUS LAST        FIRST    STREET       CITY         ST ZIP_C   BALANCE  CRI
--- ----------  -------  -----------  ----------   -- -----   -------- ---
124 Adams       Sally    481 Oak      Lansing      MI 49224    818.75
256 Jones ◄     Ann      215 Pete     Grant        MI 49219     21.5
311 Charles     Don      48 College   Ira          MI 49034    825.75
315 Daniels     Tom      914 Cherry   Kent         MI 48391    770.75
405 Williams    Al       519 Watson   Grant        MI 49219    402.75
412 Adams                             Lansing      MI 49224   1817.5
522 Nelson                            Ada          MI 49441     98.75
567 Dinh                              Harper       MI 48421    402.4
587 Galvez                            Ada          MI 49441    114.6
622 Martin                            Grant        MI 49219   1045.75

10 rows selected.

SQL>
```

Table to update

Column to
change

New value

Condition

Updated value
in table

Figure 5.1 Updating a table

If you determine that the update was done incorrectly, you can use the
ROLLBACK command to return the data to its original state. As shown in Figure 5.2,
the name of customer number 256 has been returned to its original value (Samuels).

```
Oracle SQL*Plus                                          _ □ ×
File  Edit  Search  Options  Help
SQL> ROLLBACK; ◄

Rollback complete.

SQL>
SQL>
SQL> SELECT *
  2  FROM CUSTOMER;

CUS LAST        FIRST    STREET       CITY         ST ZIP_C   BALANCE  CRI
--- ----------  -------  -----------  ----------   -- -----   -------- ---
124 Adams       Sally    481 Oak      Lansing      MI 49224    818.75
256 Samuels ◄   Ann      215 Pete     Grant        MI 49219     21.5
311 Charles     Don      48 College   Ira          MI 49034    825.75
315 Daniels     Tom      914 Cherry   Kent         MI 48391    770.75
405 Williams    Al       519 Watson   Grant        MI 49219    402.75
412 Adams       Sally    16 Elm       Lansing      MI 49224   1817.5
522 Nelson      Mary     108 Pine     Ada          MI 49441     98.75
567 Dinh        Tran     808 Ridge    Harper       MI 48421    402.4
587 Galvez      Mara     512 Pine     Ada          MI 49441    114.6
622 Martin      Dan      419 Chip     Grant        MI 49219   1045.75

10 rows selected.

SQL>
```

ROLLBACK
command

Change is
reversed

Figure 5.2 Using the ROLLBACK command

If, on the other hand, you verified that the updates you made are correct,
you can use the COMMIT command to make the update permanent. You do this by
typing the COMMIT command, followed by a semicolon, after running the update.
However, you should note that the COMMIT command is permanent; running the
ROLLBACK command cannot reverse the update.

Note	Normally you would use the ROLLBACK command only to correct a problem with an update. If you execute the commands in the body of this chapter, you should execute a rollback after each UPDATE, INSERT, or DELETE command so your data returns to its original state before you complete the exercises at the end of the chapter. You also will need to execute rollbacks when you complete the end of chapter exercises.

Example 2:	For each customer with a $1,000 credit limit whose balance does not exceed the credit limit, increase the credit limit to $1,200.

The only difference between this example and Example 1 is that this example uses a compound condition to identify the rows that will change. The UPDATE command and its results are shown in Figure 5.3.

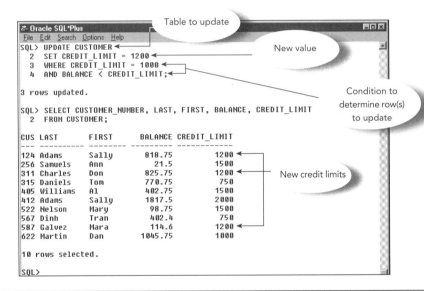

Figure 5.3 Using a compound condition to update a table

You also can use the previous value in a column in the update. For example, if you needed to increase the credit limit by 10% instead of changing it to a specific value, you can multiply the previous credit limit by 1.10. The SET clause to do this would be as follows:

SET CREDIT_LIMIT = CREDIT_LIMIT * 1.10

ADDING NEW ROWS TO AN EXISTING TABLE

In Chapter 2, you used the INSERT command to add data to the database. You also can use the INSERT command as a way of updating the data in a table.

Example 3:   Add sales rep number 14 to the SALES_REP table. Her name is Ann Crane, she lives at 123 River in Alpen, MI, and her ZIP code is 49114. Her commission rate is 5% (.05), but she has not yet earned any commission.

You can add new data using the INSERT command, as shown in Figure 5.4.

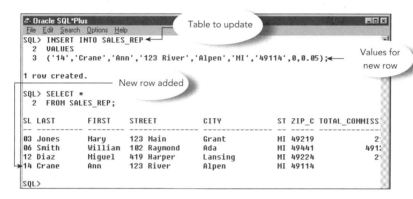

Figure 5.4 Inserting a row

DELETING EXISTING ROWS FROM A TABLE

When rows are no longer needed, you should remove them. For example, if Al Williams moved and is not a customer of Premiere Products any longer, you should remove his row from the CUSTOMER table.

Example 4:   Delete from the database the customer information for Al Williams.

To delete data from the database, use the DELETE command. The format for the DELETE command is DELETE <table name> WHERE <column name> = <value>. The command shown in Figure 5.5 deletes from the customer table any row with a value of "Williams" in the LAST column.

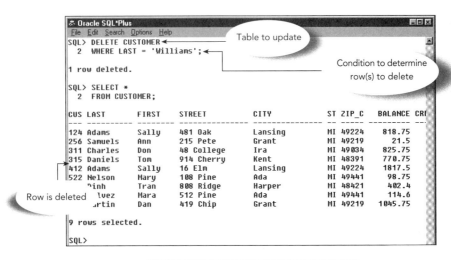

Figure 5.5 Deleting rows

Deleting rows can be dangerous. If there is more than one customer in the table whose last name is Williams, that customer also is deleted by the DELETE command. The safest way to delete data is to use a condition that involves the value in the primary key. Because the primary key value is a unique value by definition, you can be certain that you will not delete any other rows in the table accidentally.

Question	What happens if you run a DELETE command that does not contain a WHERE clause?
Answer	Without a condition to specify which row to delete, all rows would be deleted from the table.

CREATING A NEW TABLE FROM AN EXISTING TABLE

It is possible to create a new table by using some of the data in an existing table, as illustrated in the following two examples.

Example 5: Create a new table named SMALL_CUST containing the same columns as the CUSTOMER table, then insert in the new table only those rows for which the credit limit is $1,200 or less.

The first task is to describe the new table SMALL_CUST using the CREATE TABLE command as shown in Figure 5.6. Then you can use the INSERT command to add data to the table. Here, however, you can use a SELECT command to indicate which rows from the existing table (CUSTOMER) to insert into the new table. The INSERT command is shown in Figure 5.6.

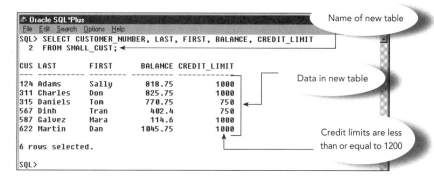

Figure 5.6 Creating a table from an existing table

The SELECT command shown in Figure 5.7 shows the resulting data in the SMALL_CUST table.

Figure 5.7 Results of table creation

Note	Recall Example 2 in which an UPDATE command was used to change certain credit limits to 1200. Those changes are not reflected in the data shown in Figure 5.7, because you executed a rollback after the update. If you are executing the updates in the body of the chapter, but you are not executing a rollback, your results will be different from those shown in Figure 5.7.

When you create a table from an existing table, you do not have to include the same columns as in the existing table. This is illustrated in the next example.

Example 6:   Create a new table named CUST_OF_03 containing the customer number, last name, first name, and balance of every customer assigned to sales rep number 03.

The CREATE TABLE command for this new table is shown in Figure 5.8. The INSERT command to add the data from the existing CUSTOMER table and the resulting data in the new table are shown in Figure 5.9.

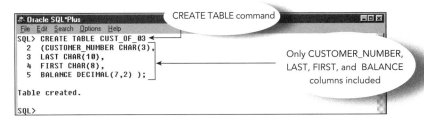

Figure 5.8 Creating a table that does not contain all the columns

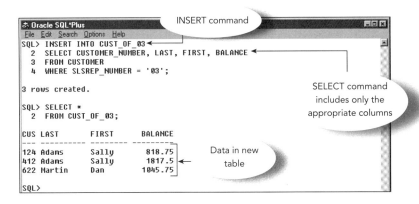

Figure 5.9 Inserting rows

CHANGING A VALUE IN A COLUMN TO NULL

There are some special issues involved when dealing with nulls. You already have seen how to add a row in which some of the values are null and how to select rows in which a given column is null. You also must be able to change the value in a column in an existing row to null, as illustrated in Example 7. Remember that in order to make this type of change, the affected column must be able to accept nulls. If you specified NOT NULL for the column when you created the table, then changing a value in a column to null is prohibited.

Example 7:	Change the address of customer number 124 to null.

The command for changing the value to null is exactly what it would be for changing any other value. Simply use the value NULL as the replacement value, as shown in Figure 5.10. Notice that the NULL command is *not* enclosed in single quotation marks. If it were, the command would change the street address to the word NULL.

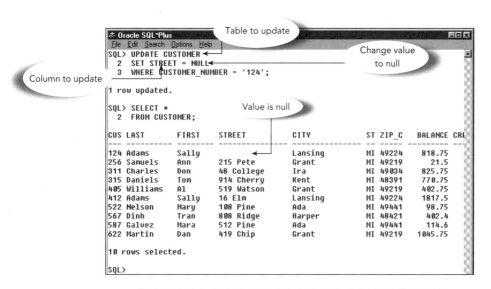

Figure 5.10 Setting a column to null

CHANGING THE TABLE STRUCTURE

One of the nicest features of a relational DBMS is the ease with which you can change the table structure. You can use the CREATE TABLE command to add new tables, delete tables that are no longer required, add new columns to a table, and change the physical characteristics of existing columns. Next, you will see how to accomplish these changes.

Altering the Structure of an Existing Table

Using SQL to alter the structure of an existing table is easy. In contrast, altering the structure of an existing table in a nonrelational system is a much more complex process. In a nonrelational database system you have to change the description of the structure using utility programs that unload the data from the current structure and then reload it with the new structure.

With SQL you can change a table's structure using the ALTER table command, as illustrated in the following examples.

Example 8:	Premiere Products decides to maintain a customer type for each customer in the database. These types are R for regular customers, D for distributors, and S for special customers. Add this information as a new column in the CUSTOMER table.

To add a new column, use the ADD clause of the ALTER command. The format for the command is ALTER TABLE <table name> ADD <column name> <characteristics>. Figure 5.11 shows the appropriate ALTER TABLE command for this example.

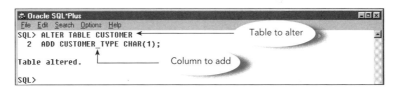

Figure 5.11 Adding a column using ALTER

The CUSTOMER table now contains a new column named CUSTOMER_TYPE. Any new rows added to the table must include values for the new column. Effective immediately, all existing rows contain this new column. The data in any existing row will be changed to reflect the new column the next time the row is updated. However, any time a row is selected for any reason, the system treats the row as though the column is actually present. Thus, to the user, it will feel as though the structure was changed immediately.

For existing rows, some value of CUSTOMER_TYPE must be assigned. The simplest approach (from the point of view of the DBMS, not the user) is to assign the value NULL as a CUSTOMER_TYPE in all existing rows. This process requires the CUSTOMER_TYPE column to accept null values, and some systems actually insist on this. That is, any column added to a table definition *must* accept nulls; the user has no choice. A more flexible approach, and one that is supported by some systems, is to allow the user to specify an initial value. For example, if most customers are of type R, we might set all the types for existing customers to R, and then later change distributors to type D and special customers to type S. The command to change the structure and set the value of CUSTOMER_TYPE to R for all existing records would be as follows:

ALTER TABLE CUSTOMER
ADD CUSTOMER_TYPE CHAR(1) INIT = 'R';

If a system will set new columns only to null, as is the case in Oracle, the previous initialization still can be accomplished by following the ALTER command with an UPDATE command as shown in Figure 5.12.

CHAPTER 5

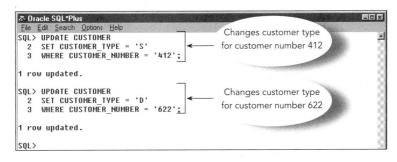

```
☼ Oracle SQL*Plus                                            _ □ x
 File  Edit  Search  Options  Help
SQL> UPDATE CUSTOMER
  2    SET CUSTOMER_TYPE = 'R';◄─────────────────        CUSTOMER_TYPE
                                          ◄              values will be
10 rows updated.                                         changed to R

SQL> SELECT CUSTOMER_NUMBER, LAST, FIRST, CUSTOMER_TYPE
  2    FROM CUSTOMER;
                                            Because there is no
CUS LAST         FIRST      C                  WHERE clause, all
--- ----------   --------   -                rows will be updated
124 Adams        Sally      R
256 Samuels      Ann        R
311 Charles      Don        R
315 Daniels      Tom        R
405 Williams     Al         R
412 Adams        Sally      R
522 Nelson       Mary       R
567 Dinh         Tran       R
587 Galvez       Mara       R          All values have been
622 Martin       Dan        R             changed to R

10 rows selected.          ▲
                           └──────
SQL>
```

Figure 5.12 Making the same entry in all rows

Example 9: Two customers have a type other than R. The type for customer number 412 should be S, and the type for customer number 622 should be D.

The previous example assigned type R as the type for every customer. To change individual types to something other than type R, use the UPDATE command. The appropriate UPDATE commands to make these changes are shown in Figure 5.13.

```
☼ Oracle SQL*Plus                                            _ □ x
 File  Edit  Search  Options  Help
SQL> UPDATE CUSTOMER                           Changes customer type
  2    SET CUSTOMER_TYPE = 'S'     ◄────────    for customer number 412
  3    WHERE CUSTOMER_NUMBER = '412';

1 row updated.

SQL> UPDATE CUSTOMER                           Changes customer type
  2    SET CUSTOMER_TYPE = 'D'     ◄────────    for customer number 622
  3    WHERE CUSTOMER_NUMBER = '622';

1 row updated.

SQL>
```

Figure 5.13 Changing individual values

Figure 5.14 shows the results of these UPDATE commands. The customer type for customer number 412 is S and the type for customer number 622 is D. The type for all other customers is R.

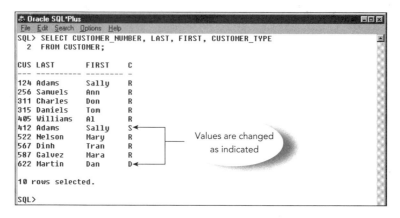

Figure 5.14 Results of changes

Example 10: The length of the STREET column is too short. Increase its length to 20 characters.

Characteristics of existing columns can be changed using the MODIFY clause of the ALTER TABLE command. The ALTER TABLE command used to change the length of the STREET column from 15 to 20 characters is shown in Figure 5.15. The DESCRIBE command in the figure shows the current structure of the CUSTOMER table.

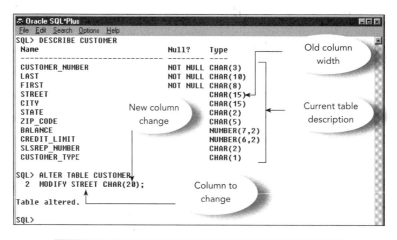

Figure 5.15 Changing column width

Example 11:	Currently the CITY column is allowed to accept nulls. Change the CITY column so that nulls are no longer allowed. Currently the FIRST column is not allowed to accept nulls. Change the FIRST column so that nulls are allowed.

You can use the MODIFY clause of the ALTER TABLE command to change a column that currently allows nulls to NOT NULL. You also can change a column that doesn't allow nulls to NULL. Both changes are shown in Figure 5.16. Now the DBMS rejects any attempt to store a null value in the CITY column. An attempt to store a null value in the FIRST column, however, is allowed.

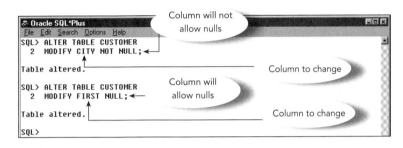

Figure 5.16 Changing columns to NOT NULL or NULL

If there were existing rows in the CUSTOMER table in which the CITY column was already null, the modification to the CITY column in Figure 5.16 would be rejected. The DBMS would display an error message indicating that this alteration was not possible. To make the change at that point, you must use an UPDATE command to change all values that were null to some other value. Then you could alter the table structure. Figure 5.17 shows a description of the structure of the CUSTOMER table after the changes have been made.

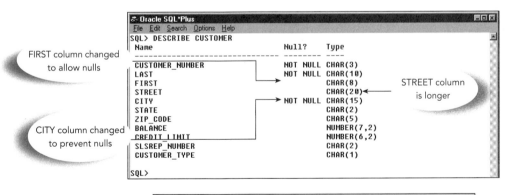

Figure 5.17 Changes to table structure

Making Complex Changes

In some cases, you might wish to make a change to a table structure that is beyond the capabilities of your DBMS. Perhaps you need to eliminate a column, change the column order, or combine data from two tables into one, but your system does not allow these types of changes. For example, some systems, including Oracle, do not allow you to reduce the size of a column or to change a data type. In these situations, you can use the CREATE TABLE command to describe the new table, and then insert values into it using the INSERT command combined with an appropriate SELECT clause.

Dropping a Table

As you learned in Chapter 2, a table that is no longer needed can be deleted using the DROP command. For example, if the SALES_REP table is not needed in the Premiere Products database, you can delete it with the following command (do not execute this command, however):

DROP TABLE SALES_REP

Once the command is executed, the SALES_REP table and all its data is deleted permanently from the database.

In this chapter you learned how to use the UPDATE command to change the data in a table. You learned to use the INSERT command to add new rows and used the DELETE command to delete existing rows. You created a new table that contained some of the data from an existing table and set a column to null. You used the ALTER command to change the structure of a table by adding new columns, deleting columns, and changing the characteristics of columns. Finally, you used the DROP command to delete an entire table. In the next chapter, you will use SQL commands for database administration tasks, such as creating views and using the system catalog.

SUMMARY

1.   Use the UPDATE command to change existing data in a table.

2.   Use the COMMIT command to make updates permanent; use the ROLLBACK command to cancel any updates that have not been committed.

3.   Use the INSERT command to add new rows to a table.

4.   Use the DELETE command to delete rows from a table.

5.   To create a new table from an existing table, first create the new table using the CREATE TABLE command. Then use an INSERT command containing a SELECT clause to select the desired data to be included from the existing table.

6.   To change all values in a column to null, the clause is SET <column name> = NULL. To change a specific value in a column to null, use a condition to select the row.

7.   To add a column to a table, use the ALTER TABLE command with the ADD option.

8.   To remove a column from a table, use the ALTER TABLE command with the DELETE option.

9.   To change the characteristics of a column, use the ALTER TABLE command with the MODIFY option.

10. Use the DROP TABLE command to delete a table.

EXERCISES (PREMIERE PRODUCTS)

Use SQL to make the following changes to the Premiere Products database. After each change, execute an appropriate query to determine whether the correct change was made correctly. Remember to execute a rollback after each step in the exercise.

If you are using Oracle for these exercises and wish to print a copy of your commands and results, type SPOOL followed by the name of a file and then press the Enter key. All the commands from that point on will be saved in the file that you named. For example, to save the commands and results to a file named CHAPTER5.SQL on drive A, the command is as follows:

SPOOL A:CHAPTER5.SQL

When you have finished, type SPOOL OFF, and then press the Enter key to stop saving commands to the file. Then you can start any program that opens *.txt files, open the file that you saved, and print it using the Print command on the File menu.

1. Change the description of part BT04 to Oven.

2. Add $100 to the credit limit of every customer represented by sales rep number 06.

3. Add order 12600 (order date: 9/6/98, customer number: 311) to the database. Add two order lines for this order. On the first line, the part number is AX12, the number ordered is 5, and the quoted price is $13.95. On the second line, the part number is BA74, the number ordered is 3, and the quoted price is $4.50.

4. Write the command to delete every customer whose balance is $0 and who is represented by sales rep number 12. Do not execute the command.

5. Create a new table named SPGOOD to contain the columns PART_NUMBER, DESCRIPTION, and UNIT_PRICE. Then insert into this new table the part number, part description, and unit price from the PART table for every part whose item class is SG.

6. Change the street address of sales rep number 03 to null.

7. Add a column named ALLOCATION to the PART table. The allocation is a three-digit number representing the number of units of each part that have been allocated to each customer. Set all values of ALLOCATION to zero. Calculate the number of units of BT04 currently on order. Change the value of ALLOCATION for part number BT04 to this number.

8. Write the command to delete the ITEM_CLASS column from the PART table. Do not execute the command.

9. Increase the length of the PART_DESCRIPTION column to 30 characters.

10. Write the command to remove the PART table from the Premiere Products database. Do not execute the command.

EXERCISES (HENRY BOOKS)

Use SQL to make the following changes to the Henry Books database. After each change, execute an appropriate query to determine whether the correct change was made correctly. Remember to execute a rollback after each step in the exercise.

1. Change the number of units on hand to 5 for all books located in branch number 1.

2. Bantam Books (BB) has decreased the price of its books by 3 percent. Update the prices in the database.

3. Insert a new book into the database. The book code is 9700, the title is Using Microsoft Access 97, the publisher code is BF, the book type is CS, the price is 19.97, and the book is available only in paperback. The author number is 07 and there are four books on hand in branch number 1. The sequence number is 2.

4. Write the command to delete the author named Stephen King from the database. Make sure that your command will not delete any additional rows. Do not execute the command.

5. Create a new table named FICTION using the data in the book code, book title, and book price columns in the BOOK table. Select only those books of type FIC and insert them into the new table.

6. Increase the price of all books in the FICTION table by 12 percent.

7. The price of the book titled "Amerika" in the FICTION table has increased. Change the value to null while you are waiting for the publisher to give you the new price.

8. Add to the FICTION table a new character column that is one character in length named BEST_SELLER. The default value for all columns is N.

9. Change the BEST_SELLER column in the FICTION table to Y for the book titled "Kane and Abel."

10. Change the length of the BOOK_TITLE column in the FICTION table to 50.

11. Change the BEST_SELLER column in the FICTION table to reject nulls.

12. Change the BEST_SELLER column in the FICTION table to accept nulls.

13. Delete the FICTION table from the database.

CHAPTER 6

Database Administration

OBJECTIVES

- Understand, create, and drop views
- Recognize the benefits of using views
- Grant and revoke database privileges to users
- Create, use, and drop an index
- Understand the purpose, advantages, and disadvantages of using an index
- Understand and obtain information from the system catalog
- Use integrity constraints to control data entry

INTRODUCTION

There are some special issues involved in managing a database. This process, often called **database administration**, is especially important when the database is used by more than one person. In a business organization, a person or an entire group known as the **database administrator** is charged with managing the database.

In Chapter 5 you learned about one function of the database administrator — changing the structure of a database. In this chapter you will learn about additional tasks of the database administrator. You will see how each user can be given his or her own view of the database. You will use the GRANT and REVOKE commands to assign different database privileges to different users. You will use indexes to improve database performance. You will see how SQL keeps information about the database structure in a special object called the system catalog. Using the system catalog, the database administrator can obtain helpful information concerning the database structure, and specify integrity constraints to establish rules that the data in the database must satisfy.

■　■　■　■　■

VIEWS

Most database management systems, including Oracle, are capable of giving each user his or her own picture of the data in the database. In SQL this is done using views. The existing, permanent tables in a relational database are called **base tables**. A **view** is a derived table because the data in the view is derived from the base table. It appears to the user to be an actual table. In many cases, a user can interact with the database using a view. Because a view usually includes less information than the full database, using a view can represent a great simplification. Views also provide a measure of security, because omitting sensitive tables or columns from a view renders them unavailable to anyone who is accessing the database through the view.

To illustrate the idea of a view, suppose that Juan is interested in the part number, part description, units on hand, and unit price of parts in item class HW. He is not interested in any other columns in the PART table, nor is he interested in any of the rows that correspond to parts in other item classes. Whereas Juan cannot change the structure of the PART table and omit some of its rows for his purposes, he can do the next best thing. He can create a view that consists of only the rows and columns that he needs.

A view is defined by creating a defining query. The **defining query** is a SQL command that indicates the rows and columns that will appear in the view. The command to create the view for Juan, including the defining query, is illustrated in Example 1.

Example 1:	Define a view named HOUSEWARES that consists of the part number, part description, units on hand, and unit price of all parts in item class HW.

The CREATE VIEW command shown in Figure 6.1 creates a view of the PART table that contains only the specified columns that match the selection condition.

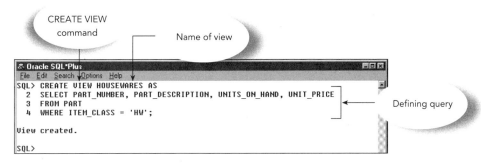

CREATE VIEW command

Name of view

Defining query

```
Oracle SQL*Plus
File  Edit  Search  Options  Help
SQL> CREATE VIEW HOUSEWARES AS
  2    SELECT PART_NUMBER, PART_DESCRIPTION, UNITS_ON_HAND, UNIT_PRICE
  3    FROM PART
  4    WHERE ITEM_CLASS = 'HW';

View created.

SQL>
```

Figure 6.1 Creating the HOUSEWARES view

Given the current data in the Premiere Products database, this view contains the data shown in Figure 6.2.

HOUSEWARES

PART_NUMBER	PART_DESCRIPTION	UNITS_ON_HAND	UNIT_PRICE
AX12	Iron	104	$24.95
BH22	Cornpopper	95	$24.95
CA14	Griddle	78	$39.99
CX11	Blender	112	$22.95

Figure 6.2 HOUSEWARES view

Note	If you did not rollback the data in Chapter 5, your results will be different from those shown in Figure 6.2.

The data does not actually exist in this form, however, nor will it *ever* exist in this form. When this view is used, it is tempting to think that the query will be executed and produce some sort of temporary table, named HOUSEWARES, that the user can access at any time. This is *not* what happens. Instead, the query acts as a sort of "window" into the database (see Figure 6.3). As far as a user of this view is concerned, the whole database consists of the shaded portion of the PART table.

PART

PART_NUMBER	PART_DESCRIPTION	UNITS_ON_HAND	ITEM_CLASS	WAREHOUSE_NUMBER	UNIT_PRICE
AX12	Iron	104	HW	3	$ 24.95
AZ52	Dartboard	20	SG	2	$ 12.95
BA74	Basketball	40	SG	1	$ 29.95
BH22	Cornpopper	95	HW	3	$ 24.95
BT04	Gas Grill	11	AP	2	$149.99
BZ66	Washer	52	AP	3	$399.99
CXA14	Griddle	78	HW	3	$ 39.99
CB03	Bike	44	SG	1	$299.99
CX11	Blender	112	HW	3	$ 22.95
CZ81	Treadmill	68	SG	2	$349.95

Figure 6.3 Premiere Products sample data

The way in which the view is implemented is clever. Suppose, for example, that a user of this view runs the query shown in Figure 6.4.

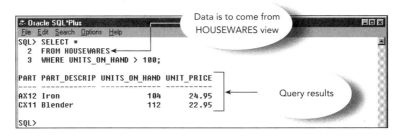

Figure 6.4 Using the HOUSEWARES view

Rather than being executed directly, the query first is merged with the query that defines the view, producing the following statement:

```
SELECT PART_NUMBER, PART_DESCRIPTION, UNITS_ON_HAND, UNIT_PRICE
FROM PART
WHERE ITEM_CLASS = 'HW'
AND UNITS_ON_HAND > 100
```

Notice that the selection is from the PART table rather than from the HOUSEWARES view; the asterisk is replaced by just those columns in the HOUSE-WARES view; and the condition includes the condition in the query entered by the user together with the condition stated in the view definition. This new query is the one that the DBMS actually executes.

The user, however, is unaware that this kind of activity takes place. There is no evidence of it shown in Figure 6.4. It seems as though there actually is a table named HOUSEWARES that is being accessed.

One advantage of this approach is that because the HOUSEWARES view never exists in its own right, any update to the PART table is reflected *immediately* in the HOUSEWARES view and is apparent to anyone accessing the database through the view. If the HOUSEWARES view were an actual stored table, this immediate update would not be the case.

The formulation of a view definition is: CREATE VIEW<view name> AS <query>. The query, which is called the **defining query**, can be any legitimate SQL query.

You also can assign column names that are different from those in the base table, as illustrated in the next example.

Example 2:	Define a view named HOUSEWARES that consists of the part number, part description, units on hand, and unit price of all parts in item class HW. In this view, rename the PART_NUMBER column to NUM, the PART_DESCRIPTION column to DSC, the UNITS_ON_HAND column to OH, and the UNIT_PRICE column to PRCE.

When renaming columns, you include the new column names in parentheses following the name of the view as shown in Figure 6.5. In this case, anyone accessing the HOUSEWARES view will refer to PART_NUMBER as NUM, to PART_DESCRIPTION as DSC, to UNITS_ON_HAND as OH, and to UNIT_PRICE as PRCE. If you select all columns from the HOUSEWARES view, the new column names will display as shown in Figure 6.5.

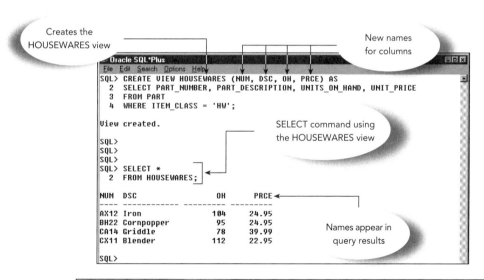

Figure 6.5 Renaming columns when creating a view

The HOUSEWARES view is an example of a **row-and-column subset view**, because it consists of a subset of the rows and columns in some base table—in this case, in the PART table. Because the query can be any SQL query, a view could involve the join of two or more tables, or it also could involve statistics. The next example illustrates a view that joins two tables.

| Example 3: | Define a view named SALES_CUST. The view consists of the sales rep number (named SNUMB), sales rep last name (named SLAST), sales rep first name (named SFIRST), customer number (named CNUMB), customer last name (named CLAST), and customer first name (named CFIRST) for all sales reps and matching customers in the SALES_REP and CUSTOMER tables. |

The command to create this view is shown in Figure 6.6.

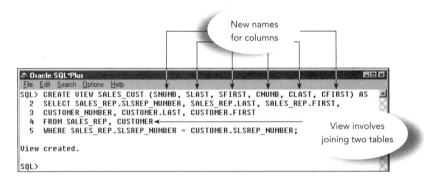

Figure 6.6 Creating the SALES_CUST view

Given the current data in the Premiere Products database, this view contains the data shown in Figure 6.7.

```
* Oracle SQL*Plus                                                    _ □ ×
File  Edit  Search  Options  Help
SQL> SELECT *
  2  FROM SALES_CUST;

SN SLAST        SFIRST    CNU CLAST       CFIRST
-- ----------   --------  --- ----------  --------
03 Jones        Mary      124 Adams       Sally
03 Jones        Mary      412 Adams       Sally
03 Jones        Mary      622 Martin      Dan
06 Smith        William   256 Samuels     Ann
06 Smith        William   315 Daniels     Tom
06 Smith        William   567 Dinh        Tran
06 Smith        William   587 Galvez      Mara
12 Diaz         Miguel    311 Charles     Don
12 Diaz         Miguel    405 Williams    Al
12 Diaz         Miguel    522 Nelson      Mary

10 rows selected.

SQL>
```

Figure 6.7 Using the SALES_CUST view

The next example involves statistics.

Example 4:	Define a view named CRED_CUST that consists of each credit limit (CREDIT_LIMIT) and the number of customers who have this credit limit (NUMBER_CUSTOMERS).

The command shown in Figure 6.8 creates this view; the current data in the Premiere Products database also displays in the figure.

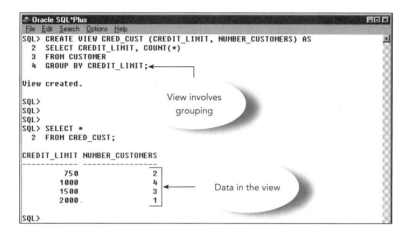

Figure 6.8 Creating the CRED_CUST view

Using views has several benefits:

1. Views provide data independence. If the database structure changes (adding columns, changing the way objects are related, etc.), the user still can access the same view. If adding extra columns to tables in the database is the only change and these columns are not required by the user, the defining query might not need to be changed. If relationships change, the defining query might be different, but this difference is unknown to the user. The user continues to access the database through the same view, as though nothing has changed. For an example of the type of change that requires modification of the defining query, suppose that customers are assigned to territories, each territory is assigned to a single sales rep, a sales rep can have more than one territory, and a customer is represented by the sales rep who covers the customer's assigned territory. To implement these changes, you might choose to restructure the database as follows:

SALES_REP(<u>SLSREP NUMBER</u>, LAST, FIRST, STREET, CITY, STATE, ZIP_CODE,
   TOTAL_COMMISSION, COMMISSION_RATE)
TERRITORY(<u>TERRITORY NUMBER</u>, TERRITORY_DESCRIPTION, SLSREP_NUMBER)
CUSTOMER(<u>CUSTOMER NUMBER</u>, LAST, FIRST, STREET, CITY, STATE, ZIP_CODE, BALANCE,
   CREDIT_LIMIT, TERRITORY_NUMBER);

Assuming that the SALES_CUST view shown earlier still is required, the defining query could be reformulated as follows:

CREATE VIEW SALES_CUST (SNUMB, SLAST, SFIRST, CNUMB, CLAST, CFIRST) AS
SELECT SALES_REP.SLSREP_NUMBER, SALES_REP.LAST, SALES_REP.FIRST,
CUSTOMER.CUSTOMER_NUMBER, CUSTOMER.LAST, CUSTOMER.FIRST
FROM SALES_REP, TERRITORY, CUSTOMER
WHERE SALES_REP.SLSREP_NUMBER = TERRITORY.SLSREP_NUMBER
AND TERRITORY.TERRITORY_NUMBER = CUSTOMER.TERRITORY_NUMBER;

The user of this view will retrieve the number and name of a sales rep together with the number and name of every customer the sales rep represents. The user will be unaware, however, of the new structure in the database.

2. Because each user has his or her own view, the same data can be viewed by different users in different ways. In other words, the data can be customized to meet each user's needs.

3. A view should contain only those columns required by a given user. This practice accomplishes two things. First, because the view usually contains fewer columns than the overall database and because the view is a single table rather than a collection of tables, a view can simplify greatly the user's perception of the database. Second, views furnish a measure of security. Columns that are not included in the view are not accessible to the user. For example, omitting the BALANCE column from the view ensures that a user of the view cannot access any customer's balance. Likewise, rows that are not included in the view are not accessible. A user of the HOUSEWARES view, for example, cannot obtain any information about sporting goods, even though both housewares and sporting goods are stored in the same base table (PART).

These benefits hold true only when views are used for retrieval purposes. When updating the database, the issues involved in updating data through a view depend on the type of view, as you will see next.

Row and Column Subsets

Consider the row and column subset view named HOUSEWARES. There are columns in the underlying base table (PART) that are not present in the view. Thus, if you attempt to add a row with the data ('BB99','PAN',50,14.95), the system must determine how to enter the data in those columns from the PART table that are not included in the HOUSEWARES view (ITEM_CLASS and WAREHOUSE_NUMBER). In this case, it is clear what data to enter in the ITEM_CLASS column. According to the view definition, all rows are item class HW. But it is not clear what data to enter in the WAREHOUSE_NUMBER column. The only possibility would be NULL. Thus, provided that every column not included in a view can accept nulls, you can add new rows using the INSERT command. There is another problem, however. Suppose the user attempts to add a row containing the data ('AZ52','POT',25,9.95). This attempt *must* be rejected, because there is a part number AZ52 that already exists in the PART table. Because this part is not in item class HW, this rejection certainly will seem strange to the user, because there is no such part in the user's view.

Updates or deletions cause no particular problem in this view. If the description of part number CA14 changes from skillet to pan, this change is made in the PART table. If part number CX11 is deleted, this deletion occurs in the PART table. One surprising change could take place, however. Suppose that ITEM_CLASS is included as a column in the HOUSEWARES view and then a user changes the item class of part number CX11 from HW to AP. Because this item would no longer satisfy the criterion for being included in the HOUSEWARES view, part number CX11 would disappear from the user's view.

Whereas some problems do have to be overcome, it seems possible to update the database through the HOUSEWARES view. This does not imply that *any* row and column subset view is updateable, however. Consider the view shown in Figure 6.9. (You use the word DISTINCT to omit duplicate rows from the view.) This view currently contains the data shown in Figure 6.9.

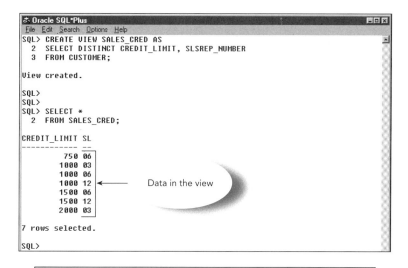

Figure 6.9 Creating the SALES_CRED view

How would you add the row (1000,'06') to this view? In the underlying base table (CUSTOMER) at least one customer must be added whose credit limit is $1000 and whose sales rep number is 06, but who is it? You can't leave the other columns null in this case, because one of them is CUSTOMER_NUMBER, which is the base table's primary key. What would it mean to change the row (1200,'12') to (2000,'12')? Would it mean changing the credit limit to $2,000 for every customer represented by sales rep number 12 who currently has a credit limit of $1,200? Would it mean changing the credit limit of one of these customers and deleting the rest? Would it mean deleting the row (750,'06')? Would it mean deleting all customers whose credit limit is $750 and whose sales rep number is 06, or would it mean assigning these customers a different sales rep or a different credit limit? Potentially, you also could set the credit limit and/or the sales rep numbers to null.

Why does the SALES_CRED view involve a number of serious problems that are not present in the HOUSEWARES view? The basic reason is that the HOUSEWARES view includes, as one of its columns, the primary key of the underlying base table and the SALES_CRED view does not. A row and column subset view that contains the primary key of the underlying base table is updateable (subject, of course, to some of the concerns we have discussed).

Joins

In general, views that involve joins of base tables can cause problems at update. Consider the relatively simple view SALES_CUST, for example, described earlier (see Figures 6.6 and 6.7). The fact that some columns in the underlying base tables are not seen in this view presents some of the same problems discussed earlier. Even assuming that these problems can be overcome through the use of nulls, there are more serious problems inherent in the attempt to update the database through this view. On the surface, changing the row ('06','Smith','William','256','Samuels','Ann') to ('06','Baker','Nancy','256','Samuels','Ann') might not appear to pose any problems other than some inconsistency in the data. (In the new version of the row, the name of sales rep number 06 is Nancy Baker; in the next row in the table, the name of sales rep number 06, *the same sales rep*, is William Smith.)

The problem is actually more serious than that—making this change is not possible. The name of a sales rep is stored only once in the underlying SALES_REP table. Changing the name of sales rep number 06 from William Smith to Nancy Baker in this one row of the view causes the change to be made to the single row for sales rep number 06 in the SALES_REP table. Because the view simply displays data from the base tables, every row in which the sales rep number is 06 now shows the name as Nancy Baker. In other words, it appears that the same change has been made in all the other rows. In this case this change probably would be a good thing. In general, however, the unexpected changes caused by an update are not desirable.

Before leaving the topic of views that involve joins, you should note that all joins do not create the preceding problem. If two base tables happen to have the same primary key and the primary key is used as the join column, updating the database is not a problem. For example, suppose the actual database contains two tables (SLSREP_DEMO and SLSREP_FIN) instead of one table (SALES_REP). Figure 6.10 shows the data in these two tables.

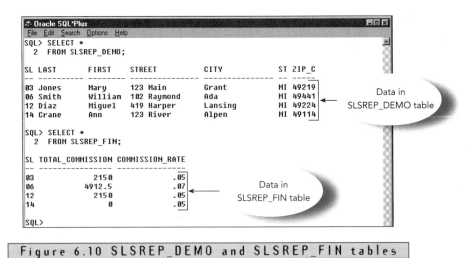

Figure 6.10 SLSREP_DEMO and SLSREP_FIN tables

In this case, what was a single table in the Premiere Products design has been divided into two separate tables. Any user who expected to see a single table could be accommodated through a view that joins these two tables together using the SLSREP_NUMBER column. The view definition is shown in Figure 6.11.

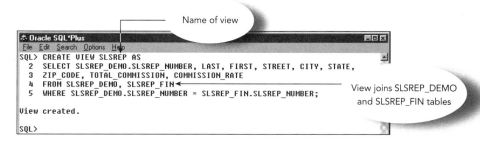

Figure 6.11 Creating the SLSREP view

The SLSREP view is shown in Figure 6.12.

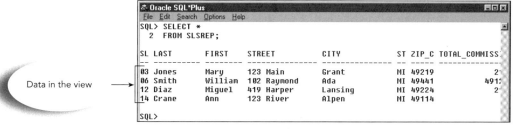

Figure 6.12 Using the SLSREP view

No difficulty is encountered in updating this view. To add a row, simply add a row to each underlying base table. To change data in a row, change the appropriate base table. To delete a row from the view, delete the corresponding rows from both underlying base tables.

Question	How would you add the row '10', 'Peters', 'Jean', '14 Brink', 'Holt', 'MI', '46223', 107.50, .05 to the SLSREP view?
Answer	Add the row ('10','Peters', 'Jean', '14 Brink', 'Holt', 'MI', '46223') to the SLSREP_DEMO table and add the row ('10',107.50,.05) to the SLSREP_FIN table.

Question	How would you change the name of sales rep number 03 to Mary Lewis?
Answer	Use an update to change the name in the SLSREP_DEMO table.

Question	How would you change Mary's commission rate to .06?
Answer	Use an update to change the rate in the SLSREP_FIN table.

Question	How would you delete sales rep number 06 from the SLSREP view?
Answer	Delete sales rep number 06 from *both* the SLSREP_DEMO *and* SLSREP_FIN tables.

The SLSREP view is updateable; updates (add, change, or delete) do not cause any problems. The main reason that this view is updateable—whereas other views involving joins are not—is that this view is derived from joining two base tables *on the primary key of each table*. In contrast, the SALES_CUST view is derived by joining two tables by matching the primary key of one table with a column that is not the primary key in the other table. Even more severe problems are encountered if neither of the join columns is a primary key column.

Statistics

A view that involves statistics calculated from one or more base tables is the most troublesome view of all. Consider the CRED_CUST view, for example (see Figure 6.8). How would you add the row (900,3) to indicate that there are three customers who each have a credit limit of $900? Likewise, changing the row (750,2) to (750,5) means you are adding three new customers with credit limits of $750 each, for a total of five customers. Clearly these are impossible tasks; you can't add rows to a view that includes calculations. You only could add appropriate data to the underlying base tables.

Dropping a View

When a view is no longer needed, you can remove it by using the DROP VIEW command.

Example 5:	The SLSREP view is no longer necessary, so remove it.

The DROP VIEW command to delete the SLSREP view is shown in Figure 6.13. The view is deleted permanently from the database, but the tables and data on which the view is based still exist. The DROP VIEW command removes only the view definition.

Figure 6.13 Dropping a view

SECURITY

Security is the prevention of unauthorized access to the database. Within an organization, the database administrator determines the types of access various users need for the database. Some users might be able to retrieve and update data in the database. Other users might be able to retrieve any data from the database but not make any changes to it. Still other users might be able to access only a portion of the database. For example, Bill can retrieve and update customer data, but cannot retrieve data for sales reps, orders, order lines, or parts. Mary can retrieve data only for parts. Sam can retrieve and update data on parts in item class HW, but cannot retrieve any data for other item classes.

Once determined, these access rules are enforced by whatever security mechanism the DBMS provides. SQL systems offer two security mechanisms. You already have seen that views furnish a certain amount of security. (If someone is accessing the database through a view, for example, he or she cannot access any data that is not part of the view.) The main mechanism, however, is the GRANT command. Here the basic idea is that different types of privileges can be granted to users and then revoked later, if necessary. These privileges include such things as the ability to select rows from a table, insert new rows, update existing rows, and so on. You can grant and revoke these privileges by using the GRANT and REVOKE commands. The following examples illustrate various uses of the GRANT command.

Note	Because the user names in the examples that follow will not be on your system, you will not be able to execute these commands in SQL.

Example 6:	User Jones must be able to retrieve data from the SALES_REP table.

The SQL statement to permit users to retrieve data includes the following SELECT statement for the table:

GRANT SELECT ON SALES_REP TO JONES;

Example 7:	Users Smith and Brown must be able to add new parts to the PART table.

The SQL statement to add data includes the user names, separated by a comma, as follows:

GRANT INSERT ON PART TO SMITH, BROWN;

Example 8:	User Anderson must be able to change the last name, first name, or street address of customers.

The SQL statement to update data includes the table name, followed by the column name(s) to update in parentheses, as follows:

GRANT UPDATE ON CUSTOMER (LAST, FIRST, STREET) TO ANDERSON;

Example 9:	User Martin must be able to delete order lines.

The SQL statement to delete rows is as follows:

GRANT DELETE ON ORDER_LINE TO MARTIN;

Example 10:	Every user must be able to retrieve part numbers, part descriptions, and item classes.

The SQL statement to indicate that all users have the privilege to retrieve data includes the special word PUBLIC, as follows:

GRANT SELECT ON PART (PART_NUMBER, PART_DESCRIPTION, ITEM_CLASS)
TO PUBLIC;

Example 11:	User Roberts must be able to create an index on the SALES_REP table.

We will discuss indexes and their uses in the next section. This example illustrates how to grant a user the ability to create an index. The SQL statement to create an index is as follows:

GRANT INDEX ON SALES_REP TO ROBERTS;

Example 12:	User Thomas must be able to change the structure of the CUSTOMER table.

The SQL statement to change a table's structure is as follows:

GRANT ALTER ON CUSTOMER TO THOMAS;

Example 13:	User Wilson must have all privileges for the SALES_REP, CUSTOMER, and ORDERS tables.

The SQL statement to indicate that a user has all privileges includes the use of the ALL privilege, as follows:

GRANT ALL ON SALES_REP, CUSTOMER, ORDERS TO WILSON

The privileges that can be granted are SELECT to retrieve data, UPDATE to change data, DELETE to delete data, INSERT to add new data, INDEX to create an index, and ALTER to change the table structure.

Privileges usually are assigned by the database administrator. Normally, when the database administrator grants a particular privilege to a user, the user cannot pass that privilege along to other users. If the user needs to be able to pass the privilege to another user, the GRANT statement must include the WITH GRANT OPTION clause. This clause grants the indicated privilege to the user and also permits the user to grant the same privileges (or a subset of them) to other users.

Any privileges granted can be revoked later by using the REVOKE command. The format of the REVOKE command is essentially the same as that of the GRANT command, but with two differences. Instead of GRANT privileges TO users, the format is REVOKE privileges FROM users. In addition, the clause WITH GRANT OPTION obviously is not meaningful as part of a REVOKE command. Incidentally, the revoke will cascade so that if Jones is granted privileges WITH GRANT OPTION and then Jones grants these same privileges to Smith, revoking the privileges from Jones revokes Smith's privileges at the same time. Example 14 illustrates the use of the REVOKE command.

Example 14: | User Jones is no longer allowed to retrieve data from the SALES_REP table.

The SQL command to revoke a privilege is as follows:

REVOKE SELECT ON SALES_REP FROM JONES

The GRANT and REVOKE commands also can be applied to views so that access is restricted to only certain rows within tables.

Example 15: | Allow sales rep number 03 (Mary Jones) to access any data concerning the customers she represents, but do not permit her to access data concerning any other customer.

The SQL statement to restrict data access is as follows:

```
CREATE VIEW SLSR3CST AS
SELECT *
FROM CUSTOMER
WHERE SLSREP_NUMBER = '03'
GRANT SELECT ON SLSR3CST TO MARY JONES
```

INDEXES

Usually when you query a database you are searching for a row (or collection of rows) that satisfies some condition. Examining every row in a table to find the desired rows often takes too much time to be practical, especially if there are thousands of records in the table. Fortunately, you can create and use an **index** to speed up the searching process significantly. An index in a DBMS is similar to an index in a book. If you want to find a discussion of a given topic in a book, you can scan the entire book from start to finish and look for references to the topic. More than likely, however, you wouldn't resort to this time-consuming method. If the book has an index, you can use it to locate the page numbers on which your topic is discussed.

For relational model systems that run on both mainframes and microcomputers, such as Oracle, the main mechanism for increasing the efficiency with which data is retrieved from the database is by using indexes. Consider Figure 6.14, for example, which shows the CUSTOMER table for Premiere Products together with one extra column named ROW_NUMBER. This extra column contains the row number of each row in the table (customer number 124 is in row 1; customer number 256 is in row 2; and so on). The DBMS uses these row numbers to go directly to a specific row. The row numbers are not used by the users of the DBMS, and that is why usually you do not see them.

CUSTOMER

ROW_NUMBER	CUSTOMER_NUMBER	LAST	FIRST	STREET	CITY	STATE	ZIP_CODE	BALANCE	CREDIT_LIMIT	SLSREP_NUMBER
1	124	Adams	Sally	481 Oak	Lansing	MI	49224	$ 818.75	$1200	03
2	256	Jones	Ann	215 Pete	Grant	MI	49219	$ 21.50	$1500	06
3	311	Charles	Don	48 College	Ira	MI	49034	$ 825.75	$1200	12
4	315	Daniels	Tom	914 Cherry	Kent	MI	48391	$ 770.75	$ 750	06
5	412	Adams	Sally	16 Elm	Lansing	MI	49224	$1817.50	$2000	03
6	522	Nelson	Mary	108 Pine	Ada	MI	49441	$ 98.75	$1500	12
7	567	Dinh	Tran	808 Ridge	Harper	MI	48421	$ 402.40	$ 750	06
8	587	Galvez	Mara	512 Pine	Ada	MI	49441	$ 114.60	$1200	06
9	622	Martin	Dan	419 Chip	Grant	MI	49219	$1045.75	$1000	03

Figure 6.14 CUSTOMER table with row numbers

To access a customer on the basis of his or her customer number, you might create and use an index as shown in Figure 6.15. The index is a separate file that contains two columns. The first column contains a customer number, and the second column contains the number of the row in which the customer number is found. To find a customer, you look up the customer's number in the first column in the index. The value in the second column indicates which row to retrieve from the CUSTOMER table; then the row for the desired customer is retrieved.

CUSTOMER_NUMBER INDEX

CUSTOMER_NUMBER	ROW_NUMBER
124	1
256	2
311	3
315	4
412	5
522	6
567	7
587	8
622	9

CUSTOMER

ROW_NUMBER	CUSTOMER_NUMBER	LAST	FIRST	STREET	CITY	STATE	ZIP_CODE	BALANCE	CREDIT_LIMIT	SLSREP_NUMBER
1	124	Adams	Sally	481 Oak	Lansing	MI	49224	$ 818.75	$1200	03
2	256	Jones	Ann	215 Pete	Grant	MI	49219	$ 21.50	$1500	06
3	311	Charles	Don	48 College	Ira	MI	49034	$ 825.75	$1200	12
4	315	Daniels	Tom	914 Cherry	Kent	MI	48391	$ 770.75	$ 750	06
5	412	Adams	Sally	16 Elm	Lansing	MI	49224	$1817.50	$2000	03
6	522	Nelson	Mary	108 Pine	Ada	MI	49441	$ 98.75	$1500	12
7	567	Dinh	Tran	808 Ridge	Harper	MI	48421	$ 402.40	$ 750	06
8	587	Galvez	Mara	512 Pine	Ada	MI	49441	$ 114.60	$1200	06
9	622	Martin	Dan	419 Chip	Grant	MI	49219	$1045.75	$1000	03

Figure 6.15 Index for CUSTOMER table on CUSTOMER_NUMBER column

Because customer numbers are unique, there will be a single row number in each row in the index. If the column on which the index is created is not unique, there might be multiple numbers in the rows in the index. Suppose, for example, that you need to access all customers who have a given credit limit. You also need to access all customers who are represented by a given sales rep. In this case, you might choose to create and use an index on the CREDIT_LIMIT column and an index on the SLSREP_NUMBER column as shown in Figure 6.16. In the CREDIT_LIMIT index, the first column contains a credit limit and the second column contains the numbers of *all* rows in which that credit limit is found. The SLSREP_NUMBER index is similar, except that the first column contains a sales rep number.

CREDIT_LIMIT INDEX

CREDIT_LIMIT	ROW_NUMBERS
$ 750	4, 7
$1000	9
$1200	1, 3, 8
$1500	2, 6
$2000	5

SLSREP_NUMBER INDEX

SLSREP_NUMBER	ROW_NUMBERS
03	1, 5, 9
06	2, 4, 7, 8
12	3, 6

CUSTOMER

ROW_NUMBER	CUSTOMER_NUMBER	LAST	FIRST	STREET	CITY	STATE	ZIP_CODE	BALANCE	CREDIT_LIMIT	SLSREP_NUMBER
1	124	Adams	Sally	481 Oak	Lansing	MI	49224	$ 818.75	$1200	03
2	256	Jones	Ann	215 Pete	Grant	MI	49219	$ 21.50	$1500	06
3	311	Charles	Don	48 College	Ira	MI	49034	$ 825.75	$1200	12
4	315	Daniels	Tom	914 Cherry	Kent	MI	48391	$ 770.75	$ 750	06
5	412	Adams	Sally	16 Elm	Lansing	MI	49224	$1817.50	$2000	03
6	522	Nelson	Mary	108 Pine	Ada	MI	49441	$ 98.75	$1500	12
7	567	Dinh	Tran	808 Ridge	Harper	MI	48421	$ 402.40	$ 750	06
8	587	Galvez	Mara	512 Pine	Ada	MI	49441	$ 114.60	$1200	06
9	622	Martin	Dan	419 Chip	Grant	MI	49219	$1045.75	$1000	03

Figure 6.16 Index for CUSTOMER table on CREDIT_LIMIT column

Question	How would you use the index shown in Figure 6.15 to find every customer with a $1500 credit limit?
Answer	Look up $1500 in the CREDIT_LIMIT index to find a collection of row numbers (2 and 6). Use these row numbers to find the corresponding rows in the CUSTOMER table (Ann Jones and Mary Nelson).

Question	How would you use the index shown in Figure 6.16 to find every customer who is represented by sales rep number 06?
Answer	Look up 06 in the SLSREP_NUMBER index to find a collection of row numbers (2, 4, 7, and 8). Use these row numbers to find the corresponding rows in the CUSTOMER table (Ann Jones, Tom Daniels, Tran Dinh, and Mara Galvez).

The actual structure of these indexes is more complicated than what is shown in the figures, but this is fine for our purposes. Fortunately, you don't have to be concerned with the details of manipulating and using indexes because the DBMS manages indexes for you. You decide which columns should have indexes built on them. Typically, an index can be created and maintained for any column or combination of columns in any table. Once an index has been created, the DBMS can use it to facilitate retrieval. No reference is made to any index by the user; rather, the DBMS automatically makes the decision whether to use a particular index.

As you would expect, using an index has advantages and disadvantages. An important advantage already mentioned is that an index makes certain types of retrieval more efficient. There are two disadvantages. First, an index occupies disk space that could be used for something else. Any retrieval that you can make using an index you also can make without the index; the index just speeds up the retrieval. The process of not using an index might be less efficient, but it still is possible. An index in one sense is technically unnecessary.

Second, the index must be updated whenever corresponding data in the database is updated. Without the index, these updates would not have to be performed. The main question to ask when considering whether to create a given index is: Do the benefits derived during retrieval outweigh the additional storage required and the extra processing involved in update operations? In a very large database, you might find that indexes are essential to decrease the time required to retrieve records. However, in a small database, an index might not provide any significant additional benefits.

Indexes can be added and dropped as needed. The final decision concerning the columns or combination of columns on which indexes should be built does not have to be made at the time the database is created. If the pattern of access to the database later indicates that overall performance would benefit from the creation of a new index, an index can be added. Likewise, if it appears that an existing index is unnecessary, the index can be dropped.

Creating an Index

Suppose that the users at Premiere Products find that they frequently need to display lists of customers that are ordered by the customers' balances. Also there are occasions where the users don't know a customer's number and need to locate the customer in the database by using the customer's name (last and first). Users also need to produce a report in which customers are listed by credit limit in descending order. Within the group of customers having the same credit limit, the customer records must be ordered by last name.

Each of the above requirements is more efficient when you create the appropriate index. The command used to create an index is CREATE INDEX, as illustrated in Example 16.

Example 16:	Create an index named BALIND on the BALANCE column in the CUSTOMER table. Create an index named CUSTNAME on the combination of the LAST and FIRST columns in the CUSTOMER table. Create an index named CREDNAME on the combination of the CREDIT_LIMIT, LAST, and FIRST columns in the CUSTOMER table with the credit limits listed in descending order.

The appropriate CREATE INDEX commands to create these indexes are shown in Figure 6.17. Each command lists the name of the index and the table name on which the index is to be created. The column name(s) are listed in parentheses. If any column is to be included in descending order, the column name is followed by the word DESC.

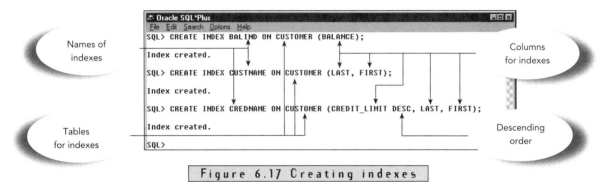

Names of indexes

Tables for indexes

Columns for indexes

Descending order

```
Oracle SQL*Plus
File  Edit  Search  Options  Help
SQL> CREATE INDEX BALIND ON CUSTOMER (BALANCE);

Index created.

SQL> CREATE INDEX CUSTNAME ON CUSTOMER (LAST, FIRST);

Index created.

SQL> CREATE INDEX CREDNAME ON CUSTOMER (CREDIT_LIMIT DESC, LAST, FIRST);

Index created.

SQL>
```

Figure 6.17 Creating indexes

If customers are listed using the CREDNAME index, the records will appear in order of descending credit limit. Within any credit limit, the customers will be ordered by name.

Dropping an Index

The command used to drop (delete) an index is DROP INDEX. To delete the CREDNAME index, for example, the command would be as follows:

DROP INDEX CREDNAME;

Once the command is executed, the index no longer exists. CREDNAME was the index the DBMS used when listing customer records in descending credit limit order and then by customer name within credit limit. The DBMS still can list customers in this order; however, it cannot do so as efficiently as when an index could be used.

Unique Indexes

When you indicate the primary key for a table, the DBMS ensures automatically that the values for the primary key are unique. An attempt to add a second customer whose number is 124, for example, would automatically be rejected because customer number 124 already exists. Thus, you don't need to take any special action to make sure that values in the primary key column are unique; the DBMS does it for you.

Occasionally, a column that is not the primary key might need unique values. For example, in the CUSTOMER table, the primary key is CUSTOMER_NUMBER. If the CUSTOMER table also contains a column for Social Security numbers, the values in this column also must be unique. Because the Social Security number column is not the table's primary key, however, you need to take special action in order for the DBMS to ensure that values in this column do not contain duplicates.

To ensure this uniqueness, create a special type of index called a **unique index** by using the CREATE UNIQUE INDEX command. To create a unique index named SSN on the SOC_SEC_NUMBER column of the CUSTOMER table, for example, the command would be as follows:

CREATE UNIQUE INDEX SSN ON CUSTOMER (SOC_SEC_NUMBER);

The unique index has all the properties of indexes already discussed along with one additional property: the DBMS refuses to accept any update that would cause a duplicate value in the column. In this case, that means the DBMS will reject the addition of a customer whose Social Security number is the same as that of another customer already in the database.

THE SYSTEM CATALOG

Information concerning tables known to the DBMS is kept in the **system catalog**, or the **data dictionary**. In the following description of the catalog, the exact structure has been simplified, but it is representative of the basic idea.

The system catalog contains several tables of its own. We will focus on three important tables to simplify this discussion. The most common names for these three tables are SYSTABLES (information about the tables known to SQL), SYSCOLUMNS (information about the columns within these tables), and SYSVIEWS (information about indexes defined on these tables). Individual implementations of SQL might use different names for these tables. In Oracle and in the examples that follow, the equivalent tables are named DBA_TABLES, DBA_TAB_COLUMNS, and DBA_VIEWS.

The system catalog is a relational database of its own. Consequently, in general, the same types of queries that are used to retrieve information from relational databases are used to retrieve information from the system catalog. The following examples illustrate this process.

Note	Usually users need special privileges to view the data in the system catalog. Thus you might not be able to execute these commands.

Example 17:	List the name of every table for which the owner (creator of the table) is PRATT.

The command to list the table names owned by PRATT is shown in Figure 6.18. The WHERE clause restricts the table names to only those tables whose owner is PRATT.

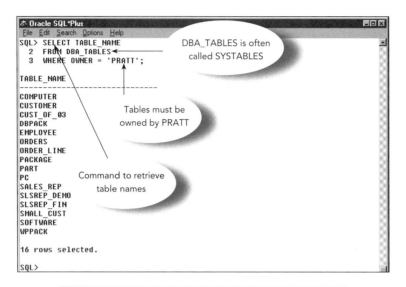

Figure 6.18 Tables owned by PRATT

Example 18: List the name of every view whose owner is PRATT.

This command is similar to the command in Example 17. Rather than TABLE_NAME, the column to be selected is named VIEW_NAME. The command is shown in Figure 6.19.

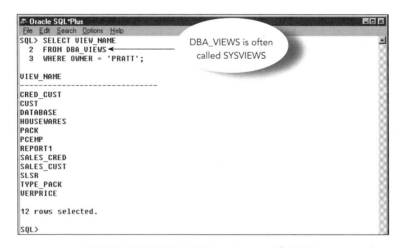

Figure 6.19 Views owned by PRATT

Example 19: List every column, and their associated data types, in the CUSTOMER table whose owner is PRATT.

The command for this example is shown in Figure 6.20. The columns to select are TABLE_NAME, COLUMN_NAME, and DATA_TYPE.

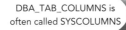

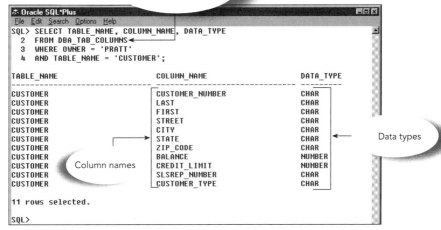

Figure 6.20 Columns in the CUSTOMER table

Example 20: List every table owned by PRATT that contains a column named CUSTOMER_NUMBER.

This command also uses the DBA_TAB_COLUMNS table as shown in Figure 6.21. In this case, the COLUMN_NAME column is used in the WHERE clause to restrict the rows to those in which the COLUMN_NAME is CUSTOMER_NUMBER.

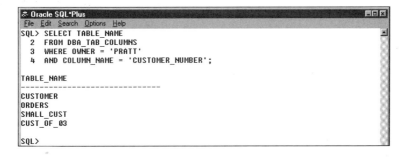

Figure 6.21 Names of tables by PRATT that include CUSTOMER_NUMBER column

You can obtain from the system catalog information about the tables in the relational database, the columns they contain, and the views built on them. You do this by using the same SQL syntax you use to query any other table.

Updating the tables in the system catalog occurs automatically when users create, alter, or drop tables or when they create or drop indexes. Users should not update the catalog directly using the update features of SQL because inconsistent results might be produced. If a user deletes the row in the SYSCOLUMNS table for the CUSTOMER_NUMBER column, for example, the system would no longer have any knowledge of this column, which is the table's primary key; yet all the rows in the database would still contain a customer number. The system might now treat those customer numbers as last names, because as far as the system is concerned, the column named LAST is the first column in the CUSTOMER table.

INTEGRITY IN SQL

An **integrity constraint** is a rule that the data in the database must follow. Examples of integrity constraints in the Premiere Products database are as follows:

1. No two sales reps can have the same sales rep number.

2. The sales rep number for a customer must match the number of a sales rep currently in the database. For example, because there is no sales rep number 20, a customer cannot be assigned to sales rep number 20.

3. Item classes for parts must be AP, HW, or SG.

If a user enters data in the database that violates any of these constraints, the database will develop serious problems. For example, two sales reps with the same number, a customer with a non-existent sales rep, or a part in a non-existent item class would cause serious difficulties for users of the database. Thus, it is important to make sure that the data does not violate any integrity constraints. To solve these types of problems, the DBMS provides integrity support. **Integrity support** means that you can specify integrity constraints when creating your database and the DBMS enforces these constraints. SQL has clauses to support three types of integrity constraints that can be specified within a CREATE TABLE command or an ALTER TABLE command. The only difference between these two commands is that an ALTER TABLE command is preceded by the word ADD to indicate that the constraint is to be added to any constraints that are already in place. To change an integrity constraint after it has been created, just enter the new constraint; the new constraint takes the place of the original.

The types of constraints supported in SQL are as follows:

1. **Legal values**. The CHECK clause ensures that only values that satisfy a particular condition are allowed in a given column. For example, to ensure that the only legal values for item class are AP, HW, or SG, use one of the following clauses:

   CHECK (ITEM_CLASS IN ('AP', 'HW', 'SG'))
   or
   CHECK (ITEM_CLASS = 'AP' OR ITEM_CLASS = 'HW' OR ITEM_CLASS = 'SG')

The general form of the CHECK clause is simply the CHECK command followed by a condition. If any update to the database violates the condition, the update is rejected automatically.

2. **Primary keys.** The primary key, or the column or columns that uniquely identify a row in the table, is specified through the ADD PRIMARY KEY clause. For example, to indicate that SLSREP_NUMBER is the primary key for the SALES_REP table, the clause is as follows:

ADD PRIMARY KEY (SLSREP_NUMBER)

In general, the PRIMARY KEY clause takes the form ADD PRIMARY KEY followed by the column name in parentheses that make up the primary key. If more than one column name is included the column names are separated by commas.

3. **Foreign keys.** A foreign key is a column in one table whose values match the primary key of another table. (One example is SLSREP_NUMBER in the CUSTOMER table. Values in this column are required to match those of the primary key of the SALES_REP table.) Any foreign keys are specified through ADD FOREIGN KEY clauses. To specify a foreign key, you need to specify *both* the column that is a foreign key *and* the table it matches. In the CUSTOMER table, for example, SLSREP_NUMBER is a foreign key that must match the SLSREP_NUMBER value in the SALES_REP table. The clause to specify a foreign key is as follows:

ADD FOREIGN KEY (SLSREP_NUMBER) REFERENCES SALES_REP

The general form for assigning a foreign key is: ADD FOREIGN KEY, followed by the column name(s) that constitute the foreign key, followed by the REFERENCES clause, and then by the table name that the foreign key is required to match.

Example 21: When the SALES_REP table was created, no primary key was assigned. Assign the SLSREP_NUMBER column as the primary key.

Figure 6.22 describes the SALES_REP table and shows the command to designate the primary key.

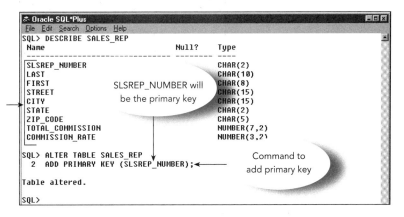

Figure 6.22 Assigning a primary key

Each foreign key to be specified requires a separate ADD FOREIGN KEY command.

Example 22:	Assign a foreign key for every table in the Premiere Products database.

These commands are shown in Figure 6.23.

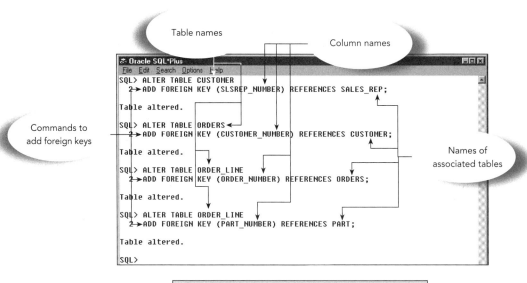

Figure 6.23 Adding foreign keys

After creating the foreign keys, the DBMS rejects any update that violates the foreign key constraint. For example, the INSERT command in Figure 6.24 attempts to add an order for which the customer number (600) does not match any customer in the CUSTOMER table; thus the insert is rejected. The DELETE command in the figure attempts to delete customer number 124. Deleting customer number 124 means that the rows in the ORDERS table for which the customer number is 124 no longer match any row in the CUSTOMER table; thus the deletion is rejected.

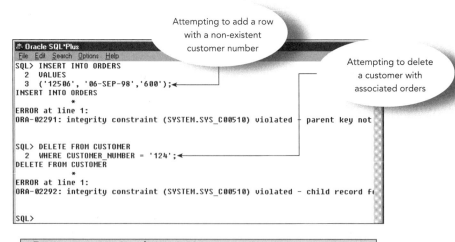

Figure 6.24 Violating foreign key constraints

Note that the error messages shown in Figure 6.24 include the words "parent" and "child." When you use a foreign key, the table containing the foreign key is the **child** and the table referenced by the foreign key is the **parent**. For example, the CUSTOMER_NUMBER column in the ORDERS table is a foreign key that references the CUSTOMER table. For this foreign key, the CUSTOMER table is the parent and the ORDERS table is the child. The first error message indicates that there is no parent for the order (i.e., there is no customer number 600). The second error message indicates that there are child records (rows) for customer number 124 (i.e., customer number 124 has orders). The DBMS rejects both updates because they violate referential integrity.

| **Example 23:** | Specify that the units on hand values in the PART table be greater than or equal to zero and less than or equal to 900. In addition, specify the item class as AP, HW, or SG. |

The commands are shown in Figure 6.25.

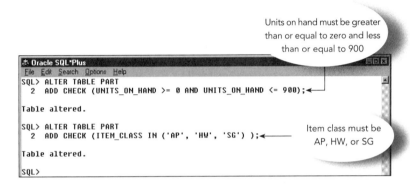

Figure 6.25 Adding additional integrity constraints

The DBMS now rejects any update that violates either constraint. For example, it would reject the update in Figure 6.26 because the command attempts to change the item class to XX, which is an illegal value.

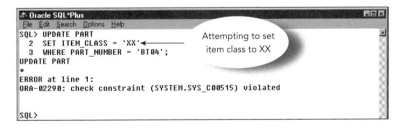

Figure 6.26 Violating an integrity constraint

In this chapter you learned about the purpose, creation, use, and benefits of views. Then you examined the features of SQL that relate to security; and you granted and revoked various privileges that controlled the types of activities that users of the database need to perform. You learned about the purpose, advantages, and disadvantages of using indexes, and how to create and drop indexes. You saw how to obtain information from the system catalog. You also learned about the importance of integrity constraints, and how to create them. In the next chapter, you will learn how to use SQL commands to create reports.

SUMMARY

1. A view is a pseudotable whose contents are derived from data in existing base tables whenever users attempt to access the view.

2. To define a view, use the CREATE VIEW statement. This statement includes a defining query that describes the portion of the database included in the view. When a user retrieves data from the view, the query entered by the user is merged with the defining query, producing the query that SQL actually executes.

3. Views provide data independence, allow database access control, and simplify the database structure for users.

4. You cannot update views that involve statistics and views with joins of non-primary key columns. In this case you must make all updates to the base table.

5. You delete views using the DROP VIEW command.

6. Use the GRANT command to give users access privileges concerning various portions of the database.

7. Use the REVOKE command to terminate previously granted privileges.

8. You can use an index to make data retrieval more efficient.

9. Use the CREATE INDEX command to create an index. Use the CREATE UNIQUE INDEX command to enforce a rule so that only unique values are allowed in a non-primary key column.

10. Use the DROP INDEX command to delete an index.

11. The DBMS, not the user, makes the choice of which index to use to accomplish a given task.

12. In the system catalog the DBMS maintains information about the tables, columns, indexes, and other system elements. Information about tables is kept in the SYSTABLES table; information about columns is kept in the SYSCOLUMNS table; and information about views is kept in the SYSVIEWS table. In Oracle these same tables are named DBA_TABLES, DBA_TAB_COLUMNS, and DBA_VIEWS.

13. Use the SELECT command to obtain information from the system catalog. The DBMS updates the system catalog continuously; users do not update the catalog directly.

14. Integrity constraints are rules that the data in the database must follow to ensure that only legal values are accepted in specified columns, or that primary and foreign key values match between tables. To specify a general integrity constraint, use the CHECK clause. To specify a primary key, use the ADD PRIMARY KEY clause. To specify a foreign key, use the ADD FOREIGN KEY clause.

EXERCISES (PREMIERE PRODUCTS)

Use SQL to make the following changes to the Premiere Products database.

If you are using Oracle for these exercises and wish to print a copy of your commands and results, type SPOOL followed by the name of a file and then press the Enter key. All the commands from that point on will be saved in the file that you named. For example, to save the commands and results to a file named CHAPTER6.SQL on drive A, the command is as follows:

SPOOL A:CHAPTER6.SQL

When you have finished, type SPOOL OFF, and then press the Enter key to stop saving commands to the file. Then you can start any program that opens *.txt files, open the file that you saved, and print it using the Print command on the File menu.

1. Define a view named SMALLCST. It consists of the customer number, last name, first name, street address, balance, and credit limit for every customer whose credit limit is $1,000 or less.

    a. Write the view definition for SMALLCST.

    b. Write a query to retrieve the customer number, last name, and first name of every customer in the SMALLCST view whose balance is over the credit limit.

    c. Write the query that the DBMS actually executes.

    d. Are any problems created by updating the database through this view? If so, what are they? If not, why not?

2. Define a view named CUSTORD. It consists of the customer number, last name, first name, balance, order number, and order date for every order currently on file.

    a. Write the view definition for CUSTORD.

    b. Write a query to retrieve the customer number, last name, first name, order number, and order date for every order in the CUSTORD view for each customer whose balance is more than $500.

    c. Write the query that the DBMS actually executes.

d. Are any problems created by updating the database through this view? If so, what are they? If not, why not?

3. Define a view named ORDTOT. It consists of the order number and order total for each order currently on file. (The order total is the sum of the number ordered times the quoted price on each of the order lines for the order.)

   a. Write the view definition for ORDTOT.

   b. Write a query to retrieve the order number and order total for every order whose total is over $500. Order the results by order number.

   c. Write the query that the DBMS actually executes.

   d. Are any problems created by updating the database through this view? If so, what are they? If not, why not?

4. Write the SQL commands to grant the following privileges, but do not execute the commands.

   a. User Stillwell must be able to retrieve data from the PART table.

   b. Users Webb and Bradley must be able to add new orders and order lines.

   c. User McKee must be able to change the number of units on hand for all parts.

   d. User Thompson must be able to delete customers.

   e. All users must be able to retrieve each customer's number, last name, first name, street address, city, state, and ZIP code.

   f. User Pool must be able to create an index on the ORDERS table.

   g. User Locke must be able to change the structure of the PART table.

   h. User Scott must have all privileges on the ORDERS, ORDER_LINE, and PART tables.

   i. User Richards must be permitted to access any data concerning housewares but not to access data concerning any other parts.

5. Write the SQL command to revoke user Stillwell's privilege, but do not execute the command.

6. Write the SQL commands to create the following indexes, but do not execute the commands.

   a. Create an index named PARTIND on the PART_NUMBER column in the ORDER_LINE table.

   b. Create an index named PARTIND2 on the ITEM_CLASS column in the PART table.

    c.   Create an index named PARTIND3 on the ITEM_CLASS and WARE-HOUSE_NUMBER columns in the PART table.

    d.   Create an index named PARTIND4 on the ITEM_CLASS and WARE-HOUSE_NUMBER columns in the PART table and list units on hand in descending order.

7.   Write the SQL command to delete the index named PARTIND3; it is no longer necessary.

8.   Write the SQL commands to obtain the following information from the system catalog.

    a.   List every table that you own.

    b.   List every column in the PART table and its associated data type.

    c.   List every table that contains a column named PART_NUMBER.

    d.   List the name of every view in the system that is owned by you.

    e.   List the table name, column name, and data type for the columns named STREET, CITY, STATE, ZIP_CODE. Order the results by table name.

9.   Assume that the CUSTOMER table has been created, but there are no integrity constraints. Write an ALTER TABLE command for the CUSTOMER table to ensure that the only values entered into the CREDIT_LIMIT column are 750, 1000, 1500, and 2000. The ALTER TABLE command should also indicate that the CUSTOMER_NUMBER column is the primary key and that the SLSREP_NUMBER column is a foreign key that must match the primary key of the table named SALES_REP.

EXERCISES (HENRY BOOKS)

Use SQL to make the following changes to the Henry Books database.

1.   Define a view named BANTAM. It consists of the book code, book title, book type, and book price for every book published by Bantam Books (code BB).

    a.   Write the view definition for BANTAM.

    b.   Write a query to retrieve the book code, book title, and book price for every book with a price of less than $10.

    c.   Write the query that the DMBS actually executes.

    d.   Are there any problems created by updating the database through this view? If so, what are they? If not, why not?

2.   Define a view named HARDBACK. It consists of the book code, book title, publisher name, and book price for every book that is not available in paperback.

    a.   Write the view definition for HARDBACK.

    b.   Write a query to retrieve the book title and publisher name for every book in the HARDBACK view that is priced at more than $20.

    c.   Write the query that the DMBS actually executes.

    d.   Are there any problems created by updating the database through this view? If so, what are they? If not, why not?

3.   Define a view named VALUE. It consists of a count of all books on hand for each branch.

    a.   Write the view definition for VALUE.

    b.   Write a query to retrieve the total count for the number of books in stock for each branch.

    c.   Write the query that the DMBS actually executes.

    d.   Are there any problems created by updating the database through this view? If so, what are they? If not, why not?

4.   Write SQL commands to grant the following privileges, but do not execute the commands.

    a.   User Lopez must be able to retrieve data from the BOOK table.

    b.   Users Bowen and Merrill must be able to add new books and publishers to the database.

    c.   Users Jenkins and Sherman must be able to change the units on hand value.

    d.   All users must be able to retrieve the book title, book code, and book price for every book.

    e.   User Scout must be able to add and delete publishers.

    f.   User Verner must be able to create an index for the BOOK table.

    g.   Users Verner and Scout must be able to change the structure of the AUTHOR table.

    h.   User Scout must have all privileges on all tables in the Henry Books database.

    i.   User Chambers must be able to change the units on hand for books in branch number 2 but not to access data in any other branch.

5. User Verner has left the company. Write the SQL command to revoke all of her privileges.

6. Write SQL commands to create the following indexes.

    a. Create an index named BOOKIND on the BOOK_TITLE column in the BOOK table.

    b. Create an index named BOOKIND2 on the BOOK_TYPE column in the BOOK table.

    c. Create an index named BOOKIND3 on the PUBLISHER_CODE and PUBLISHER_NAME columns in the PUBLISHER table and list the publisher codes in descending order.

7. Write the SQL command to delete the index named BOOKIND3; it is no longer necessary.

8. Write the SQL commands to obtain the following information from the system catalog.

    a. List every table that you own that contains a column named BOOK_CODE or BRANCH_NUMBER. Order the results by table name.

    b. List every column in the PUBLISHER table and its associated data type.

    c. List every table that contains a column named PUBLISHER_CODE.

    d. List the name of every view that you own.

    e. List the table name, column name, and data types for the columns named BOOK_CODE, BOOK_TITLE, and BOOK_PRICE. Order the results by column name.

9. Write the SQL commands to specify the following integrity constraints.

    a. Book types must be PSY, FIC, HOR, MYS, ART, POE, SUS, SFI, MUS, or CS.

    b. The PAPERBACK column can accept only values of Y or N.

    c. The only branch numbers are 1, 2, 3, and 4.

    d. The only sequence numbers are 1 and 2.

10. Write the SQL commands to add the following foreign keys to the Henry Books database.

    a. Publisher code is a foreign key in the BOOK table.

    b. Author number is a foreign key in the WROTE table.

CHAPTER 7

Reports

OBJECTIVES

- Use concatenation in a query
- Create a view for a report
- Create a query for a report
- Change column headings and formats in a report
- Add a title to a report
- Group data in a report
- Include totals and subtotals in a report
- Send a report to a file that can be printed

INTRODUCTION

In addition to the sorting and statistical functions available by using the SELECT command, many implementations of SQL include report formatting commands. In this chapter, you will learn about these commands by examining the report formatting commands found in Oracle.

In a sense, you can think of the output of a SELECT command as a very simple report that follows a rigid format. In many cases, this format is fine if you are concerned only about the particular data that appears in the result, and you are not concerned about the way the data is formatted.

If you need to generate a formatted report, however, you can't use a SELECT command. Fortunately, you can use other SQL commands to reformat the report in a variety of ways, and then you can rerun the query so the results display in the desired format.

■ ■ ■ ■ ■

CONCATENATING COLUMNS

Before creating a report, you need to understand the process of combining two or more character columns into a single expression because you will use this feature in the report that you will create later in this chapter. This process is called **concatenation**. To concatenate columns, you type two vertical lines (‖) between the column names, as illustrated in Example 1.

Example 1:	List the sales rep number and name of every sales rep. The name should be a concatenation of the FIRST and LAST columns.

The command and its results are shown in Figure 7.1. The double vertical line between the column names in the SELECT command indicates a concatenation. The first and last names now appear as a single column in the query results.

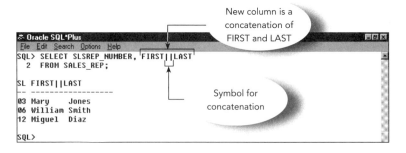

Figure 7.1 Using concatenation

When the first name doesn't include sufficient characters to fill the width of the column (as is the case with Mary Jones and Miguel Diaz), SQL inserts extra spaces. To remove these extra spaces, you use the RTRIM (right trim) function. When you apply this function to the value in a column, SQL displays the original value and removes any spaces inserted at the end of the value. To use RTRIM in this query, the command is as follows:

SELECT SLSREP_NUMBER, RTRIM(FIRST)||' '||RTRIM(LAST)
FROM SALES_REP;

For sales rep number 03, for example, this command trims the first name to "Mary," concatenates it with a single space, and then concatenates the last name to "Jones."

Question	Why is it necessary to insert a single space character in quotation marks in the query?
Answer	Without the space character, there would be no space between the first and last names. The name of sales rep number 03, for example, would display as "MaryJones."

Question	Is it necessary to trim the last name?
Answer	It is technically unnecessary to trim the end of the expression because you can't tell visually whether blanks are trimmed. However, trimming the last name in this case can be beneficial, especially when using the report formatting commands later in this chapter.

CREATING AND USING SCRIPTS

When entering report formatting commands, it's a good idea to save the commands for future use. Otherwise, you must re-enter the commands every time you want to produce the same report. Every version of SQL allows you to save commands. In this chapter, you will see how commands are saved in Oracle.

In Oracle a file containing SQL commands is called a **script**. You create a script by typing the EDIT command followed by the name of the script. For example, one of the scripts in this chapter is named FMT_RPT1. To create or edit this script, you would type EDIT FMT_RPT1 and then press the Enter key. (You can type the command in either uppercase or lowercase letters.)

The first time you type the EDIT command, the editor starts and asks if you want to create the file for the script. If you indicate Yes, the file is created and you can begin typing the necessary commands in the editor. If the file already exists, the file's contents display, and then you can edit the file. In either case, when you close the editor, you are prompted to save your work. To run the commands in the script, type @ followed by the script filename.

Saving your commands in a script has another advantage—doing so allows you to develop your report in stages. You can create a file with an initial set of commands to format the report, and then see what the report looks like. If necessary, you can change the commands in the script to improve the report's appearance and view the report again. You can make additional changes and view the report until you are satisfied with its appearance.

CREATING A VIEW FOR THE REPORT

The data for a report can come from either a table or a view. It often is better to use a view, particularly if the report involves data from more than one table.

The report you create in this chapter involves data from the SALES_REP and CUSTOMER tables. The report also concatenates two column names, as illustrated in Example 1. Therefore, it is advisable to create a view for the report. Example 2 creates this view.

Example 2:   Create a view for the report. The view should contain a column named SLSR that is the concatenation of the sales rep number, first name, and last name. There should be a hyphen between the sales rep number and name. The first and last names should be separated by a single space. (For example, the resulting value in the SLSR column for the first sales rep should be "03-Mary Jones.") A second column named CUST should be formatted in the same way and display the customer number, first name, and last name. The view also should contain a column named BAL that contains the balance, a column named CRED that contains the credit limit, and a column named AVAIL that contains the available credit (CREDIT_LIMIT - BALANCE).

The command to create this view is shown in Figure 7.2. The first line indicates that the view will consist of five columns named SLSR, CUST, BAL, CRED, and AVAIL. The third and fourth lines in the query specify a single column, SLSR, that uses concatenation and the RTRIM function. The fifth and sixth lines concatenate data into a single column named CUST. The remainder of the command is similar to many commands you have seen before.

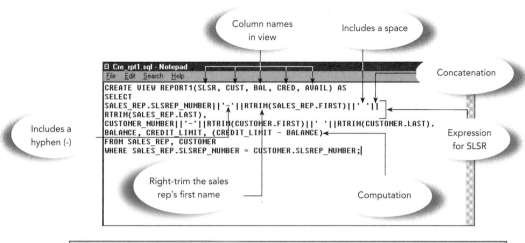

Figure 7.2 Command to create the view for the report

The command shown in Figure 7.3 creates a view named REPORT1. Once the CREATE VIEW command is executed, the view is ready to use.

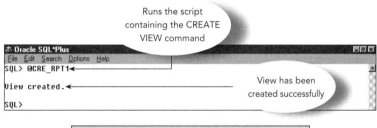

Figure 7.3 Creating the view

EXECUTING A SELECT COMMAND

To produce a report, you must run an appropriate SELECT command to create the data to use in the report. As a basis for our discussion on report formatting, we will use the query specified in Example 3.

Example 3:	List all the data in the REPORT1 view. The rows should be ordered by the SLSR column.

The command to list the rows, which is stored in a script, is shown in Figure 7.4.

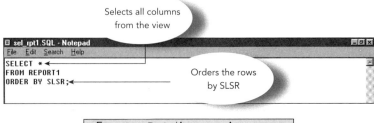

Figure 7.4 Using the view

The query results are shown in Figure 7.5. In the next examples, you will modify the format of the report to change the column headings, add a title, change the format of the numbers, and add totals and subtotals.

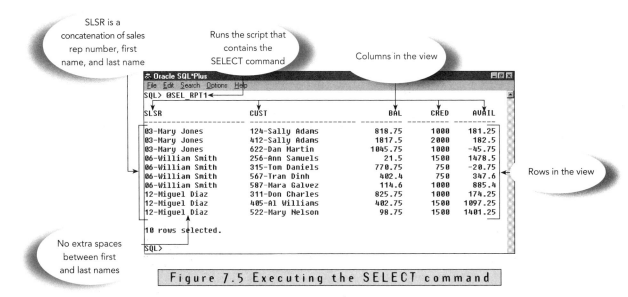

Figure 7.5 Executing the SELECT command

CHANGING COLUMN HEADINGS

The column headings in Figure 7.5 are not very descriptive of the columns' contents. You can change the headings to improve readability.

Example 4: Change the column headings in the report so they are more descriptive of the columns' contents.

To change a column heading, type the COLUMN command followed by the name of the column heading you want to change. Then use the HEADING clause to assign a new heading. If the heading is to extend over two lines, separate the two portions of the heading with a single vertical line (|). The commands to change the column headings are shown in Figure 7.6.

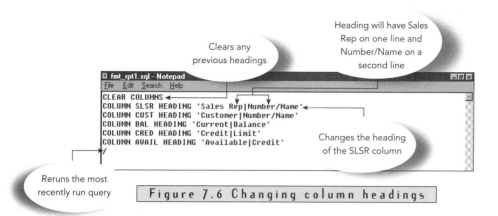

Clears any
previous headings

Heading will have Sales
Rep on one line and
Number/Name on a
second line

Changes the heading
of the SLSR column

Reruns the most
recently run query

Figure 7.6 Changing column headings

You can include the CLEAR COLUMNS command as a safety feature to clear any previous column changes. Without this command, any previous changes that you made to column headings or formats would still be in place. The next commands make the required changes to the column headings. The slash (/) on the final line reruns the last query. This time, however, the results will reflect the changes to the column headings. The result of running the script containing these commands is shown in Figure 7.7. Notice the new column headings.

Runs script to change
column headings

New column
headings

Figure 7.7 Column headings changed

CHANGING COLUMN FORMATS IN A REPORT

You can use the COLUMN command to change more than just the column headings. You also can use the COLUMN command to change the width of the column or the way the entries appear in the column. Example 5 illustrates these types of formatting changes.

Example 5:	Change the format of the columns so the SLSR and CUST columns contain 18 characters each. The data in the other columns should display with dollar signs and two decimal places.

The appropriate commands are shown in Figure 7.8. The first two COLUMN commands change the format of the SLSR and CUST columns to A18. The letter A indicates that the column is alphanumeric (another name for character); the 18 indicates that the column is to be 18 characters long.

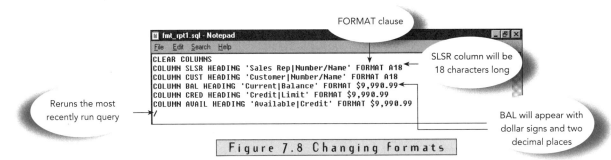

Figure 7.8 Changing Formats

The next three COLUMN commands change the format of the three numeric columns in the view. In each case, the new format is $9,990.99. The 9s indicate that the value is numeric. The two 9s to the right of the decimal point indicate that each number will display with two decimal places. The total number of 9s indicates the size of the column by representing the largest number that can be displayed. The dollar sign indicates that the values will display as currency. Finally, the zero immediately to the left of the decimal point indicates that a value of zero will display as $0.00. If you use all nines ($9,999.99), a value of zero will not display; zero values would be left blank.

One way to construct the appropriate format for the numeric columns is to write the largest number the column can display. If the amount can be over $10,000 but must be less than $100,000, for example, the format would be $99,999.99. If the amount must be less than $1,000 but more than $100, the format would be $999.99. The final step is to determine whether a value of zero should display. If you want a zero value to display, change the nine immediately to the left of the decimal to zero.

The result of running the script containing these commands is shown in Figure 7.9. Notice the new format of the columns.

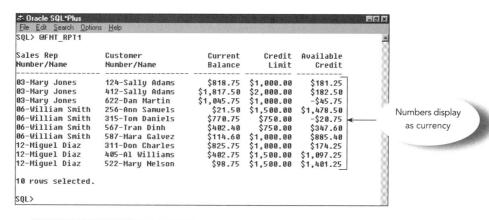

Figure 7.9 Report with formatting changes

ADDING A TITLE TO A REPORT

The next step is to add a title to the report, as illustrated in Example 6.

Example 6: Add a title to the report. The title should extend over two lines. The first line is "Customer Financial Report." The second line is "Organized by Sales Rep."

To add a title at the top of the report, use the TTITLE (top) command as shown in Figure 7.10. (To add a title at the bottom of the report, you use the BTITLE command.) Then you include the desired title in the TTITLE command. If the title will extend over two lines, separate the two portions by a vertical line as shown in Figure 7.10.

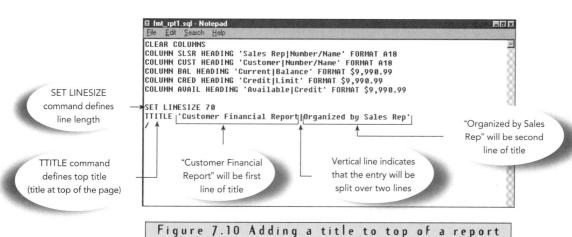

Figure 7.10 Adding a title to top of a report

In order for the title to display appropriately, you can adjust the line size by using the SET LINESIZE command. The **line size** determines where the title appears when it is centered across the line. In Figure 7.10, the SET LINESIZE command is used to set the line size to 70 characters. In this report, a line size of 70 characters is appropriate and places the title in the correct position on the line. In general, you can experiment with the line size to determine the best size for your report.

The resulting report is shown in Figure 7.11. Notice that the page number and date appear automatically along with the title.

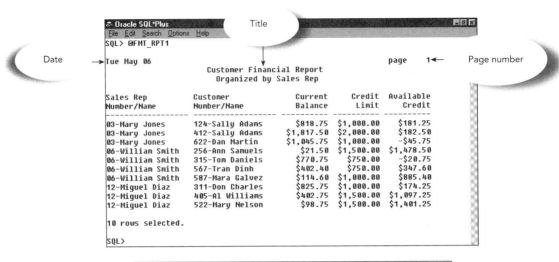

Figure 7.11 Title added to top of report

GROUPING DATA IN A REPORT

Just as you can group data by using SQL queries, you also can group data in reports by using the BREAK command. You use the BREAK command to identify a column (or collection of columns) on which to group the data. The value in the column displays only at the beginning of the group. In addition, you can specify a number of lines to skip after each group. Example 7 illustrates the BREAK command in grouping data. The example also removes the message "10 rows selected." from the end of the report.

Example 7: Group the rows in the display by the SLSR column. In addition, remove the message at the end of the report that indicates the number of rows selected.

To group rows by the SLSR column, the command is BREAK ON SLSR, as shown in Figure 7.12.

In order for the BREAK ON command to work properly, you need to sort the data on the indicated column. In this example, the data is sorted correctly because the SELECT command that produced the data included an ORDER BY SLSR clause.

The SKIP 1 clause at the end of the command indicates that one blank line should appear between groups. The SET FEEDBACK OFF command ensures that the message indicating the number of rows selected by the query will not display.

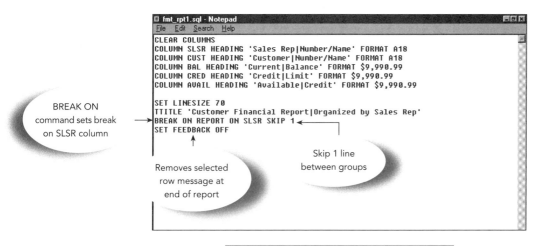

BREAK ON command sets break on SLSR column

Removes selected row message at end of report

Skip 1 line between groups

Figure 7.12 Adding a break

The results of executing these commands are shown in Figure 7.13. Notice that the rows are grouped by sales rep, with the sales rep number and name appearing only once. Notice also that there is a blank line separating the groups. The message indicating the number of rows selected does not display.

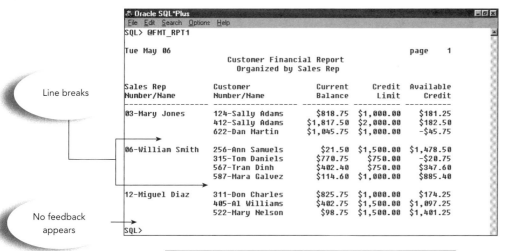

Line breaks

No feedback appears

Figure 7.13 Breaks added to report

INCLUDING TOTALS AND SUBTOTALS IN A REPORT

A total that appears after each group is called a **subtotal**. In order to calculate subtotals, you must include a BREAK command to group the rows. Then use a COMPUTE command to indicate the computation for the subtotal, as shown in Example 8.

Example 8: Include totals and subtotals for the BAL and AVAIL columns in the report.

The COMPUTE command uses **statistical functions** to calculate values to include in the report. The SQL statistical functions are shown in Table 7.1.

Table 7.1 Statistical Functions

STATISTICAL FUNCTION	RESULT OF CALCULATION
AVG	Average of values in a column
COUNT	Number of rows in a table
MAX	Largest value in a column
MIN	Smallest value in a column
STDEV	Standard deviation of values in a column
SUM	Sum of values in a column
VARIANCE	Variance of values in a column

In Example 8, SUM is the appropriate function to use. The script in Figure 7.14 shows the four COMPUTE commands needed to include totals and subtotals in the report.

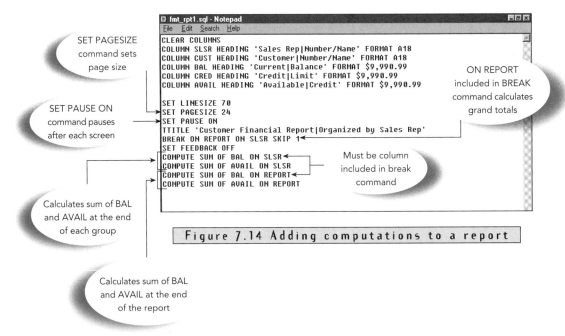

SET PAGESIZE command sets page size

SET PAUSE ON command pauses after each screen

ON REPORT included in BREAK command calculates grand totals

Must be column included in break command

Calculates sum of BAL and AVAIL at the end of each group

Calculates sum of BAL and AVAIL at the end of the report

```
CLEAR COLUMNS
COLUMN SLSR HEADING 'Sales Rep|Number/Name' FORMAT A18
COLUMN CUST HEADING 'Customer|Number/Name' FORMAT A18
COLUMN BAL HEADING 'Current|Balance' FORMAT $9,990.99
COLUMN CRED HEADING 'Credit|Limit' FORMAT $9,990.99
COLUMN AVAIL HEADING 'Available|Credit' FORMAT $9,990.99

SET LINESIZE 70
SET PAGESIZE 24
SET PAUSE ON
TTITLE 'Customer Financial Report|Organized by Sales Rep'
BREAK ON REPORT ON SLSR SKIP 1
SET FEEDBACK OFF
COMPUTE SUM OF BAL ON SLSR
COMPUTE SUM OF AVAIL ON SLSR
COMPUTE SUM OF BAL ON REPORT
COMPUTE SUM OF AVAIL ON REPORT
```

Figure 7.14 Adding computations to a report

Notice that the commands in Figure 7.14 contain an OF clause that includes the desired computation and column name on which the computation is to take place. The ON clause indicates the point at which the computation is to occur. The ON clause must contain the column name (or the word REPORT) that is included in the BREAK command.

The computations that end with ON REPORT represent computations that display once at the end of the report. In this report, the computations represent grand totals. The computations associated with the other breaks occur at the end of the indicated group. In this report, the computations represent subtotals that display after the group of customers of a particular sales rep.

There are two other commands in Figure 7.14 that are useful if the report will be displayed on the screen: SET PAGESIZE and SET PAUSE. In this example, the SET PAGESIZE command sets the number of lines that display on a single page of the report to 24 (the screen line size). The SET PAUSE ON command causes the display of the report to pause after each screen. To display the next screen, press the Enter key. The result is shown in Figure 7.15.

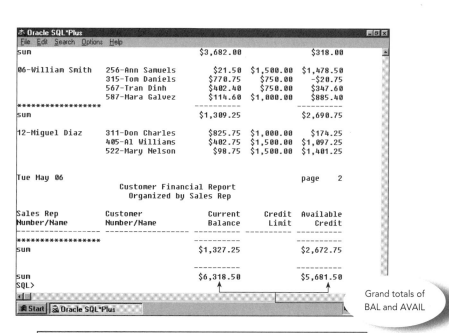

Break (end of records for sales rep number 06)

Subtotals of BAL and AVAIL

Grand totals of BAL and AVAIL

Figure 7.15 Totals and subtotals included

The report includes subtotals to indicate the balances and available credit limits for every customer of each sales rep. Subtotals represent a subset of the overall total. Grand totals of the balance and available credit amounts for all customers appear at the end of the report.

SENDING THE REPORT TO A FILE

In many cases, viewing the results of a query on the screen is sufficient. In other cases, you might want to print a copy; this is especially true for reports. The exact manner in which you print the report depends on the DBMS. If you have any questions about printing, consult your DBMS documentation.

To print a report using Oracle, you first send the output of the query to a file by using the SPOOL command. (The process of sending printed output to a file rather than directly to a printer is called **spooling** and this is where the command gets its name.) After spooling you can print the contents of the file just as you would print the contents of any other file.

Example 9:   Send the report created in the previous examples to the file named REPORT1.SQL.

The SPOOL REPORT1.SQL command in Figure 7.16 begins sending the output of the subsequent commands to the file named REPORT1.SQL. The final command (SPOOL OFF) turns off spooling and stops any further output from being sent to the REPORT1.SQL file.

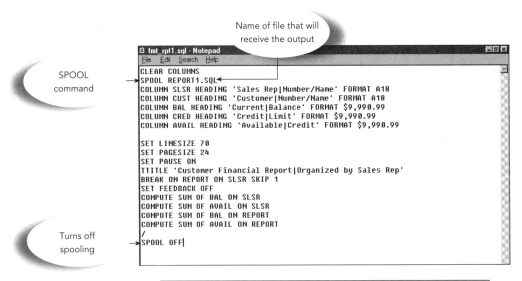

Figure 7.16 Sending the report to a file

When you run the new script, the report displays again on the screen. As it displays on the screen (see Figure 7.17) it also is being placed in the file. After completing the spooling process, the report is stored in the REPORT1.SQL file. Then you can print the file, edit it, include it in a document, or use it as needed in other ways.

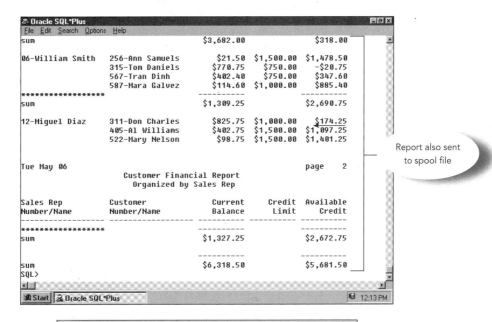

Figure 7.17 Running the final report

A COMPLETE SCRIPT TO PRODUCE THE REPORT

You can include additional commands to the script to complete it. These commands are shown in Figure 7.18.

The first command, CLEAR COLUMNS, clears any previous column definitions. The next two commands have the same purpose. The CLEAR COMPUTE command clears any previously specified computations, and the CLEAR BREAK command clears any previous breaks. The TTITLE OFF command turns off any previously specified title.

The SQL query for the report is included next in the script. Without this query a user who runs this script would have to execute the query first and then run the script. The script will not work if you don't execute the query, so it is a good idea to include the query execution command in the script to avoid this problem.

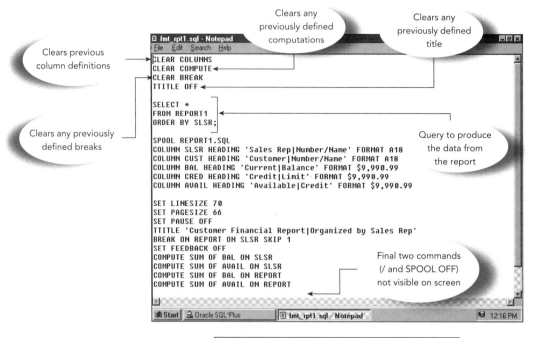

Clears previous column definitions

Clears any previously defined computations

Clears any previously defined title

Clears any previously defined breaks

Query to produce the data from the report

Final two commands (/ and SPOOL OFF) not visible on screen

Figure 7.18 Completed script

Because this report will be printed, it is appropriate to adjust the SET PAGESIZE and SET PAUSE commands. Change the page size to 66 (the length of a printed page) rather than 24 (the length of the screen). In addition, there is no reason for the display to pause for a report that will be printed, so change the SET PAUSE ON command to SET PAUSE OFF.

The remaining commands in the script are the same as those encountered earlier. Running the script shown in Figure 7.18 produces the report shown in Figure 7.19.

```
Tue May 06                                              page    1
                       Customer Financial Report
                         Organized by Sales Rep

Sales Rep          Customer            Current      Credit   Available
Number/Name        Number/Name         Balance       Limit      Credit
-----------------  -----------------  ----------  ----------  ----------
03-Mary Jones      124-Sally Adams       $818.75  $1,000.00     $181.25
                   412-Sally Adams     $1,817.50  $2,000.00     $182.50
                   622-Dan Martin      $1,045.75  $1,000.00     -$45.75
*******************                    ----------              ----------
sum                                    $3,682.00                $318.00

06-William Smith   256-Ann Samuels        $21.50  $1,500.00   $1,478.50
                   315-Tom Daniels       $770.75    $750.00     -$20.75
                   567-Tran Dinh         $402.40    $750.00     $347.60
                   587-Mara Galvez       $114.60  $1,000.00     $885.40
*******************                    ----------              ----------
sum                                    $1,309.25              $2,690.75

12-Miguel Diaz     311-Don Charles       $825.75  $1,000.00     $174.25
                   405-Al Williams       $402.75  $1,500.00   $1,097.25
                   522-Mary Nelson        $98.75  $1,500.00   $1,401.25
*******************                    ----------              ----------
sum                                    $1,327.25              $2,672.75

                                       ----------              ----------
sum                                    $6,318.50              $5,681.50
```

Figure 7.19 Completed report

In this chapter, you learned about several important commands to create and format reports. These commands and their descriptions are outlined in Table 7.2.

Table 7.2 Reporting command summary

COMMAND	DESCRIPTION
BREAK ON	Groups data in a report on a specified column
BTITLE	Adds a title at the bottom of a report
BTITLE OFF	Clears any previously specified title at the bottom of a report
CLEAR BREAK	Clears any previously specified report breaks
CLEAR COLUMNS	Clears any previous column changes
CLEAR COMPUTE	Clears any previously specified report computations
COLUMN	Changes the name of a column
COMPUTE	Calculates a count, minimum, maximum, sum, average, standard deviation, or a variance on the values in a column in a report
HEADING	Assigns a new column heading
ON REPORT	Indicates that a calculation is to be performed on all values in the report
RTRIM	Deletes extra spaces that appear after a value in column
SET FEEDBACK OFF	Turns off the message indicating the number of rows selected by a query in a report
SET LINESIZE	Indicates the maximum number of characters on a line
SET PAGESIZE	Indicates the number of lines on a page
SET PAUSE	Indicates whether the screen display pauses after each screen of data
SKIP 1	Inserts one blank line between groups in a report
SPOOL	Sends query output to a file that can be printed
TTITLE	Adds a title at the top of a report
TTITLE OFF	Clears any previously specified title at the top of a report

SUMMARY

1. To concatenate columns in report, separate the column names with two vertical lines (||). Use the RTRIM command to delete any extra spaces that follow the values.

2. You use a script to save the commands used to create a report, so you can make modifications to the report at a later time. To save commands in a script, type EDIT followed by the script name. To run a script, type @ followed by the script name.

3. Reports are based on tables or views that contain the report data.

4. Use the COLUMN command to change a column heading. The HEADING clause is used to assign a new heading name. Type a single vertical line (|) to break a column heading over two lines.

5. You can use the COLUMN command to change the format of column values.

6. Use the TTITLE or BTITLE commands to add a title to the top or bottom of a report, respectively.

7. Use the BREAK command to group data in a report.

8. Use the BREAK and COMPUTE commands and an appropriate statistical function to calculate data in a report such as totals and subtotals.

9. Use the SET PAUSE and SET PAGESIZE commands to pause a report after each screen of data, or to change the number of report lines to display.

10. Use the SPOOL command to send a report to a file for printing.

EXERCISES (PREMIERE PRODUCTS)

Use SQL to make the following changes to the Premiere Products database.

If you are using Oracle for these exercises and wish to print a copy of your commands and results, type SPOOL followed by the name of a file and then press the Enter key. All the commands from that point on are saved in the file that you named. For example, to save the commands and results to a file named CHAPTER7.SQL on drive A, the command is as follows:

SPOOL A:CHAPTER7.SQL

When you have finished, type SPOOL OFF, and then press the Enter key to stop saving commands to the file. Then you can start any program that opens *.txt files, open the file that you saved, and print it using the Print command on the File menu.

1. Use SQL to produce a query that lists the name, street address, and city, state, and ZIP code for every customer. Concatenate the first and last name data, and the city, state, and ZIP code data into single expressions. Insert a comma between the city and state data and trim the columns so that only one space displays between column data.

2. Create a view named REPORT2 for the query that you produced in Exercise 1. Change the column headings to NAME, ADDRESS, CITY.

3. Change the column headings to CUSTOMER NAME, CUSTOMER ADDRESS, and CUSTOMER CITY/STATE/ZIP so the word "CUSTOMER" appears on the first line and the other part of the heading appears on the second line.

4. Change the format of each column to 25 alphanumeric characters.

5. Create a view named REPORT3 that lists a trimmed concatenation of every customer's first and last name, along with his or her credit limit and current balance. The credit limit and balance should display as currency.

6. Add the title "CUSTOMER CREDIT LIMITS AND BALANCES" to the report. The title should display on two lines, with the words "AND BALANCES" on the second line.

7. Change the report so the feedback about the number of rows selected does not display.

8. Create the following report: List the number and name of every sales rep together with the number, name, and balance of every customer represented by the sales rep. Column headings for these columns are SNUM, SNAME, CNUM, CNAME, and BAL, respectively. Sort the report by customer number within sales rep number. Format the BALANCE column with two decimal places and total it by sales rep. The heading for the report is "SALES REP REPORT." Format the report so it can be printed with 66 lines on the page and no screen pauses.

EXERCISES (HENRY BOOKS)

Use SQL to make the following changes to the Henry Books database.

1. Create the following report: For each branch and each book published, list the branch number, book title, publisher name, publisher location (a concatenation of the publisher's city and state, separated by a comma and a space), the book price, and the number of units of the book that are currently on hand in the branch. The column headings for these columns are BRANCH NUMBER, BOOK TITLE, PUBLISHER NAME, PUBLISHER LOCATION, PRICE, and UNITS ON HAND. The title of the report is INVENTORY LIST on one line and HENRY BOOKS on the second line. Format columns that contain currency with dollar signs and two decimals places, so values of zero display as $0.00. Group the data in the report by branch number, with one blank line between groups. The report should contain subtotals of the units on hand by branch number and a grand total of the number of units on hand for all branch numbers at the end of the report. Format the report so it can be printed on paper. Experiment with different settings for the column width, pagesize, and linesize commands when producing your report. (*Hint:* Some of the data in the BOOK_TITLE column will need to print on more than one line, but you cannot control where the line break will occur, so the data might be split in a random location. You should set the linesize and pagesize first, trim the concatenated column, and then format the column widths to the smallest size possible to hold the data in order to fit the report on the printed page.)

CHAPTER 8

Embedded SQL

OBJECTIVES

- Embed SQL commands in COBOL
- Retrieve single rows using embedded SQL
- Update a table using embedded INSERT, UPDATE, and DELETE commands
- Use cursors to retrieve multiple rows in embedded SQL
- Update a database using cursors
- Learn how to handle errors in programs containing embedded SQL commands

INTRODUCTION

SQL is a very powerful non-procedural language in which you communicate tasks to the computer using simple commands. As in other non-procedural languages, you can accomplish many tasks using a single, relatively simple command. By contrast, a procedural language is one in which you must give the computer the step-by-step process for accomplishing tasks. To accomplish a task in a procedural language might require many lines of code. COBOL is an example of a procedural language. In this chapter, we will use COBOL to illustrate how you can embed SQL commands into another language.

Even though SQL and other non-procedural languages are well-equipped to store and query data, sometimes you might need to complete tasks that are beyond the capabilities of SQL. In such cases, you need to use a procedural language. Fortunately, you can embed SQL commands into a procedural language to capitalize on the advantages of SQL. You can use SQL for some tasks, and then include embedded SQL commands in the procedural language to accomplish tasks that are beyond the capabilities of SQL.

In this chapter, you learn how to embed SQL commands in COBOL. The process of embedding SQL in other programming languages, such as C or PL/SQL, is very similar. Because the focus of this chapter is not on the COBOL language but rather is on the use of SQL within COBOL, we will use simple ACCEPT and DIS-PLAY statements within the COBOL programs for input and output.

A COBOL program in which SQL commands are embedded will have additional statements beyond the standard COBOL statements in both the DATA and PROCEDURE divisions. In both cases, these new statements are preceded by EXEC SQL and followed by END-EXEC, so that the COBOL compiler can distinguish embedded SQL commands from standard COBOL statements.

Note   Your instructor might inform you of other requirements about the way you embed SQL commands.

In the DATA DIVISION (in particular, in the WORKING-STORAGE SECTION), the new statements declare the tables that will be used in processing the database as well as define a communications area for SQL. The **communications area** includes items that allow SQL to communicate various aspects of processing with the program. The main item you use in the communications area is SQLCODE. After executing any SQL statement, SQLCODE contains a code indicating the fate of the executed statement. If the execution is normal, SQLCODE is zero. If the execution is not normal, the value in SQLCODE indicates the problem that occurred (for example, not finding any rows that satisfy the condition in a WHERE clause). Programs should contain statements that check the value of SQLCODE after each SQL statement is executed.

In the PROCEDURE DIVISION, the new statements will be SQL statements, with some slight variations. The examples that follow illustrate how to use SQL to retrieve a single row, insert new rows, and update and delete existing rows. Finally, you will learn how to retrieve multiple rows. Executing a SELECT statement that retrieves more than one row presents a problem for a language like COBOL, which is oriented toward processing one record at a time. Thus, you must take some special action in such situations.

■ ■ ■ ■ ■

DATA DIVISION

Any tables to be processed in COBOL must be declared in WORKING-STORAGE, the portion of the program where you declare your variables. To do this, you use the DECLARE TABLE command, which is similar to the SQL CREATE TABLE command. To process the SALES_REP table, for example, the code is written as follows:

```
EXEC SQL
        DECLARE SALES_REP TABLE
                        (SLSREP_NUMBER          DECIMAL (2),
                        LAST                    CHAR (10),
                        FIRST                   CHAR (8),
                        STREET                  CHAR (15),
                        CITY                    CHAR (15),
                        STATE                   CHAR (2),
                        ZIP_CODE                CHAR (5),
                        TOTAL_COMMISSION        DECIMAL (7,2),
                        COMMISSION_RATE         DECIMAL (3,2) )
END-EXEC.
```

Optionally, if the description of the SALES_REP table is stored in a special location, often called a **library**, under the name DECSALES_REP, the code is written as follows:

```
EXEC SQL
        INCLUDE DECSALES_REP
END-EXEC.
```

When processing this table, you will need to use regular COBOL variables corresponding to the columns in the table. For the SALES_REP table, for example, the COBOL code is written as follows:

```
01 W-SALES-REP.
        03 W-SLSREP-NUMBER          PIC S9(2) COMP-3.
        03 W-LAST                   PIC X(10).
        03 W-FIRST                  PIC X(8).
        03 W-STREET                 PIC X(15).
        03 W-CITY                   PIC X(15).
        03 W-STATE                  PIC X(2).
        03 W-ZIP-CODE               PIC X(5).
        03 W-TOTAL-COMMISSION       PIC S9(5)V9(2) COMP-3.
        03 W-COMMISSION-RATE        PIC S9V9(2) COMP-3.
```

Because this description is standard COBOL, you do not precede the code with EXEC SQL.

Note The programs in this chapter use a naming approach in which the work variables begin with the letter "W" and are followed by a hyphen. This naming convention emphasizes that the variables are work variables and not items from the database.

Finally, the system uses the **SQL communication area (SQLCA)** to provide feedback to the program using SQLCODE. You include the SQLCA by coding the command as follows:

```
EXEC SQL
        INCLUDE SQLCA
END-EXEC.
```

There is only one other new type of entry—a cursor—that appears in the DATA DIVISION. You use a **cursor** for the multiple-row SELECT statements mentioned earlier. Cursors and the problems associated with multiple-row retrieval are discussed later in this chapter.

PROCEDURE DIVISION

Before looking at examples of SQL statements in the PROCEDURE DIVISION, some general comments are necessary. First, you can use normal COBOL variables in SQL statements. Such variables are called **host variables**; they are variables in the host language, in this case COBOL. When used, you must precede the variable with a colon. If you use W-LAST *within a SQL statement*, for example, you must enter it as :W-LAST. For any other use, it can appear as W-LAST. Second, you must place the results of SQL queries in host variables in the INTO clause, which is written as follows:

```
SELECT LAST
        INTO :W-LAST
        FROM SALES_REP
        WHERE SLSREP_NUMBER = '03'
```

Note	When naming host variables, you must follow the naming rules in the host language. In COBOL, for example, hyphens are allowed, but underscores are not. One way to avoid problems is to use hyphens in the host variable wherever there is an underscore in the corresponding SQL column name. For example, the host variable corresponding to the SQL ZIP_CODE column becomes W-ZIP-CODE. Notice that the underscore separating the words ZIP and CODE has changed to a hyphen in COBOL, and that the COBOL variable is preceded by "W-".

Finally, you must make provisions for exceptional conditions. Such conditions occur when no data is found to satisfy a condition or when no space is available to add a new row on the disk. The specific condition determines which action occurs. Mechanisms to check for and handle these conditions are discussed after the following examples.

Retrieve a Single Row and Column

Example 1 illustrates using embedded SQL to retrieve a single row and column from a table.

Example 1:	Obtain the last name of sales rep number 03 and place it in W-LAST.

Because this retrieval is based on the primary key (SLSREP_NUMBER), it does not pose any problem for a record-at-a-time language like COBOL. If SQL is used in a stand-alone mode, the statement is written as follows:

```
SELECT LAST
      FROM SALES_REP
      WHERE SLSREP_NUMBER = '03'
```

In COBOL, the statement is written as follows:

```
EXEC SQL
      SELECT LAST
            INTO :W-LAST
            FROM SALES_REP
            WHERE SLSREP_NUMBER = '03'
END-EXEC.
```

The only difference between the statements—other than the required EXEC SQL and END-EXEC codes—is the addition of the INTO clause indicating that the result should be placed in the host. The W-LAST variable now can be used in any way it could be used in any other COBOL program. Its value could be printed in a report, displayed on screen, compared with some other name, and so on.

Retrieve a Single Row and All Columns

There are two differences between Example 2 and Example 1. First, Example 2 requires retrieving all columns. Second, the sales rep number is not given in this example; it is stored in a host (COBOL) variable.

Example 2:	Obtain all information about the sales rep whose number is stored in the host variable W-SLSREP-NUMBER.

To fill in W-SLSREP-NUMBER, you can use an appropriate COBOL statement, such as MOVE. This statement copies the value in one variable into another. You also can use ACCEPT, which obtains input from a user and places it in a variable. Then you can use the following embedded SQL command:

```
EXEC SQL
    SELECT LAST, FIRST, STREET, CITY, STATE, ZIP_CODE,
        TOTAL_COMMISSION, COMMISSION_RATE
        INTO :W-LAST, :W-FIRST, :W-STREET, :W-CITY, :W-STATE,
            :W-ZIP-CODE, :W-TOTAL-COMMISSION, :W-COMMISSION-RATE
        FROM SALES_REP
        WHERE SLSREP_NUMBER = :W-SLSREP-NUMBER
END-EXEC.
```

In this formulation, several columns are listed in the SELECT statement, and the corresponding host variables that will receive the values are listed in the INTO statement. In addition, the host variable W-SLSREP-NUMBER is used in the WHERE clause. Note that there was no need to select SLSREP_NUMBER and place it in W-SLSREP-NUMBER, because W-SLSREP-NUMBER already contains the desired number.

Figure 8.1 shows a complete COBOL program to accomplish the task. SQL command are shaded. Let's look at the numbered portions of the program.

1. This program contains a loop. The user can display sales reps repeatedly. The data item named ARE-WE-DONE is a flag that indicates that the user does not wish to display any more sales reps. (The user indicates that he or she is finished by entering a sales rep number of zero.)

2. The record named W-SALES-REP contains the host variables that store the sales rep data. Within W-SALES-REP, there is a field for each column in the SALES_REP table. The approach used here for naming these fields is to precede the name of the column in the table with "W-".

3. This statement is the declaration of the SALES_REP table. Note that it is very similar to the SQL CREATE TABLE command.

4. This statement is used to include the SQL communication area in the program.

5. This is the main loop where the user is asked to enter the number of the desired sales rep or enter zero if no more sales reps are desired. If the user enters zero, the flag ARE-WE-DONE is set to YES, indicating that the process should terminate. If not, the program performs the paragraph named FIND-AND-DISPLAY-SALES_REP.

6. This embedded SELECT statement selects the desired sales rep and places the information about the sales rep in the indicated host variables.

7. If SQLCODE contains the number zero, the desired sales rep was found successfully, in which case the information displays. If not, the sales rep is not in the database and an appropriate error message displays.

```
                    IDENTIFICATION DIVISION.
                    PROGRAM-ID.      DSPSLS.

                    ENVIRONMENT DIVISION.

                    DATA DIVISION.

                    WORKING-STORAGE SECTION.

1      01  STATUS-FLAGS.
           03  ARE-WE-DONE                  PIC X(3).
               88  WE-ARE-DONE                          VALUE 'YES'.

2      01  W-SALES-REP.
           03  W-SLSREP-NUMBER             PIC X(2).
           03  W-LAST                      PIC X(10).
           03  W-FIRST                     PIC X(8).
           03  W-STREET                    PIC X(15).
           03  W-CITY                      PIC X(15).
           03  W-STATE                     PIC X(2).
           03  W-ZIP-CODE                  PIC X(5).
           03  W-TOTAL-COMMISSION          PIC S9(5)V9(2).
           03  W-COMMISSION-RATE           PIC SV9(2).

3          EXEC SQL
             DECLARE SALES_REP TABLE
                  (SLSREP_NUMBER      CHAR (2),
                   LAST               CHAR (10),
                   FIRST              CHAR (8),
                   STREET             CHAR (15),
                   CITY               CHAR (15),
                   STATE              CHAR (2),
                   ZIP_CODE           CHAR (5),
                   TOTAL_COMMISSION   DECIMAL (7,2),
                   COMMISSION_RATE    DECIMAL (3,2) )
           END-EXEC.

4          EXEC SQL
               INCLUDE SQLCA
           END-EXEC.

       PROCEDURE-DIVISION.

       MAIN-PROGRAM.
           MOVE 'NO' TO ARE-WE-DONE.
           PERFORM MAIN-LOOP
               UNTIL WE-ARE-DONE.
           STOP RUN.

       MAIN-LOOP.
5          DISPLAY 'SALES REP NUMBER OR ** TO END PROGRAM: '.
           ACCEPT W-SLSREP-NUMBER.
           IF W-SLSREP-NUMBER = '**'
               MOVE 'YES' TO ARE-WE-DONE
             ELSE
               PERFORM FIND-AND-DISPLAY-SALES_REP.

       FIND-AND-DISPLAY-SALES_REP.
6          EXEC SQL
               SELECT LAST, FIRST, STREET, CITY, STATE, ZIP_CODE,
                      TOTAL_COMMISSION, COMMISSION_RATE
               INTO :W-LAST, :W-FIRST, :W-STREET, :W-CITY, :W-STATE,
                    :W-ZIP_CODE, :W-TOTAL-COMMISSION,
                    :W-COMMISSION-RATE
               FROM SALES_REP
               WHERE SLSREP_NUMBER = :W-SLSREP-NUMBER
           END-EXEC.
7          IF SQLCODE = 0
               DISPLAY '      LAST NAME: ', W-LAST,
               DISPLAY '     FIRST NAME: ', W-FIRST
               DISPLAY '         STREET: ', W-STREET,
               DISPLAY '           CITY: ', W-CITY,
               DISPLAY '          STATE: ', W-STATE,
               DISPLAY '       ZIP CODE: ', W-ZIP-CODE
               DISPLAY 'TOTAL COMMISSION: ', W-TOTAL-COMMISSION
               DISPLAY ' COMMISSION RATE: ', W-COMMISSION-RATE
             ELSE
               DISPLAY 'THERE IS NO SUCH SALES REP'.
```

Figure 8.1 Program to display sales rep information

Figure 8.2 represents a slightly different version of the same program. The only difference here occurs on line 1. Instead of including the specific table declaration for SALES_REP in the program, as in the previous version, the INCLUDE DECSALES_REP statement is included. This statement assumes that the declaration has been created already and is stored in the file DECSALES_REP.

```
                    IDENTIFICATION DIVISION.
                    PROGRAM-ID.    DSPSLS.

                    ENVIRONMENT DIVISION.

                    DATA DIVISION.

                    WORKING-STORAGE SECTION.

                    01  STATUS-FLAGS.
                        03  ARE-WE-DONE          PIC X(3).
                            88  WE-ARE-DONE                      VALUE 'YES'.

                    01  W-SALES-REP.
                        03  W-SLSREP-NUMBER       PIC X(2).
                        03  W-LAST                PIC X(10).
                        03  W-FIRST               PIC X(8).
                        03  W-STREET              PIC X(15).
                        03  W-CITY                PIC X(15).
                        03  W-STATE               PIC X(2).
                        03  W-ZIP-CODE            PIC X(5).
                        03  W-TOTAL-COMMISSION    PIC S9(5)V9(2).
                        03  W-COMMISSION-RATE     PIC SV9(2).

          1           EXEC SQL
                          INCLUDE DECSALES_REP
                      END-EXEC.

                      EXEC SQL
                          INCLUDE SQLCA
                      END-EXEC.

                    PROCEDURE-DIVISION.

                    MAIN-PROGRAM.
                        MOVE 'NO' TO ARE-WE-DONE.
                        PERFORM MAIN-LOOP
                            UNTIL WE-ARE-DONE.
                        STOP RUN.

                    MAIN-LOOP.
                        DISPLAY 'SALES REP NUMBER OR ** TO END PROGRAM: '.
                        ACCEPT W-SLSREP-NUMBER.
                        IF W-SLSREP-NUMBER = '**'
                            MOVE 'YES' TO ARE-WE-DONE
                          ELSE                          .
                            PERFORM FIND-AND-DISPLAY-SALES_REP.

                    FIND-AND-DISPLAY-SALES_REP.
                        EXEC SQL
                            SELECT LAST, FIRST, STREET, CITY, STATE, ZIP_CODE,
                                TOTAL_COMMISSION, COMMISSION_RATE
                            INTO :W-LAST, :W-FIRST, :W-STREET, :W-CITY, :W-STATE,
                                :W-ZIP_CODE, :W-TOTAL-COMMISSION,
                                :W-COMMISSION-RATE
                            FROM SALES_REP
                            WHERE SLSREP_NUMBER = :W-SLSREP-NUMBER
                        END-EXEC.
                        IF SQLCODE = 0
                            DISPLAY '        LAST NAME: ', W-LAST,
                            DISPLAY '       FIRST NAME: ', W-FIRST
                            DISPLAY '           STREET: ', W-STREET,
                            DISPLAY '             CITY: ', W-CITY,
                            DISPLAY '            STATE: ', W-STATE,
                            DISPLAY '         ZIP CODE: ', W-ZIP-CODE
                            DISPLAY 'TOTAL COMMISSION: ', W-TOTAL-COMMISSION
                            DISPLAY ' COMMISSION RATE: ', W-COMMISSION-RATE
                          ELSE
                            DISPLAY 'THERE IS NO SUCH SALES REP'.
```

Figure 8.2 Program to display sales rep information (version 2)

Retrieve a Single Row from a Join

An embedded SQL command can be used to join tables, as illustrated in Example 3.

Example 3: Obtain the last name, first name, and address of the customer whose customer number is stored in the host variable, W-CUSTOMER-NUMBER, as well as the number, last name, and first name of the sales rep who represents this customer.

This query involves joining the CUSTOMER and SALES_REP tables. Because the restriction involves the primary key of the CUSTOMER table and each customer is related to exactly one sales rep, the result of the query will be a single row. The method for handling this query is similar to that for the preceding queries. The SELECT command is written as follows:

```
EXEC SQL
        SELECT CUSTOMER.LAST, CUSTOMER.FIRST, CUSTOMER.STREET,
                CUSTOMER.CITY, CUSTOMER.STATE, CUSTOMER.ZIP_CODE,
                CUSTOMER.SLSREP_NUMBER, SALES_REP.LAST, SALES_REP.FIRST
        INTO :W-LAST OF :W-CUSTOMER, :W-FIRST OF :W-CUSTOMER,
                :W-STREET OF :W-CUSTOMER, :W-CITY OF :W-CUSTOMER,
                :W-STATE OF :W-CUSTOMER, :W-ZIP-CODE OF :W-CUSTOMER,
                :W-SLSREP-NUMBER OF :W-CUSTOMER, :W-LAST OF :W-SALES-REP,
                :W-FIRST OF :W-SALES-REP
        FROM SALES_REP, CUSTOMER
        WHERE SALES_REP.SLSREP_NUMBER = CUSTOMER.SLSREP_NUMBER
        AND CUSTOMER.CUSTOMER_NUMBER = :W-CUSTOMER-NUMBER
END-EXEC.
```

Note

Any qualification of host variables must follow the rules of the host language rather than the rules of SQL. In COBOL, for example, this means following the name of the variable with the OF command and then by the record name. For example, to indicate the last name of a customer, the expression is :W-LAST OF :W-CUSTOMER. To indicate the last name of a sales rep, the expression is :W-LAST OF :W-SALES-REP.

Insert a Row into a Table

When you are updating SQL databases from within COBOL programs, you need to use appropriate SQL commands to update the database. For example, to add a row to a table in the database, you do not use the COBOL WRITE statement that normally is used when updating files. Instead, you use the SQL INSERT command as illustrated in Example 4.

Example 4:

Add a row to the SALES_REP table. The sales rep number, last name, first name, address, total commission, and credit limit already have been placed in the variables W-SLSREP-NUMBER, W-LAST, W-FIRST, W-STREET, W-CITY, W-STATE, W-ZIP-CODE, W-TOTAL-COMMISSION, and W-COMMISSION-RATE, respectively.

To insert a row into a table, use the INSERT command. The values are contained in host variables, whose names must be preceded by colons. The command is written as follows:

```
EXEC SQL
        INSERT
                INTO SALES_REP
                VALUES (:W-SLSREP-NUMBER, :W-LAST, :W-FIRST, :W-STREET,
                        :W-CITY, :W-STATE, :W-ZIP-CODE, :W-TOTAL-COMMISSION,
                        :W-COMMISSION-RATE)
END-EXEC.
```

The values currently in the host variables included in the INSERT statement are used to add a new row to the SALES_REP table.

Figure 8.3 shows a complete COBOL program to add sales reps. Let's examine the numbered portions of the program.

```
                IDENTIFICATION DIVISION.
                PROGRAM-ID.      ADDSLS.

                ENVIRONMENT DIVISION.

                DATA DIVISION.

                01  STATUS-FLAGS.
                    03  ARE-WE-DONE            PIC X(3).
                        88  WE-ARE-DONE                      VALUE 'YES'.
                    03  IS-DATA-VALID          PIC X(3).
                        88  DATA-IS-VALID                    VALUE 'YES'.

                01  W-SALES-REP.
                    03  W-SLSREP-NUMBER            PIC X(2).
                    03  W-LAST                     PIC X(10).
                    03  W-FIRST                    PIC X(8).
                    03  W-STREET                   PIC X(15).
                    03  W-CITY                     PIC X(15).
                    03  W-STATE                    PIC X(2).
                    03  W-ZIP-CODE                 PIC X(5).
                    03  W-TOTAL-COMMISSION         PIC S9(5)V9(2).
                    03  W-COMMISSION-RATE          PIC SV9(2).

                    EXEC SQL
                        INCLUDE DECSALES_REP
                    END-EXEC.

                    EXEC SQL
                        INCLUDE SQLCA
                    END-EXEC.

                PROCEDURE-DIVISION.

                MAIN-PROGRAM.
                    MOVE 'NO' TO ARE-WE-DONE.
                    PERFORM MAIN-LOOP
                        UNTIL WE-ARE-DONE.
                    STOP RUN.

                MAIN-LOOP.
                    DISPLAY 'SALES REP NUMBER OR ** TO END PROGRAM: '.
                    ACCEPT W-SLSREP-NUMBER.
                    IF W-SLSREP-NUMBER = '**'
                        MOVE 'YES' TO ARE-WE-DONE
                      ELSE
1                       PERFORM OBTAIN-REMAINING-DATA.
2                       PERFORM VALIDATE-DATA.
3                       IF DATA-IS-VALID
                            PERFORM ADD-SALES_REP.

                OBTAIN-REMAINING-DATA.
4                   DISPLAY 'ENTER LAST NAME: '.
                    ACCEPT W-LAST.
                    DISPLAY 'ENTER FIRST NAME: '
                    ACCEPT W-FIRST.
                    DISPLAY 'ENTER STREET: '.
                    ACCEPT W-STREET.
                    DISPLAY 'ENTER CITY: '.
                    ACCEPT W-CITY.
                    DISPLAY 'ENTER STATE: '.
                       ACCEPT W-STATE.
                       DISPLAY 'ENTER ZIP CODE: '.
                       ACCEPT W-ZIP_CODE.
                       DISPLAY 'ENTER TOTAL COMMISSION: '.
                       ACCEPT W-TOTAL-COMMISSION.
                       DISPLAY 'ENTER COMMISSION RATE: '.
                       ACCEPT W-COMMISSION-RATE.

                VALIDATE-DATA.
                    MOVE 'YES' TO IS-DATA-VALID.
5                   EXEC SQL
                        SELECT LAST
                            INTO :W-LAST
                            FROM SALES_REP
                            WHERE SLSREP_NUMBER = :W-SLSREP-NUMBER
                    END-EXEC.
6                   IF SQLCODE = 0
                        MOVE 'NO' TO IS-DATA-VALID
                        DISPLAY 'ERROR - DUPLICATE SALES REP'.

                ADD-SALES_REP.
7                   EXEC SQL
                        INSERT
                        INTO SALES_REP
                        VALUES (:W-SLSREP-NUMBER, :W-LAST, :W-FIRST,
                            :W-STREET, :W-CITY, :W-STATE, :W-ZIP-CODE,
                            :W-TOTAL-COMMISSION, :W-COMMISSION-RATE)
                    END-EXEC.
```

Figure 8.3 Program to add sales reps

1. This command performs the paragraph named OBTAIN-REMAINING-DATA to obtain the rest of the data concerning the sales rep from the user.

2. The paragraph named VALIDATE-DATA ensures the validity of the data entered by the user. If the data is valid, the flag named IS-DATA-VALID is set to YES. If the data is not valid, the flag is set to NO.

3. If the data is valid, the program performs the paragraph named ADD-SALES_REP to add the data to the database.

4. For each field to enter, this paragraph contains a prompt for the field (such as 'ENTER LAST NAME:') followed immediately by an ACCEPT command to obtain the desired data from the user.

5. The SELECT command determines whether there is a sales rep already in the database with the same number.

6. If SQLCODE is zero, a sales rep with the same number has been found. In this case, you should not add the sales rep. You indicate this by setting IS-DATA-VALID to NO and displaying an error message.

7. This INSERT command adds the new row to the database.

In general, the paragraph named VALIDATE-DATA is used to provide any sort of required validation. In a program to add customers, for example, this paragraph could contain logic necessary to ensure that credit limits are $750, $1,000, $1,500, or $2,000. It also could contain logic to ensure that the sales rep number entered for the customer corresponds to a sales rep number already in the database.

Change a Single Row in a Table

You used SQL commands to insert rows in a SQL database; you also need to use SQL commands to update the rows as illustrated in Example 5.

Example 5: Change the last name of the sales rep whose number currently is stored in W-SLSREP-NUMBER to the value currently stored in W-LAST.

Again, the only difference between this example and the update examples in Chapter 5 is the use of host variables. The statement is written as follows:

```
EXEC SQL
        UPDATE SALES_REP
                SET LAST = :W-LAST
                WHERE SLSREP_NUMBER = :W-SLSREP-NUMBER
END-EXEC.
```

Change Multiple Rows in a Table

A benefit of using SQL commands to update the database is that you can use a single command to update multiple rows—something you normally cannot accomplish in COBOL. Example 6 illustrates this capability.

Example 6: Add the amount stored in the host variable INCREASE-IN-RATE to the commission rate for all sales reps who currently represent any customer having a credit limit of $1,000.

To update multiple rows, the statement is written as follows:

```
EXEC SQL
      UPDATE SALES_REP
            SET COMMISSION_RATE = COMMISSION_RATE + :INCREASE-IN-RATE
            WHERE SLSREP_NUMBER IN
                  (SELECT SLSREP_NUMBER
                        FROM CUSTOMER
                        WHERE CREDIT_LIMIT = 1000)
END-EXEC.
```

Delete a Single Row from a Table

Just as you would expect, if you must use SQL commands to insert and change rows in a table, you also must use SQL commands to delete rows, as illustrated in Example 7.

Example 7: Delete the sales rep whose number currently is stored in W-SLSREP-NUMBER from the SALES_REP table.

The formulation is written as follows:

```
EXEC SQL
      DELETE
            FROM SALES_REP
            WHERE SLSREP_NUMBER = :W-SLSREP-NUMBER
END-EXEC.
```

Delete Multiple Rows from a Table

Sometimes you need to delete more than one row from a table. If you delete an order from the ORDERS table, for example, you also need to delete all associated order lines from the ORDER_LINE table, as illustrated in Example 8.

Example 8: Delete every order line for the order whose order number currently is stored in the host variable W-ORDER-NUMBER from the ORDER_LINE table.

The formulation is written as follows:

```
EXEC SQL
      DELETE
            FROM ORDER_LINE
            WHERE ORDER_NUMBER = :W-ORDER-NUMBER
END-EXEC.
```

MULTIPLE-ROW SELECT

The previous examples posed no problems for COBOL because the SELECT statements retrieved only individual rows. There was an UPDATE example in which multiple rows were updated and a DELETE example in which multiple rows were deleted, but these tasks presented no difficulty. The SQL statements were executed and the updates or deletions occurred. The program could move on to the next task.

What happens when a SELECT statement produces multiple rows? What if, for example, the SELECT statement produced the number and name of every customer represented by the sales rep whose number was stored in W-SLSREP-NUMBER? Could we formulate this query as follows:

```
EXEC SQL
        SELECT CUSTOMER_NUMBER, LAST, FIRST
                INTO :W-CUSTOMER-NUMBER, :W-LAST, :W-FIRST
                FROM CUSTOMER
                WHERE SLSREP_NUMBER = :W-SLSREP-NUMBER
END-EXEC.
```

There is a problem—COBOL can process only one record at a time, whereas this SQL command produces multiple rows (records). Whose number and name is placed in W-CUSTOMER-NUMBER, W-LAST, and W-FIRSTif 100 customers are retrieved? Should you make W-CUSTOMER-NUMBER, W-LAST, and W-FIRSTarrays capable of holding 100 customers and, if so, what should be the size of these arrays? Fortunately, you can solve this problem by using a cursor.

Cursors

A **cursor** is a pointer to a row in the collection of rows retrieved by a SQL statement. (This is *not* the same cursor that you see on your computer screen.) The cursor advances one row at a time to provide sequential, record-at-a-time access to the retrieved rows so the rows can be processed by COBOL. By using a cursor, COBOL can process the set of retrieved rows as though they are records in a sequential file.

To use a cursor, you must first declare it as illustrated in Example 9.

Example 9:	Retrieve the number, last name, and first name of every customer represented by the sales rep whose number is stored in the host variable W-SLSREP-NUMBER.

The first step in using a cursor is to declare the cursor and describe the associated query. You do this task in the WORKING-STORAGE SECTION of the DATA DIVISION. The command is written as follows:

```
EXEC SQL
        DECLARE CUSTGROUP CURSOR FOR
                SELECT CUSTOMER_NUMBER, LAST, FIRST
                FROM CUSTOMER
                WHERE SLSREP_NUMBER = :W-SLSREP-NUMBER
END-EXEC.
```

This formulation does *not* cause the query to be executed at this time; it only declares a cursor named CUSTGROUP and associates the cursor with the indicated query. Using a cursor in the PROCEDURE DIVISION involves three commands: OPEN, FETCH, and CLOSE. Opening the cursor causes the query to be executed and makes the results available to the program. Executing a fetch advances the cursor to the next row in the set of rows retrieved by the query and places the contents of the row in the indicated host variables. Finally, closing a cursor deactivates it. Data retrieved by the execution of the query is no longer available. The cursor could be opened again later and processing could begin again. If any host variables used in making the selection change, then the set of rows might change as well.

The OPEN, FETCH, and CLOSE commands used in processing a cursor are analogous to the OPEN, READ, and CLOSE commands used in processing a sequential file. Next you will examine how each of these commands is coded in COBOL.

Opening a Cursor

The formulation for the OPENcommand is written as follows:

EXEC SQL
      OPEN CUSTGROUP
END-EXEC.

Figure 8.4 shows the result of opening the CUSTGROUP cursor. In the figure, assume for purposes of the example that W-SLSREP-NUMBER is set to 12 before the open statement is executed. Note that prior to the open, no rows were available. After the open, three rows are available to the program and the cursor is positioned at the first row; that is, the next FETCH command causes the contents of the first row to be placed in the indicated host variables.

CUSTGROUP

CUSTOMER_NUMBER	LAST	FIRST		W-CUSTOMER_NUMBER	W-LAST	W-FIRST	SQLCODE
			← next row to be fetched				0

> **Figure 8.4a Before OPEN**

CUSTGROUP

CUSTOMER_NUMBER	LAST	FIRST		W-CUSTOMER_NUMBER	W-LAST	W-FIRST	SQLCODE
311	Charles	Don	← next row to be fetched				0
405	Williams	Al					
522	Nelson	Mary					

> **Figure 8.4b After OPEN, but before First FETCH**

Fetching Rows from a Cursor

To fetch (get) the next row from a cursor, use the FETCH command. The FETCH command is written as follows:

EXEC SQL
      FETCH CUSTGROUP
          INTO :W-CUSTOMER-NUMBER, :W-LAST, :W-FIRST
END-EXEC.

Note that the INTO clause is associated with the FETCH command itself and not with the query used in the definition of the cursor. The execution of that query probably produces multiple rows. The execution of the FETCH command produces only a single row, so it is appropriate that the FETCH command causes data to be placed in the indicated host variables.

Figure 8.5 shows the result of four FETCH commands. Note that the first three fetches are successful. In each case, the data from the appropriate row in the cursor is placed in the indicated host variables and SQLCODE is set to zero. The fourth FETCH command is different, however, because there is no more data to fetch. In this case, the contents of the host variables are left untouched and SQLCODE is set to 100.

CUSTGROUP

CUSTOMER_NUMBER	LAST	FIRST
311	Charles	Don
405	Williams	Al
522	Nelson	Mary

← next row to be fetched

W-CUSTOMER_NUMBER	W-LAST	W-FIRST	SQLCODE
311	Charles	Don	0

Figure 8.5a After first FETCH

CUSTGROUP

CUSTOMER_NUMBER	LAST	FIRST
311	Charles	Don
405	Williams	Al
522	Nelson	Mary

← next row to be fetched

W-CUSTOMER_NUMBER	W-LAST	W-FIRST	SQLCODE
405	Williams	Al	0

Figure 8.5b After second FETCH

CUSTGROUP

CUSTOMER_NUMBER	LAST	FIRST
311	Charles	Don
405	Williams	Al
522	Nelson	Mary

← no more rows to be fetched

W-CUSTOMER_NUMBER	W-LAST	W-FIRST	SQLCODE
522	Nelson	Mary	100

Figure 8.5d After attempting a fourth FETCH (Note SQLCODE is 100)

CUSTGROUP

CUSTOMER_NUMBER	LAST	FIRST
311	Charles	Don
405	Williams	Al
522	Nelson	Mary

← no more rows to be fetched

W-CUSTOMER_NUMBER	W-LAST	W-FIRST	SQLCODE
522	Nelson	Mary	100

Figure 8.5d After attempting a fourth FETCH (Note SQLCODE is 100)

Closing a Cursor

The CLOSE command is written as follows:

```
EXEC SQL
        CLOSE CUSTGROUP
END-EXEC.
```

Figure 8.6 shows the result of closing the cursor. The data is no longer available.

CUSTGROUP

← no rows to be fetched

Figure 8.7 shows a complete COBOL program using the cursor. Let's examine the numbered portions of the program.

```
              IDENTIFICATION DIVISION.
              PROGRAM-ID.      CUSTSLS.

              ENVIRONMENT DIVISION.

              DATA DIVISION.

              WORKING-STORAGE SECTION.

              01  STATUS-FLAGS.
                  03  ARE-WE-DONE              PIC X(3).
                      88  WE-ARE-DONE                      VALUE 'YES'.

     1        01 W-CUSTOMER.
                  03  W-CUSTOMER_NUMBER        PIC X(3).
                  03  W-LAST                   PIC X(10).
                  03  W-FIRST                  PIC X(8).
                  03  W-STREET                 PIC X(15).
                  03  W-CITY                   PIC X(15).
                  03  W-STATE                  PIC X(2).
                  03  W-ZIP_CODE               PIC X(5).
                  03  W-BALANCE                PIC S9(5)V9(2).
                  03  W-CREDIT-LIMIT           PIC S9(4).
                  03  W-SLSREP-NUMBER          PIC X(2).

     2        EXEC SQL
                  INCLUDE DECCUSTOMER
              END-EXEC.

              EXEC SQL
                  INCLUDE SQLCA
              END-EXEC.

     3        EXEC SQL
                  DECLARE CUSTGROUP CURSOR FOR
                      SELECT CUSTOMER_NUMBER, LAST, FIRST
                      FROM CUSTOMER
                      WHERE SLSREP_NUMBER = :W-SLSREP-NUMBER
              END-EXEC.

              PROCEDURE-DIVISION.

              MAIN-PROGRAM.
                  MOVE 'NO' TO ARE-WE-DONE.
                  PERFORM MAIN-LOOP
                      UNTIL WE-ARE-DONE.
                  STOP RUN.

              MAIN-LOOP.
                  DISPLAY 'SALES REP NUMBER OR ** TO END PROGRAM: '.
                  ACCEPT W-SLSREP-NUMBER.
                  IF W-SLSREP-NUMBER = '**'
                      MOVE 'YES' TO ARE-WE-DONE
                    ELSE
                      PERFORM FIND-CUSTOMERS.

              FIND-CUSTOMERS.
     4            EXEC SQL
                      OPEN CUSTGROUP
                  END-EXEC.
     5            PERFORM FIND-A-CUSTOMER
                      UNTIL SQLCODE = 100.
     6            EXEC SQL
                      CLOSE CUSTGROUP
                  END-EXEC.

              FIND-A-CUSTOMER.
     7            EXEC SQL
                      FETCH CUSTGROUP
                          INTO :W-CUSTOMER_NUMBER, :W-LAST, :W-FIRST
                  END-EXEC.
     8            IF SLQCODE = 0
                      DISPLAY 'CUSTOMER NUMBER: ', W-CUSTOMER_NUMBER
                      DISPLAY '     LAST NAME: ', W-LAST
                      DISPLAY '    FIRST NAME: ', W-FIRST.
```

1. The appropriate host variables for customer data are declared as a record named W-CUSTOMER.

2. The description of the CUSTOMER table is stored in DECCUSTOMER, so DECCUSTOMER appears in an INCLUDE statement.

3. This statement gives the declaration of the cursor (CUSTGROUP).

4. This statement opens the cursor, making the desired data available to the program.

5. This statement performs the paragraph named FIND-A-CUSTOMER until SQLCODE is set to 100. Recall that when SQLCODE is set to 100, all rows have been fetched and an attempt is made to fetch another row.

6. This statement closes the cursor.

7. This FETCH command places the information from the next row in the cursor into the indicated host variables. If no more rows exist, SQLCODE will be set to 100.

8. If SQLCODE is zero, a row was found and the data displays.

More Complex Cursors

The formulation of the query to define the cursor in Example 9 was simple. Any SQL query is legitimate in a cursor definition. In fact, the more complicated the requirements for retrieval, the more numerous the benefits derived by the programmer who uses embedded SQL. Consider the query in Example 10.

Example 10: For every order that contains an order line for the part whose part number is stored in W-PART-NUMBER, retrieve the order number, order date, order number, last name, and first name of the customer who placed the order, and the number, last name, and first name of the sales rep who represents the customer. Sort the results by customer number.

Opening and closing the cursor is done exactly as in Example 9. The only difference in the FETCH command is a different set of host variables in the INTO clause. Thus, the only real difference is the definition of the cursor itself. In this case, the cursor definition is written as follows:

```
EXEC SQL
    DECLARE ORDGROUP CURSOR FOR
        SELECT ORDERS.ORDER_NUMBER, ORDERS.ORDER_DATE,
        CUSTOMER.CUSTOMER_NUMBER, CUSTOMER.LAST, CUSTOMER.FIRST,
        SALES_REP.SLSREP_NUMBER, SALES_REP.LAST, SALES_REP.FIRST
        FROM ORDER_LINE, ORDERS, CUSTOMER, SALES_REP
        WHERE ORDER_LINE.PART_NUMBER = :W-PART-NUMBER
        AND ORDER_LINE.ORDER_NUMBER = ORDERS.ORDER_NUMBER
        AND ORDERS.CUSTOMER_NUMBER = CUSTOMER.CUSTOMER_NUMBER
        AND CUSTOMER.SLSREP_NUMBER = SALES_REP.SLSREP_NUMBER
        ORDER BY CUSTOMER.CUSTOMER_NUMBER
END-EXEC.
```

Advantages of Cursors

The retrieval requirements in Example 10 are complicated. Yet, beyond coding the preceding cursor declaration, the programmer doesn't have to worry about the mechanics of obtaining the necessary data or placing it in the right order, because this happens automatically when the cursor is opened. To the programmer, it seems as if a sequential file already exists that has precisely the right data in it, sorted in the right order. This assumption leads to three main advantages. First, the coding in the program is greatly simplified. Second, in a normal COBOL program, the programmer must determine the most efficient way to access the data. In a program using embedded SQL, a special component of the database management system called the **optimizer** determines the best way to access the data. The programmer isn't concerned with the best way to pull the data together. In addition, if an underlying structure changes (for example, an additional index is created), the optimizer determines the best way to execute the query in view of the new structure. The program does not have to change at all. Third, if the database structure changes in such a way that the necessary information still is obtainable using a different query, the only change required in the program is the cursor definition in WORKING-STORAGE. The PROCEDURE DIVISION code is not affected.

UPDATING CURSORS

You can update the rows encountered in processing cursors. In order to indicate that an update is required, you include an additional clause—FOR UPDATE OF—in the cursor definition. For example, consider the update requirement in Example 11.

Example 11: Add $100 to the credit limit for every customer represented by the sales rep whose number currently is stored in the host variable W-SLSREP-NUMBER, whose balance is not over the credit limit, and whose credit limit is $500 or less. Add $200 to the credit limit of every customer of this sales rep whose balance is not over the credit limit and whose credit limit is more than $500. Write the number, last name, and first name of every customer of this sales rep whose balance is greater than the credit limit.

The cursor declaration is written as follows:

```
EXEC SQL
        DECLARE CREDGROUP CURSOR FOR
                SELECT CUSTOMER_NUMBER, LAST, FIRST, BALANCE,
                CREDIT_LIMIT
                FROM CUSTOMER
                WHERE SLSREP_NUMBER = :W-SLSREP-NUMBER
                FOR UPDATE OF CREDIT_LIMIT
END-EXEC.
```

To update the credit limits, you must include the FOR UPDATE OF CREDIT_LIMIT clause in the cursor declaration. The PROCEDURE DIVISION code for the OPEN and CLOSE statements is the same one you used previously. The code to fetch a row, determine whether it was fetched, and then take appropriate action is written as follows:

```
EXEC SQL
     FETCH CREDGROUP
             INTO :W-CUSTOMER-NUMBER, :W-LAST, :W-FIRST,
             :W-BALANCE, :W-CREDIT-LIMIT
     END-EXEC.
     IF SQLCODE = 100
             MOVE "NO" TO ARE-THERE-MORE-CUSTOMERS
     ELSE
             PERFORM CUSTOMER-UPDATE.
CUSTOMER-UPDATE.
     IF W-CREDIT-LIMIT > W-BALANCE
         DISPLAY W-FIRST, W-LAST
     ELSE IF W-CREDIT-LIMIT > 500
         EXEC SQL
             UPDATE CUSTOMER
                     SET CREDIT_LIMIT = CREDIT_LIMIT + 200
                     WHERE CURRENT OF CREDGROUP
         END-EXEC
     ELSE
         EXEC SQL
             UPDATE CUSTOMER
                     SET CREDIT_LIMIT = CREDIT_LIMIT + 100
                     WHERE CURRENT OF CREDGROUP
         END-EXEC.
```

The preceding code is in a loop that is performed until the flag ARE-THERE-MORE-CUSTOMERS is set to NO. The FETCH command either makes the next retrieved row available to the program with the values placed in the variables W-CUSTOMER-NUMBER, W-LAST, W-FIRST, W-BALANCE, and W-CREDIT-LIMIT, or it sets SQLCODE to 100 to indicate that no more rows were retrieved. The code that comes after the FETCH command sets the flag to NO if SQLCODE is set to 100. If SQLCODE is not set to 100, then the update routine is performed.

In the update routine, the credit limit first is compared with the balance. If the balance is larger, then a message is printed. If the balance is not larger, then the credit limit is compared with $500. If the credit limit is larger, then the row is updated by adding $200 to the credit limit. If the credit limit is not larger, then the row is updated by adding $100 to the credit limit. The WHERE CURRENT OF CREDGROUP clause indicates that the update is to apply only to the row just fetched. Without this clause, and in the absence of any WHERE clause to restrict the scope of the update, *every* customer's credit limit would be updated by this command.

ERROR HANDLING

Programs must be able to handle exceptional conditions that can arise when the database is accessed. Because problems are communicated through a value in SQLCODE, one legitimate way to handle problems is to check the value in SQLCODE after each executable SQL statement and then take appropriate action based on the indicated problem. However, with all the potential conditions, this method becomes very cumbersome. Fortunately, as you will see, there is another way to handle such conditions using the WHENEVER statement.

There are two types of error conditions that need to be addressed. The first type consists of unusual but normal conditions, such as not retrieving any data to match a given condition, attempting to store a row that violates a duplicates clause, and so on. The value in SQLCODE for such conditions is a positive number. The appropriate action is to print an error message and continue processing. The appropriate action for the END OF DATA(SQLCODE 100) message probably is termination of some loop and continuation with the rest of the program. No error message is required.

The other type of condition is far more serious, because it consists of the abnormal and unexpected conditions or, in a very real sense, the fatal ones. Examples of this type include lack of space in the database, a damaged database, and so on. The value in SQLCODE for such conditions is a negative number. The appropriate action usually is to print a final message that indicates the problem that occurred, and then terminate the program.

The WHENEVER statement can be used to handle these errors in a global way. The following example of the WHENEVER statement illustrates a typical way of handling these conditions in a program. The WHENEVER statement is written as follows:

```
EXEC SQL
        WHENEVER SQLERROR GOTO ERROR-PROCESSING-ROUTINE
END-EXEC.
EXEC SQL
        WHENEVER SQLWARNING CONTINUE
END-EXEC.
EXEC SQL
        WHENEVER NOT FOUND CONTINUE
END-EXEC.
```

In the WHENEVER statement, SQLERROR represents the abnormal or fatal conditions (SQLCODE < 0), SQLWARNING represents the unusual but normal conditions (SQLCODE > 0), and NOT FOUND represents the special warning END OF DATA (SQLCODE = 100). The WHENEVER statement ends either with GOTO followed by a section or paragraph name or with the word CONTINUE. The WHENEVER statement indicates how each of these conditions should be handled if and when they occur.

In the preceding WHENEVER statements, if a fatal condition occurs, the program is to proceed immediately to a paragraph (or section) named ERROR-PROCESSING-ROUTINE. This paragraph probably has been constructed by the organization and will be the same in each program that uses embedded SQL. Typically, this paragraph contains statements to display the SQLCODE together with any other useful information that identifies the problem, followed by a STOP RUN command. With this paragraph in place, the remainder of the program does not have to check continually for all possible errors of this type.

If an unusual but normal condition arises, or if the special NOT FOUND condition arises, however, processing should continue without any special action. This means that appropriate tests of SQLCODE must be included at appropriate places. While these tests also can be accomplished using the WHENEVER clause, doing the testing yourself provides a cleaner structure for the program. The built-in GOTOstatement of the WHENEVER clause can cause problems even in well-structured programs.

In this chapter you learned how to embed SQL commands in a procedural language. You learned how to distinguish between column names in SQL and COBOL host variables. You used embedded SQL commands to retrieve single rows, insert new rows, change existing rows, and delete rows. Then you examined the difficulties associated with embedded SQL commands that retrieved multiple rows and saw how to use cursors to address these difficulties and update a database. Finally you learned how to handle errors in COBOL programs that contain embedded SQL commands.

SUMMARY

1. To embed SQL commands in a COBOL program, precede the SQL command with EXEC SQLand follow the command with END-EXEC.

2. Statements to define the tables to be accessed must appear in the DATA DIVISION.

3. The DATA DIVISION must contain the INCLUDE SQLCA statement, which allows access to the SQL communication area.

4. Host language variables (variables that are not columns within a table) can be used in embedded SQL commands, by preceding the variable name with a colon.

5. You can use SELECT statements as embedded SQL commands in COBOL programs only when a single row is retrieved.

6. To place the results of a SELECT statement into host language variables, use the INTOclause in the SELECT command.

7. INSERT, UPDATE, and DELETE statements can be used in COBOL programs even when they affect more than one row.

8. If a SELECT statement is to retrieve more than one row, it must be used to define a cursor that will be used to select one row at a time.

9. To activate a cursor, use the OPEN command to execute the query in the cursor definition.

10. To select the next row in COBOL, use the FETCH command.

11. To deactivate a cursor, use the CLOSE command. The rows initially retrieved will no longer be available to COBOL.

12. Data in the tables on which a cursor is based can be updated by including the WHERE CURRENT OF clause cursor name in the update statement. This clause updates only the current (most recently fetched) row.

13. To see if an error has occurred, examine the value in SQLCODE.

14. Rather than checking SQLCODE in every place in the program where errors occur, use the WHENEVERclause.

EXERCISES (PREMIERE PRODUCTS)

Note	Your instructor may substitute another language for COBOL in the following exercises.

1. Assuming that the appropriate entries have been made in the DATA DIVISION of a COBOL program, give the procedure division code for each of the following:

    a. Obtain the description and unit price of the part whose part number currently is stored in W-PART-NUMBER. Place these values in the variables W-PART-DESCRIPTION and W-UNIT-PRICE, respectively.

    b. Obtain the order date, customer number, and name for the order whose number currently is stored in W-ORDER-NUMBER. Place these values in the variables W-ORDER-DATE, W-CUSTOMER-NUMBER, W-LAST, and W-FIRST, respectively.

    c. Add a row to the PART table. The data currently is stored in the columns within the W-PART record.

    d. Change the description of the part whose number is stored in W-PART-NUMBER to the value currently found in W-PART-DESCRIPTION.

    e. Increase the price of every part in item class HW by five percent.

    f. Delete the part whose number is stored in W-PART-NUMBER.

2. Retrieve the part number, part description, item class, and unit price of every part located in the warehouse whose number is stored in W-WAREHOUSE-NUMBER. In addition, you need to be able to update the unit price.

    a. Write an appropriate cursor description.

    b. Write all of the statements that will be included in the PROCEDURE DIVISION and that relate to processing the database through this cursor.

    c. Write the additional PROCEDURE DIVISION code that will update every part that is in item class HW by adding five percent to the unit price and every part in item class SG by adding ten percent to the unit price. (*Hint:* You must use the cursor in your answer.)

3. If you have access to embedded SQL, write and run the programs created in Exercises 1 and 2.

EXERCISES (HENRY BOOKS)

Note	Your instructor may substitute another language for COBOL in the following exercises.

1. Assuming that the appropriate entries have been made in the DATA DIVISION of a COBOL program, give the procedure division code for each of the following:

   a. Obtain the name and city of the publisher whose publisher code currently is stored in W-PUBLISHER-CODE. Place these values in the variables W-PUBLISHER-NAMEand W-PUBLISHER-CITY, respectively.

   b. Obtain the book title, publisher code, and publisher name for every book whose code currently is stored in W-BOOK-CODE. Place these values in the variables W-BOOK-TITLE, W-PUBLISHER-CODE, and W-PUBLISHER-NAME, respectively.

   c. Add a row to the BRANCH table. The data currently is stored in the fields within the W-BRANCHrecord.

   d. Change the title of the book whose code is stored in W-BOOK-CODE to the value currently found in W-BOOK-TITLE.

   e. Increase the price by three percent for every book whose publisher code is BB.

   f. Delete the book whose code is stored in W-BOOK-CODE.

2. Retrieve the book code, book title, publisher code, and book price for every book whose book type is stored in W-BOOK-TYPE. In addition, you need to be able to update the book price.

   a. Write an appropriate cursor description.

   b. Write all of the statements that will be included in the PROCEDURE DIVISION and that relate to processing the database through this cursor.

c. Write the additional PROCEDURE DIVISION code that will increase the book price by four percent for every book whose publisher code is PB, and by three percent for every book whose publisher code is BF. (*Hint:* You must use the cursor in your answer.)

3. If you have access to embedded SQL, write and run the programs created in Exercises 1 and 2.

Appendix A
Introduction to the Oracle Forms Designer

INTRODUCTION

You have learned to accomplish a wide variety of tasks using SQL. You know how to update tables by adding new rows, changing existing rows, and deleting rows. You can create simple and complex queries involving data from one or more tables or views. You can change the structure of your tables, create indexes, and assign security privileges. You can create formatted reports based on the data from one or more tables or views. You also know how to embed SQL commands in other programming languages.

For many of these activities, using an appropriate SQL command is the simplest way to accomplish the desired task. In some cases, however, using an appropriate form is a preferable approach. If you have ever used a data entry form, for example, you know that completing a form—instead of creating an appropriate SQL INSERT command—often is an easier way to add a row to a table.

The Oracle Forms Designer is a tool that allows you to develop such forms. You can use these forms for displaying data, querying the database, and updating data by changing an existing row, adding new rows, and deleting rows. You can use a form as an alternate to using SQL to execute some of the same tasks. Changes that you make using a form are reflected immediately in the base table on which the form is based.

In this appendix, you will learn how to create a form to update the CUSTOMER table. The form will contain all the columns in the table except the CUSTOMER_TYPE column that was added in Chapter 5. In this form, the BALANCE and CREDIT_LIMIT columns will display on the screen, but users cannot change data in them. (This form would be appropriate for an employee at Premiere Products who is allowed to view balances and credit limits, but who does not have the authority to change the values in these columns.)

After creating the form, you will use it to display data, create a query, change an existing row, add a new row, and delete a row from the table.

■ ■ ■ ■ ■

Note	If you want to create the form shown in this appendix, you should complete the bulleted steps in this chapter at the computer.

| Note | Within the Forms Designer, Oracle uses the terms *record* and *field* rather than row and column. |

> **Note** The steps in this appendix are illustrated using Microsoft Windows 95. If you are running Oracle on another platform and are unfamiliar with Windows 95, don't worry. The process for using another platform is very similar. Your instructor will inform you of any necessary changes.

CREATING A FORM

The first step in creating a form is to start the Forms Designer. The method you use to start the Forms Designer depends on the environment in which you are working. The steps in this appendix assume that you are running Microsoft Windows 95. If you are not running Microsoft Windows 95, your instructor will provide you with alternate steps.

 Click the **Start** button on the Microsoft Windows 95 taskbar.

 Point to **Programs** on the Start menu.

 Point to **Developer 2000 for Win95**.

Click **Forms Designer**.

After starting the Forms Designer, you need to connect to the database and identify yourself as a legitimate user.

 Click **File** on the menu bar, and then click **Connect**.

Type your User Name, press the **Tab** key, and then type your Password. You should not have to enter a database name unless your instructor instructs you to do so.

 Click the **Connect** button.

Creating a New Form

First you must use the New command on the File menu to create a generic form. Then you can change the default form name to whatever you like. Next you will create a new form and then change its name to CUSTOMER, to represent a form based on the CUSTOMER table.

1 Click **File** on the menu bar, and then point to **New**. A menu opens listing the types of objects you can create (see Figure A.1).

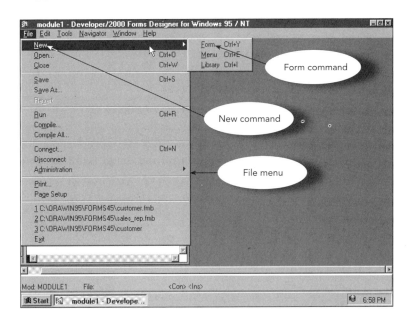

Figure A.1 Creating a new form

2 Click **Form**. The new form is created with the name MODULE2 (your module number might be different), as shown in Figure A.2. The items appearing under the form name are the various objects associated with the form. You will deal with only one of them—blocks.

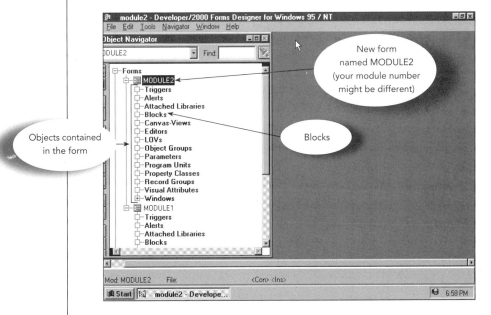

Figure A.2 New Form

3 Click **MODULE2** (again, your number might be different) so its background changes to blue indicating it is selected, type **CUSTOMER** to change the name of your form, and then press the **Enter** key.

Creating a Block

Forms are created in sections called **blocks**. The form you create will contain only a single block. More complex forms can have several blocks. The background of the form onto which you place these blocks is called a **canvas**. The following steps create a block named CUSTOMER for the CUSTOMER table. The block also will be called CUSTOMER. The name of the canvas on which the block will be placed is CUST_CAN.

1 Click **Tools** on the menu bar to open the Tools menu (see Figure A.3), and then point to **New Block**.

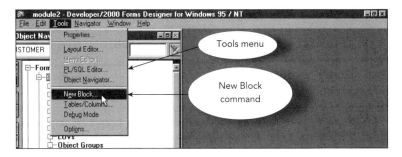

Figure A.3 Creating a new block

2 Click **New Block**. The CUSTOMER: New Block Options dialog box opens (see Figure A.4). You use this dialog box to indicate the name of the table, block, and canvas for the form. Typically, you assign the block the same name as the table. Rather than typing the name of the table, you can select it from a list by clicking the Select button.

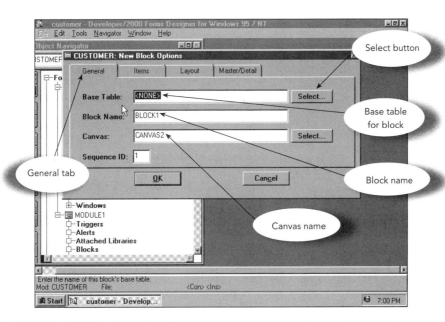

Figure A.4 Specifying general characteristics of the block

3 Click the **Select** button for the Base Table, as shown in Figure A.4.

The Tables dialog box opens, as shown in Figure A.5. You use this dialog box to select the table or view on which to base the form.

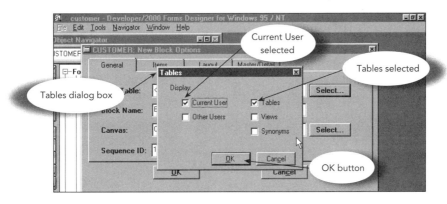

Figure A.5 Selecting the table

1 Make sure that both the Current User and Tables boxes are checked, and then click the **OK** button.

2 Click **CUSTOMER** in the list that appears, and then click the **OK** button.

3 Select the text in the **Canvas** text box, and then type **CUST_CAN**. See Figure A.6.

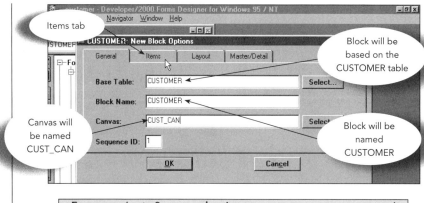

Figure A.6 General characteristics entered

④ Click the **Items** tab, and then click the **Select Columns** button to open the list of available fields.

⑤ Click the **BALANCE** field in the list of available fields to select it.

⑥ Click the **Type** list arrow. See Figure A.7.

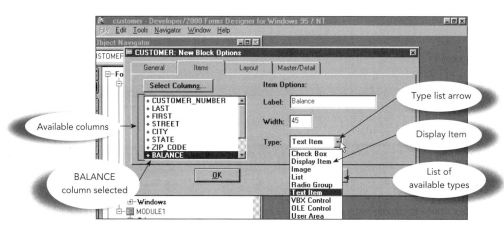

Figure A.7 Specifying items

The available columns for the form appear in the list box on the left side of the dialog box. The BALANCE field is selected. The list of available types appears. Currently, the Text Item type is selected. Using this type allows the user to make updates to the BALANCE field by using the form. If you change the type to Display Item, the field will appear on the form, but you cannot change it.

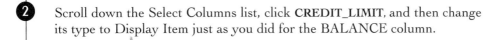

1. Click **Display Item** as the type for the BALANCE column.

2. Scroll down the Select Columns list, click **CREDIT_LIMIT**, and then change its type to Display Item just as you did for the BALANCE column.

3. Scroll down the list of columns, and then click **CUSTOMER_TYPE**. (You should have added the CUSTOMER_TYPE column in Chapter 5. If you didn't add this column to the CUSTOMER table, skip this step and the next step.)

4. Click the **Include** check box to remove the check mark. See Figure A.8.

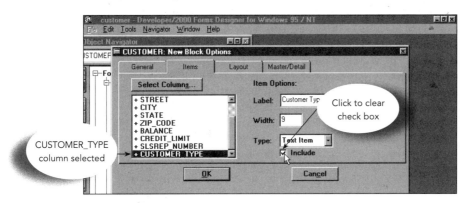

Figure A.8 Omitting a column from the form

The symbol in front of the CUSTOMER_TYPE column changes from a plus sign (+) to a minus sign (-) to indicate that it will not be included in the form. See Figure A.9.

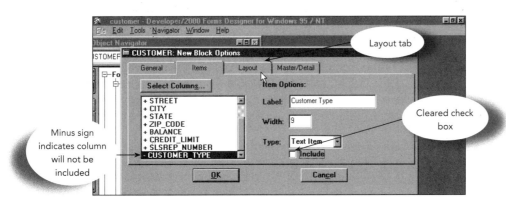

Figure A.9 Column omitted from form

Now you will indicate the layout for your form by specifying the form's appearance. You will indicate that it is to be laid out as a form, rather than as a table. You also will indicate that the form is to contain special-purpose buttons that will be used to view and manipulate data on the form.

1 Click the **Layout** tab.

2 Click the **Style** list arrow indicated in Figure A.10.

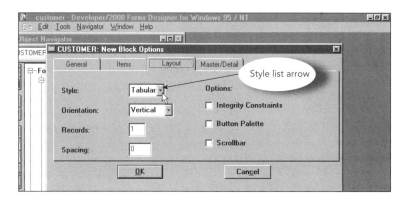

Figure A.10 Specifying the layout

3 Click **Form** in the list that appears.

4 Click the **Button Palette** check box to select it, as shown in Figure A.11.

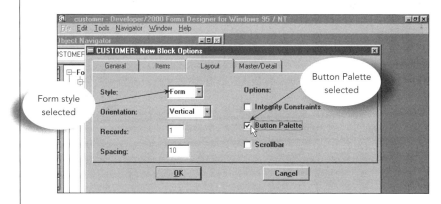

Figure A.11 Layout specified

5 Click the **OK** button to create the form.

Viewing the Form

You can view the form you just created by clicking the Run command on the File menu.

1 Click **File** on the menu bar, and then click **Run**.

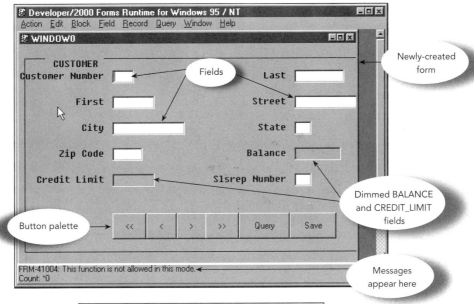

Figure A.12 Viewing the Form

Note	The messages that appear at the bottom of the window might be different depending on where the insertion point is positioned in the form. Your messages might be different.

The form displays with the fields that you selected, as shown in Figure A.12. Notice that the CUSTOMER_TYPE field is not included. Also notice that the BALANCE and CREDIT_LIMIT fields are dim, indicating that the values in these fields will display but they cannot be changed. The default collection of buttons displays on the form because you selected the Button Palette check box when you specified the form layout.

Now you can close the form.

1 Click **Action** on the menu bar, and then click **Exit**.

Saving the Form

To save the form, use the Save command on the File menu.

Click **File** on the menu bar, and then click **Save**.

 Make sure the name of the form in the File name text box is **customer**. (If it isn't, select the text in the File name text box, and then type customer.)

 Select a location in which to save the file if the location displayed is not correct. You should save the file to a floppy disk unless your instructor asks you to save it elsewhere.

 Click the **Save** button.

Now the form is saved and ready for use.

USING A FORM

To use a form you first must open it on your screen. Then you can use the form to display records, change records, insert new records, or delete records.

Running a Form

Whenever you want to use your form, you need to run it using the Forms Runtime developer tool. The steps that follow assume that you are running Microsoft Windows 95. If you are not running Microsoft Windows 95, your instructor will provide alternate instructions.

 Click the **Start** button on the Microsoft Windows 95 taskbar.

 Point to **Programs** on the Start menu.

 Point to **Developer 2000 for Win95**.

 Click **Forms Runtime**. The Forms Runtime Options dialog box opens.

 Click the **Browse** button to open the Open dialog box. If necessary, change to your Student Disk, then select **customer.fmx** (see Figure A.13), and then click the Open button. (Your instructor might provide alternate instructions if your file is stored in a different folder.)

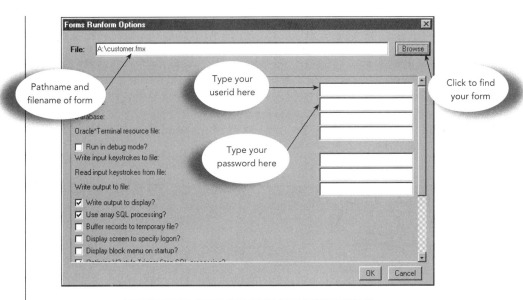

Figure A.13 Running the form

6 Click the Userid box, and then type your userid.

7 Press the **Tab** key, type your password in the Password text box, and then click the **OK** button.

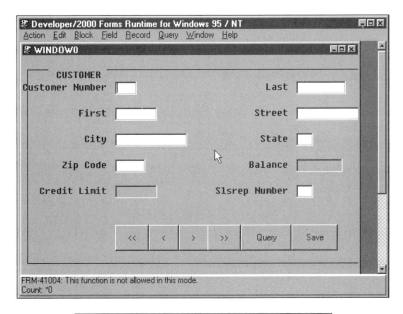

Figure A.14 Displaying records

The form opens, as shown in Figure A.14. Now you are ready to display the records from the CUSTOMER table.

Displaying Records

To display the records in the table, click the Query button on the button palette or click the Execute command on the Query menu. The first record in the table appears first. Then you can use the buttons on the form to go to other records.

1 Click the **Query** button on the button palette, or click **Query** on the menu bar and then click **Execute**. The first record from the table appears in the form. See Figure A.15.

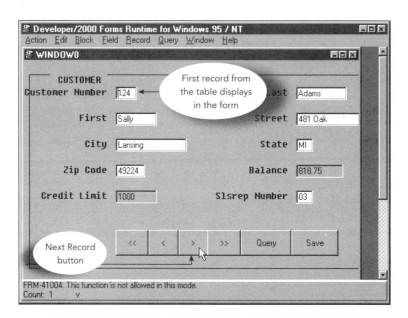

Figure A.15   Viewing the first record

2 Click the **Next Record** button (see Figure A.15) to display the second record in the form.

| Note | If you didn't include the button palette on your form, you can display the next record by clicking Record on the menu bar, and then clicking Next. |

You also can use the Query menu to create a new query by clicking Enter on the Query menu. If you click Execute without first creating a query, all records appear one at a time. As you will see in the next set of steps, if you create a query first, only those records that satisfy the query appear.

Creating a Query

Sometimes you might want to view records that satisfy some condition, such as records for the customers of sales rep number 06, instead of displaying all records in the table. You can do this by creating a query, specifying the desired condition, and then executing the query. Next you will create a query to display the records for the customers who are represented by sales rep number 06.

1. Click the **Query** button on the button palette.

2. Click the **Slsrep Number** field, and then type **06** as shown in Figure A.16.

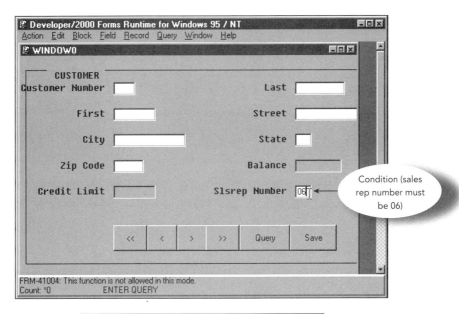

Figure A.16 Entering a query

3. Click the **Query** button again.

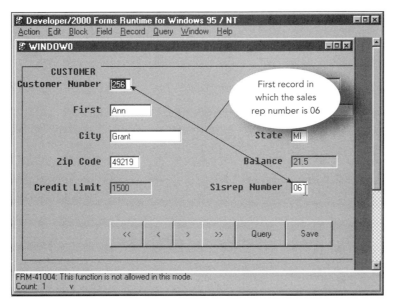

Figure A.17 Viewing the query results

The record for the first customer represented by sales rep number 06 appears in the form, as shown in Figure A.17.

1   Click the **Next Record** button on the button palette.

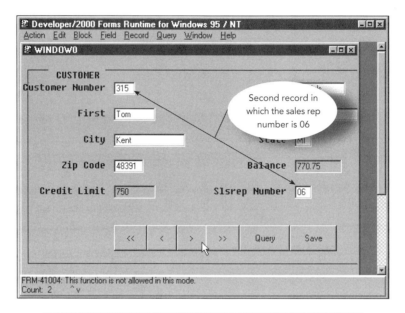

Figure A.18 Viewing additional results

The record for the second customer represented by sales rep number 06 appears in the form, as shown in Figure A.18.

Note	If you click Count hits instead of Execute on the Query menu, you see the total number of customers for sales rep number 06 rather than the actual records for the individual customers.

Note	Before entering a new query, it is a good idea to click Action on the menu bar, and then click Clear all to clear any entries from a previous query. If you don't do this, your new entries could be combined with entries from a previous query and your results might be inaccurate.

Updating a Record

You also can use a form to update the contents of the table, just as you can use the SQL UPDATE command to change rows in a table. To update a record, you first enter and execute an appropriate query to display the record. Then you can make the appropriate changes to the field(s) displayed in the form and click the Save button to save the changes. Next you will change the street value for customer number 412.

1 Click **Action** on the menu bar, and then click **Clear all** to clear the previous query.

2 Click the **Query** button on the button palette to create a new query.

3 Click the **Customer Number** field, and then type **412**.

4 Click the **Query** button a second time to display the record for customer number 412. See Figure A.19.

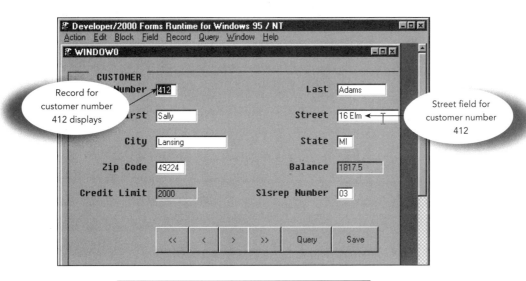

Figure A.19 Updating a record

Now that the record appears in the form, you can change the value in the Street field.

1 Click the **Street** field after the letter "m" to position the insertion point. (When you click the Street field, your form might shift to the left. After making your changes, press the Tab key and the form shifts back to its original position.)

2 Press the **Spacebar** and then type **Street** to change the value from 16 Elm to 16 Elm Street. Press the **Tab** key to complete the entry and move to the next field. See Figure A.20.

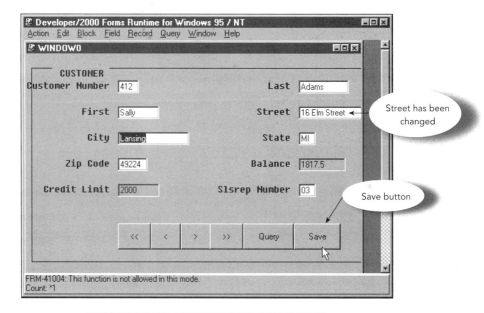

Figure A.20 Record updated

3 Click the **Save** button on the button palette to save the change. A message appears at the bottom of the form indicating that the record is saved.

Note	If you do not click the Save button after making changes, Oracle will ask you later if you want to save them. Click the Yes button to save your changes. Always save your changes as you make them to prevent unexpected data loss.

Inserting a Record

Adding a record using a form is the equivalent of adding a row to a table using the SQL INSERT command. The record also is added to the table automatically. To insert a record, use the Insert command on the Record menu.

1 Click **Record** on the menu bar, and then click **Insert**.

2 Type the data for the new record as shown in Figure A.21.

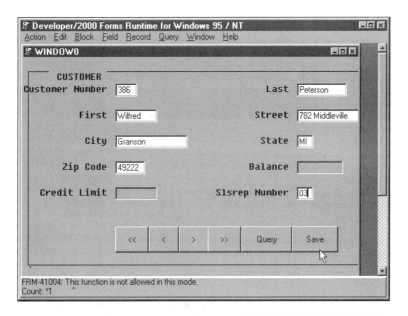

Figure A.21 Adding (inserting) a new record

3 Click the **Save** button to save the changes. A message appears at the bottom of the window to indicate that the record has been added.

Deleting a Record

When you delete a record using a form, you really are deleting it from the table in which it is saved. Deleting a record using a form is the equivalent of deleting it using the SQL DELETE command. To delete a record, first enter and execute an appropriate query to display the record on the screen. Then click Remove on the Record menu to delete the record, and then click the Save button. Next you will delete customer number 386 (the one you just added) from the table.

1 Click **Action** on the menu bar, and then click **Clear all**.

2 Click the **Query** button on the button palette to create a new query.

3 Click the **Customer Number** field, and then type **386**.

4 Click the **Query** button again. The record for customer number 386 appears in the form.

5 Click **Record** on the menu bar, and then click **Remove** to delete the current record.

6 Click the **Save** button to save the change (that is, to delete the record).

After clicking the Save button, the record is removed permanently from the table. If you don't want to remove the record, you can close the form without saving it; do not save your changes when Oracle prompts you to do so. The system then performs a rollback, thus restoring the record. In the process, of course, it also rolls back any changes you made since your most recent save. For this reason, it is a good idea to click the Save button after each update.

Exiting the Form

When you have finished using the form, you can close it by clicking the Exit command on the Action menu.

1 Click **Action** on the menu bar, and then click **Exit**.

2 If a dialog box opens asking if you want to save your changes, click the **Yes** button. The form and the Forms Runtime window close.

3 Click **File** on the menu bar , and then click **Exit** to close the Forms Designer.

Now you know an alternate method of adding, updating, and deleting records by using a form. You also used a form to create and execute queries. In order to use a form for these purposes, you must first create the form using the Forms Designer. In addition to the Forms Designer, there are a variety of other developer tools available in Oracle to assist you in creating reports and other objects. These developer tools provide much more flexibility than simply using SQL commands to create the reports and other objects.

SUMMARY

1. You can use the Oracle Forms Designer to create a form based on any base table or view in the database. You can use a form to display data, query the database, and add, delete, or update records in the database.

2. After creating a form you must create a block and place it on the canvas of the form by clicking Tools on the menu bar, and then clicking New Block.

3. Click the Items tab of the New Block Options dialog box to change the way fields appear on the form.

4. Click the Layout tab of the New Block Options dialog box to change the layout of the form.

5. Click File on the menu bar, and then click Run to view the form. Click File on the menu bar, and then click Save to name the form and save it.

6. You must create and run a query to display records on the screen. Then you can use the commands on the menu bar to make changes to the data on the form.

EXERCISES (PREMIERE PRODUCTS)

1. Start the Forms Designer and connect to the database.

2. Create a form named PART based on the PART table that contains one block. The form will be similar to the one created in the Appendix.

3. Name the canvas PART_CAN.

4. Click the Items tab. Display all fields on the form, except the ALLOCATION field. Change the display type for the UNIT PRICE field to Display Item.

5. Click the Layout tab, change the style to a form, and make sure that the button palette will display on the form, and then click the OK button.

6. Run the form and then save it using the filename "Part."

7. Start the Forms Runtime program.

8. Create a query to display every record in the PART table. How many records are in the table? (*Hint:* Use the buttons on the form to display each record.)

9. Create a new query to display the part whose number is CX11, and then change the number of units on hand to 125 and save changes.

10. Add a new part to the database. Its part number is VG34, part description is Toaster oven, number of units on hand is 28, item class is HW, and its warehouse number is 2.

11. Create a query to display the record that you added in Exercise 10, and then delete it.

12. Save your changes and then close the form.

EXERCISES (HENRY BOOKS)

1. Start the Forms Designer and connect to the database.

2. Create a form named BOOK based on the BOOK table that contains one block. The form will be similar to the one created in the Appendix.

3. Name the canvas BOOK_CAN.

4. Make sure that all fields and the buttons display on the form.

5. Run the form and then save it using the filename "Book."

6. Start the Forms Runtime program.

7. Create a query to display every record in the BOOK table. What is the price of book number 5790?

8. Click the Book Code field, click Query on the menu bar, and then click Count hits. What message appears in the status bar at the bottom of the window? What do you think this message means?

9. Create a new query to display the book whose code is 3743, and then change the book price to 13.95 and save changes.

10. Add a new book to the database. Its book code is 9534, book title is A Guide to SQL, publisher code is BF, book type is CS, book price is 34.88, and it is available only in paperback.

11. Create a query to display the record that you added in Exercise 10, and then delete it.

12. Save your changes and then close the form.

Appendix B
Answers to Odd-Numbered Exercises

CHAPTER 1 — Premiere Products

1. Ann Samuels, Al Williams, Sally Adams, and Mary Nelson

3. BT04, Gas Grill, $1649.89; and BZ66, Washer, $20,799.48

5. Four

7. 12489, 9/02/98, 124, Sally Adams; 12491, 9/02/98, 311, Don Charles;
    12494, 9/04/98, 315, Tom Daniels; 12495, 9/04/98, 256, Ann Samuels;
    12498, 9/05/98, 522, Mary Nelson; 12500, 9/05/98, 124, Sally Adams;
    12504, 9/05/98, 522, Mary Nelson

9. 03, Mary Jones; 12, Miguel Diaz; 06; William Smith

Henry Books

1. Arcade Publishing, Bantam Books, McPherson and Co., Pocket Books,
    Random House, Rizzoli, Schoken Books, Signet, Thames and Hudson,
    W.W. Norton and Co.

3. 0378, Dunwich Horror and Others; 1351, Cujo; 7443, Carrie

5. 0189, Kane and Abel; 0378, Dunwich Horror and Others; 079X,
    Smokescreen; 0808, Knockdown; 1351, Cujo; 1382, Marcel Duchamp;
    2281, Prints of the 20th Century; 2766, Prodigal Daughter; 3350, Higher
    Creativity; 3743, First Among Equals; 6128, Evil Under the Sun; 7443,
    Carrie; 7559, Risk

7. 0180, Shyness, $6.89; 0189, Kane and Abel, $5.00; 0200, Stranger, $7.88;
    0378, Dunwich Horror and Others, $17.78; 079X, Smokescreen, $4.10; etc.
    To figure the remaining prices, multiply the current price in the
    BOOK_PRICE field by .90.

9. 0189, Kane and Abel; 0200, Stranger; 079X, Smokescreen; 0808,
    Knockdown; 1382, Marcel Duchamp; 138X, Death on the Nile; 2281,
    Prints of the 20th Century; 2766, Prodigal Daughter; 3743, First Among
    Equals; 6128, Evil Under the Sun; 7559, Risk; 8092, Magritte; 8720,
    Castle; 9611, Amerika

11. $11.05

13. 1, 0180, Shyness, 2; 2, 0189, Kane and Abel, 2; 1, 0200, Stranger, 1; 2,
    0200, Stranger, 3; 2, 079X, Smokescreen, 1; 3, 079X, Smokescreen, 2; 4,
    079X, Smokescreen, 3; 1, 1351, Cujo, 1; 2, 1351, Cujo, 4; 3, 1351, Cujo, 2;
    2, 138X, Death on the Nile, 3; 1, 2226, Ghost from the Grand Banks, 3; 3,
    2226, Ghost from the Grand Banks, 2; 4, 2226, Ghost from the Grand

Banks, 1; 4, 2281, Prints of the 20th Century, 3; 3, 2766, Prodigal Daughter, 2; 1, 2908, Hymns in the Night, 3; 4, 2908, Hymns in the Night, 1; 1, 3350, Higher Creativity, 2; 2, 3906, Vortex, 1; 3, 3906, Vortex, 2; 1, 5163, Organ, 1; 4, 5790, Database Systems, 2; 2, 6128, Evil Under the Sun, 4; 3, 6128, Evil Under the Sun, 3; 2, 6328, Vixen 07, 2; 1, 669X, A Guide to SQL, 1; 2, 6908, DOS Essentials 2; 3, 7405, Night Probe, 2; 2, 7559, Risk, 2; 2, 7947, dBASE Programming, 2; 3, 8092, Magritte, 1; 1, 8720, Castle, 3; 1, 9611, Amerika, 2

CHAPTER 2 — Premiere Products

Use SQL to input the specified data.

Henry Books

Use SQL to input the specified data.

CHAPTER 3 — Premiere Products

1. SELECT PART_NUMBER, PART_DESCRIPTION
    FROM PART;
    AX12 Iron
    AZ52 Dartboard
    BA74 Basketball
    BH22 Cornpopper
    BT04 Gas Grill
    BZ66 Washer
    CA14 Griddle
    CB03 Bike
    CX11 Blender
    CZ81 Treadmill

3. SELECT LAST, FIRST
    FROM CUSTOMER
    WHERE CREDIT_LIMIT >= 800;

Adams	Sally
Samuels	Ann
Charles	Don
Williams	Al
Adams	Sally
Nelson	Mary
Galvez	Mara
Martin	Dan

5. SELECT CUSTOMER_NUMBER, LAST, FIRST
   FROM CUSTOMER
   WHERE SLSREP_NUMBER = '03' OR SLSREP_NUMBER = '12';
   124 Adams   Sally
   311 Charles   Don
   405 Williams   Al
   412 Adams   Sally
   522 Nelson   Mary
   622 Martin   Dan

7. SELECT PART_NUMBER, PART_DESCRIPTION
   FROM PART
   WHERE UNITS_ON_HAND >100 AND UNITS_ON_HAND < 200;
   AX12 Iron
   CX11 Blender

   SELECT PART_NUMBER, PART_DESCRIPTION
   FROM PART
   WHERE UNITS_ON_HAND BETWEEN 100 AND 200;
   AX12 Iron
   CX11 Blender

9. SELECT PART_NUMBER, PART_DESCRIPTION, (UNITS_ON_HAND *
   UNIT_PRICE)
   FROM PART
   WHERE (UNITS_ON_HAND * UNIT_PRICE) >= 1000;
   AX12 Iron   2594.8
   BA74 Basketball   1198
   BH22 Cornpopper   2370.25
   BT04 Gas Grill   1649.89
   BZ66 Washer   20799.48
   CA14 Griddle   3119.22
   CB03 Bike   13199.56
   CX11 Blender   2570.4
   CZ81 Treadmill   23796.6

11. SELECT CUSTOMER_NUMBER, LAST, FIRST
    FROM CUSTOMER
    WHERE FIRST LIKE 'D%';
    311 Charles   Don
    622 Martin   Dan

13.   SELECT *
FROM PART
ORDER BY PART_NUMBER, ITEM_CLASS;

AX12 Iron	104	HW	3	24.95
AZ52 Dartboard	20	SG	2	12.95
BA74 Basketball	40	SG	1	29.95
BH22 Cornpopper	95	HW	3	24.95
BT04 Gas Grill	11	AP	2	149.99
BZ66 Washer	52	AP	3	399.99
CA14 Griddle	78	HW	3	39.99
CB03 Bike	44	SG	1	299.99
CX11 Blender	112	HW	3	22.95
CZ81 Treadmill	68	SG	2	349.95

15.   SELECT SUM(BALANCE)
FROM CUSTOMER
WHERE SLSREP_NUMBER = '12' AND BALANCE < CREDIT_LIMIT;
1327.25

17.   SELECT MIN(UNIT_PRICE)
FROM PART;

19.   SELECT COUNT(*)
FROM CUSTOMER;

21.   SELECT ITEM_CLASS, SUM(UNITS_ON_HAND * UNIT_PRICE)
FROM PART
GROUP BY ITEM_CLASS;

AP	22449.37
HW	10654.67
SG	38453.16

Henry Books

1.   SELECT BOOK_CODE, BOOK_TITLE
FROM BOOK;

0180 Shyness
0189 Kane and Abel
0200 Stranger
0378 Dunwich Horror and Others
079X Smokescreen
0808 Knockdown
1351 Cujo

1382 Marcel Duchamp
138X Death on the Nile
2226 Ghost from the Grand Banks
2281 Prints of the 20th Century
2766 Prodigal Daughter
2908 Hymns to the Night
3350 Higher Creativity
3743 First Among Equals
3906 Vortex
5163 Organ
5790 Database Systems
6128 Evil Under the Sun
6328 Vixen 07
669X A Guide to SQL
6908 DOS Essentials
7405 Night Probe
7443 Carrie
7559 Risk
7947 dBASE Programming
8092 Magritte
8720 Castle
9611 Amerika

3. SELECT PUBLISHER_NAME
    FROM PUBLISHER
    WHERE PUBLISHER_STATE = 'NY';
    Arcade Publishing
    Bantam Books
    McPherson and Co.
    Pocket Books
    Random House
    Rizzoli
    Schoken Books
    Signet
    Thames and Hudson
    W.W. Norton and Co.

5. SELECT BRANCH_NAME
    FROM BRANCH
    WHERE NUMBER_EMPLOYEES >= 10;
    Henry Downtown
    Henry Brentwood

7.   SELECT BOOK_CODE, BOOK_TITLE
     FROM BOOK
     WHERE BOOK_TYPE = 'HOR' AND PAPERBACK = 'Y';
     1351 Cujo
     7443 Carrie

9.   SELECT BOOK_CODE, BOOK_TITLE, BOOK_PRICE
     FROM BOOK
     WHERE BOOK_PRICE BETWEEN 10 AND 20;
     OR WHERE BOOK_PRICE > 10
     AND BOOK_PRICE < 20;
     0378 Dunwich Horror and Others   19.75
     1382 Marcel Duchamp   11.25
     2226 Ghost from the Grand Banks   19.95
     2281 Prints of the 20th Century   13.25
     5163 Organ   16.95
     8720 Castle   12.15
     9611 Amerika   10.95

11. SELECT BOOK_CODE, BOOK_TITLE, (BOOK_PRICE * .85)
     FROM BOOK;
     0180 Shyness   6.5025
     0189 Kane and Abel   4.7175
     0200 Stranger   7.4375
     0378 Dunwich Horror and Others   16.7875
     079X Smokescreen   3.8675
     0808 Knockdown   4.0375
     1351 Cujo   5.6525
     1382 Marcel Duchamp   9.5625
     138X Death on the Nile   3.3575
     2226 Ghost from the Grand Banks   16.9575
     2281 Prints of the 20th Century   11.2625
     2766 Prodigal Daughter   4.6325
     2908 Hymns to the Night   5.7375
     3350 Higher Creativity   8.2875
     3743 First Among Equals   3.3575
     3906 Vortex   4.6325
     5163 Organ   14.4075
     5790 Database Systems   46.7075
     6128 Evil Under the Sun   3.7825
     6328 Vixen 07   4.7175
     669X A Guide to SQL   20.3575
     6908 DOS Essentials   17.425
     7405 Night Probe   4.8025

7443 Carrie	5.7375	
7559 Risk	3.3575	
7947 dBASE Programming	33.915	
8092 Magritte	18.6575	
8720 Castle	10.3275	
9611 Amerika	9.3075	

13. SELECT BOOK_CODE, BOOK_TITLE, BOOK_TYPE
FROM BOOK
WHERE BOOK_TYPE IN ('FIC','MYS','ART');

0189 Kane and Abel	FIC
079X Smokescreen	MYS
0808 Knockdown	MYS
1382 Marcel Duchamp	ART
138X Death on the Nile	MYS
2281 Prints of the 20th Century	ART
2766 Prodigal Daughter	FIC
3743 First Among Equals	FIC
6128 Evil Under the Sun	MYS
7559 Risk	MYS
8092 Magritte	ART
8720 Castle	FIC
9611 Amerika	FIC

15. SELECT BOOK_CODE, BOOK_TITLE, BOOK_TYPE
FROM BOOK
WHERE BOOK_TYPE IN ('FIC','MYS','ART')
ORDER BY BOOK_CODE DESC;

9611 Amerika	FIC
8720 Castle	FIC
8092 Magritte	ART
7559 Risk	MYS
6128 Evil Under the Sun	MYS
3743 First Among Equals	FIC
2766 Prodigal Daughter	FIC
2281 Prints of the 20th Century	ART
138X Death on the Nile	MYS
1382 Marcel Duchamp	ART
0808 Knockdown	MYS
079X Smokescreen	MYS
0189 Kane and Abel	FIC

17. SELECT COUNT(DISTINCT(BOOK_TYPE))
     FROM BOOK;
     10

19. SELECT BOOK_TYPE, AVG(BOOK_PRICE)
     FROM BOOK
     GROUP BY BOOK_TYPE;
     ART   15.483333
     CS   34.825
     FIC   7.61
     HOR   10.475
     MUS   16.95
     MYS   4.33
     POE   6.75
     PSY   8.7
     SFI   19.95
     SUS   5.55

21. SELECT BOOK_TITLE
     FROM BOOK
     WHERE BOOK_PRICE =
     (SELECT MAX(BOOK_PRICE)
     FROM BOOK);

23. SELECT BRANCH_NAME
     FROM BRANCH
     WHERE NUMBER_EMPLOYEES IN
     (SELECT MIN(NUMBER_EMPLOYEES)
     FROM BRANCH);

CHAPTER 4 — Premiere Products

1. SELECT ORDER_NUMBER, ORDER_DATE,
    CUSTOMER.CUSTOMER_NUMBER, LAST, FIRST
    FROM ORDERS, CUSTOMER
    WHERE ORDERS.CUSTOMER_NUMBER =
    CUSTOMER.CUSTOMER_NUMBER;
    12489 02-SEP-98 124 Adams   Sally
    12491 02-SEP-98 311 Charles   Don
    12494 04-SEP-98 315 Daniels   Tom
    12495 04-SEP-98 256 Samuels   Ann
    12498 05-SEP-98 522 Nelson   Mary

12500 05-SEP-98 124 Adams   Sally
12504 05-SEP-98 522 Nelson   Mary

3.   SELECT ORDERS.ORDER_NUMBER, ORDER_DATE,
    PART.PART_NUMBER, NUMBER_ORDERED, QUOTED_PRICE
    FROM ORDERS, ORDER_LINE, PART
    WHERE ORDERS.ORDER_NUMBER =
    ORDER_LINE.ORDER_NUMBER
    AND PART.PART_NUMBER = ORDER_LINE.PART_NUMBER;

12489	02-SEP-98	AX12	11	21.95
12491	02-SEP-98	BT04	1	149.99
12491	02-SEP-98	BZ66	1	399.99
12494	04-SEP-98	CB03	4	279.99
12495	04-SEP-98	CX11	2	22.95
12498	05-SEP-98	AZ52	2	12.95
12498	05-SEP-98	BA74	4	24.95
12500	05-SEP-98	BT04	1	149.99
12504	05-SEP-98	CZ81	2	325.99

5.   SELECT CUSTOMER_NUMBER, LAST, FIRST
    FROM CUSTOMER
    WHERE EXISTS
    (SELECT *
    FROM ORDERS
    WHERE ORDERS.CUSTOMER_NUMBER =
    CUSTOMER.CUSTOMER_NUMBER
    AND ORDER_DATE = '05-SEP-98');

124 Adams   Sally
522 Nelson   Mary

7.   SELECT ORDER_LINE.ORDER_NUMBER, ORDER_DATE,
    PART.PART_NUMBER, PART_DESCRIPTION, ITEM_CLASS
    FROM ORDER_LINE, ORDERS, PART
    WHERE ORDER_LINE.ORDER_NUMBER =
    ORDERS.ORDER_NUMBER
    AND ORDER_LINE.PART_NUMBER = PART.PART_NUMBER;

12489 02-SEP-98 AX12 Iron   HW
12491 02-SEP-98 BT04 Gas Grill   AP
12491 02-SEP-98 BZ66 Washer   AP
12494 04-SEP-98 CB03 Bike   SG
12495 04-SEP-98 CX11 Blender   HW
12498 05-SEP-98 AZ52 Dartboard   SG
12498 05-SEP-98 BA74 Basketball   SG

```
       12500 05-SEP-98 BT04 Gas Grill      AP
       12504 05-SEP-98 CZ81 Treadmill      SG
```

9. SELECT SLSREP_NUMBER, LAST, FIRST
    FROM SALES_REP
    WHERE SLSREP_NUMBER IN
    (SELECT SLSREP_NUMBER
    FROM CUSTOMER
    WHERE CREDIT_LIMIT IN
    (SELECT CREDIT_LIMIT
    FROM CUSTOMER
    WHERE CREDIT_LIMIT = 2000));
    03 Jones   Mary

11. SELECT CUSTOMER.CUSTOMER_NUMBER, LAST, FIRST
    FROM CUSTOMER, ORDER_LINE, ORDERS, PART
    WHERE CUSTOMER.CUSTOMER_NUMBER =
    ORDERS.CUSTOMER_NUMBER
    AND ORDERS.ORDER_NUMBER = ORDER_LINE.ORDER_NUMBER
    AND PART.PART_NUMBER = ORDER_LINE.PART_NUMBER
    AND PART_DESCRIPTION = 'Iron';
    124 Adams Sally

13. SELECT PART.PART_DESCRIPTION, PART.PART_NUMBER,
    ORDERS.ORDER_NUMBER, ORDER_DATE
    FROM ORDERS, ORDER_LINE, CUSTOMER, PART
    WHERE PART.PART_NUMBER = ORDER_LINE.PART_NUMBER
    AND ORDERS.ORDER_NUMBER = ORDER_LINE.ORDER_NUMBER
    AND CUSTOMER.CUSTOMER_NUMBER =
    ORDERS.CUSTOMER_NUMBER
    AND CUSTOMER.LAST = 'Nelson'
    AND CUSTOMER.FIRST = 'Mary'
    AND PART_DESCRIPTION = 'Treadmill';
    Treadmill   CZ81 12504 05-SEP-98

15. SELECT ORDER_NUMBER, ORDER_DATE
    FROM ORDERS, CUSTOMER
    WHERE ORDERS.CUSTOMER_NUMBER =
    CUSTOMER.CUSTOMER_NUMBER
    AND LAST = 'Nelson'
    UNION

SELECT ORDERS.ORDER_NUMBER, ORDER_DATE
FROM ORDERS, ORDER_LINE, PART
WHERE ORDERS.ORDER_NUMBER =
ORDER_LINE.ORDER_NUMBER
AND PART.PART_NUMBER = ORDER_LINE.PART_NUMBER
AND PART_DESCRIPTION = 'Iron';
12489 02-SEP-98
12498 05-SEP-98
12504 05-SEP-98

17. SELECT ORDER_NUMBER, ORDER_DATE
FROM ORDERS, CUSTOMER
WHERE ORDERS.CUSTOMER_NUMBER =
CUSTOMER.CUSTOMER_NUMBER
AND LAST = 'Nelson'
AND FIRST = 'Mary'
MINUS
SELECT ORDERS.ORDER_NUMBER, ORDER_DATE
FROM ORDERS, ORDER_LINE, PART
WHERE ORDERS.ORDER_NUMBER =
ORDER_LINE.ORDER_NUMBER
AND ORDER_LINE.PART_NUMBER = PART.PART_NUMBER
AND PART_DESCRIPTION = 'Iron';
12498 05-SEP-98
12504 05-SEP-98

19. SELECT PART_NUMBER, PART_DESCRIPTION, UNIT_PRICE,
ITEM_CLASS
FROM PART
WHERE UNIT_PRICE > ALL
(SELECT UNIT_PRICE
FROM PART
WHERE ITEM_CLASS = 'HW');

BT04	Gas Grill	149.99	AP
BZ66	Washer	399.99	AP
CB03	Bike	299.99	SG
CZ81	Treadmill	349.95	SG

The question asks for the list of parts that have a unit price that is greater than all parts in item class HW.

Henry Books

1. SELECT BOOK.BOOK_CODE, BOOK_TITLE,
    PUBLISHER.PUBLISHER_CODE, PUBLISHER_NAME
    FROM BOOK, PUBLISHER
    WHERE PUBLISHER.PUBLISHER_CODE = BOOK.PUBLISHER_CODE;

0180 Shyness	BB	Bantam Books
0189 Kane and Abel	PB	Pocket Books
0200 Stranger	BB	Bantam Books
0378 Dunwich Horror and Others	PB	Pocket Books
079X Smokescreen	PB	Pocket Books
0808 Knockdown	PB	Pocket Books
1351 Cujo	SI	Signet
1382 Marcel Duchamp	PB	Pocket Books
138X Death on the Nile	BB	Bantam Books
2226 Ghost from the Grand Banks	BB	Bantam Books
2281 Prints of the 20th Century	PB	Pocket Books
2766 Prodigal Daughter	PB	Pocket Books
2908 Hymns to the Night	BB	Bantam Books
3350 Higher Creativity	PB	Pocket Books
3743 First Among Equals	PB	Pocket Books
3906 Vortex	BB	Bantam Books
5163 Organ	SI	Signet
5790 Database Systems	BF	Best and Furrow
6128 Evil Under the Sun	PB	Pocket Books
6328 Vixen 07	BB	Bantam Books
669X A Guide to SQL	BF	Best and Furrow
6908 DOS Essentials	BF	Best and Furrow
7405 Night Probe	BB	Bantam Books
7443 Carrie	SI	Signet
7559 Risk	PB	Pocket Books
7947 dBASE Programming	BF	Best and Furrow
8092 Magritte	SI	Signet
8720 Castle	BB	Bantam Books
9611 Amerika	BB	Bantam Books

3. SELECT BOOK_TITLE, BOOK.BOOK_CODE
    FROM BOOK, PUBLISHER
    WHERE BOOK.PUBLISHER_CODE = PUBLISHER.PUBLISHER_CODE
    AND BOOK_PRICE > 10
    AND PUBLISHER_NAME = 'Bantam Books';

Ghost from the Grand Banks	2226
Castle	8720
Amerika	9611

5. SELECT BOOK_TITLE
FROM BOOK, PUBLISHER
WHERE PUBLISHER. PUBLISHER.CODE = BOOK. PUBLISHER_CODE
AND BOOK_TYPE = 'ART'
AND PUBLISHER_NAME = 'Best and Furrow';
no rows selected

7. SELECT BOOK_TITLE
FROM BOOK
WHERE EXISTS
(SELECT *
FROM WROTE
WHERE BOOK.BOOK_CODE = WROTE.BOOK_CODE
AND AUTHOR_NUMBER = '01');
Kane and Abel
Prodigal Daughter
First Among Equals

9. SELECT F.PUBLISHER_CODE, F.PUBLISHER_NAME,
S.PUBLISHER_CODE, S.PUBLISHER_NAME
FROM PUBLISHER F, PUBLISHER S
WHERE F.PUBLISHER_CITY = S.PUBLISHER_CITY
AND F.PUBLISHER_CODE < S.PUBLISHER_CODE;

AP Arcade Publishing	BB Bantam Books
AP Arcade Publishing	PB Pocket Books
BB Bantam Books	PB Pocket Books
AP Arcade Publishing	RH Random House
BB Bantam Books	RH Random House
PB Pocket Books	RH Random House
AP Arcade Publishing	RZ Rizzoli
BB Bantam Books	RZ Rizzoli
PB Pocket Books	RZ Rizzoli
RH Random House	RZ Rizzoli
AP Arcade Publishing	SB Schoken Books
BB Bantam Books	SB Schoken Books
PB Pocket Books	SB Schoken Books
RH Random House	SB Schoken Books
RZ Rizzoli	SB Schoken Books
AP Arcade Publishing	SI Signet

BB Bantam Books	SI Signet
PB Pocket Books	SI Signet
RH Random House	SI Signet
RZ Rizzoli	SI Signet
SB Schoken Books	SI Signet
AP Arcade Publishing	TH Thames and Hudson
BB Bantam Books	TH Thames and Hudson
PB Pocket Books	TH Thames and Hudson
RH Random House	TH Thames and Hudson
RZ Rizzoli	TH Thames and Hudson
SB Schoken Books	TH Thames and Hudson
SI Signet	TH Thames and Hudson
AP Arcade Publishing	WN W.W. Norton and Co.
BB Bantam Books	WN W.W. Norton and Co.
PB Pocket Books	WN W.W. Norton and Co.
RH Random House	WN W.W. Norton and Co.
RZ Rizzoli	WN W.W. Norton and Co.
SB Schoken Books	WN W.W. Norton and Co.
SI Signet	WN W.W. Norton and Co.
TH Thames and Hudson	WN W.W. Norton and Co.

11. SELECT UNITS_ON_HAND, BOOK_TITLE, AUTHOR_LAST
    FROM INVENT, BOOK, WROTE, AUTHOR
    WHERE INVENT.BOOK_CODE = BOOK.BOOK_CODE
    AND BOOK.BOOK_CODE = WROTE.BOOK_CODE
    AND WROTE.AUTHOR_NUMBER = AUTHOR.AUTHOR_NUMBER
    AND BRANCH_NUMBER = 4
    AND PAPERBACK = 'Y';

3 Smokescreen	Francis
3 Prints of the 20th Century	Castleman
1 Hymns to the Night	Novalis

13. SELECT BOOK.BOOK_CODE, BOOK_TITLE
    FROM BOOK, PUBLISHER
    WHERE PUBLISHER.PUBLISHER_CODE = BOOK.PUBLISHER_CODE
    AND PUBLISHER_STATE = 'NY'
    AND BOOK_PRICE > 5;

0180 Shyness
0189 Kane and Abel
0200 Stranger
0378 Dunwich Horror and Others

1351 Cujo
1382 Marcel Duchamp
2226 Ghost from the Grand Banks
2281 Prints of the 20th Century
2766 Prodigal Daughter
2908 Hymns to the Night
3350 Higher Creativity
3906 Vortex
5163 Organ
6328 Vixen 07
7405 Night Probe
7443 Carrie
8092 Magritte
8720 Castle
9611 Amerika

15. SELECT BOOK_TITLE, PUBLISHER_CODE
FROM BOOK
WHERE BOOK_PRICE > ANY
(SELECT BOOK_PRICE
FROM BOOK
WHERE BOOK_TYPE = 'CS');

Database Systems	BF
A Guide to SQL	BF
dBASE Programming	BF
Magritte	SI

CHAPTER 5 — Premiere Products

1. UPDATE PART
SET PART_DESCRIPTION = 'Oven'
WHERE PART_NUMBER = 'BT04';
1 row updated.

SELECT *
FROM PART;

AX12	Iron	104	HW	3	24.95
AZ52	Dartboard	20	SG	2	12.95
BA74	Basketball	40	SG	1	29.95
BH22	Cornpopper	95	HW	3	24.95
BT04	Oven	11	AP	2	149.99
BZ66	Washer	52	AP	3	399.99

CA14	Griddle	78	HW	3	39.99
CB03	Bike	44	SG	1	299.99
CX11	Blender	112	HW	3	22.95
CZ81	Treadmill	68	SG	2	349.95

3. INSERT INTO ORDERS
VALUES
('12600','06-SEP-98','311');
1 row created.

INSERT INTO ORDER_LINE
VALUES
('12600','AX12',5,13.95);
1 row created.

INSERT INTO ORDER_LINE
VALUES
('12600','BA74',3,4.50);
1 row created.

SELECT *
FROM ORDER_LINE;

12489	AX12	11	21.95
12491	BT04	1	149.99
12491	BZ66	1	399.99
12494	CB03	4	279.99
12495	CX11	2	22.95
12498	AZ52	2	12.95
12498	BA74	4	24.95
12500	BT04	1	149.99
12504	CZ81	2	325.99
12600	AX12	5	13.95
12600	BA74	3	4.5

SELECT *
FROM ORDERS;

12489	02-SEP-98	124
12491	02-SEP-98	311
12494	04-SEP-98	315
12495	04-SEP-98	256
12498	05-SEP-98	522
12500	05-SEP-98	124
12504	05-SEP-98	522
12600	06-SEP-98	311

5. CREATE TABLE SPGOODS
    (PART_NUMBER CHAR(4),
    PART_DESCRIPTION CHAR(12),
    UNIT_PRICE NUMBER(6,2));
    Table created.

    INSERT INTO SPGOODS
    SELECT PART_NUMBER, PART_DESCRIPTION, UNIT_PRICE
    FROM PART
    WHERE ITEM_CLASS = 'SG';
    4 rows created.

    SELECT *
    FROM SPGOODS;

AZ52	Dartboard	12.95
BA74	Basketball	29.95
CB03	Bike	299.99
CZ81	Treadmill	349.95

7. ALTER TABLE PART
    ADD ALLOCATION NUMBER(3,0);
    Table altered.

    UPDATE PART
    SET ALLOCATION = 0;
    10 rows updated.

    SELECT SUM(NUMBER_ORDERED)
    FROM ORDER_LINE
    WHERE PART_NUMBER = 'BT04';
    2

    UPDATE PART
    SET ALLOCATION = 2
    WHERE PART_NUMBER = 'BT04';
    1 row updated.

    SELECT *
    FROM PART;

AX12	Iron	104	HW	3	24.95	0
AZ52	Dartboard	20	SG	2	12.95	0
BA74	Basketball	40	SG	1	29.95	0
BH22	Cornpopper	95	HW	3	24.95	0
BT04	Oven	11	AP	2	149.99	2
BZ66	Washer	52	AP	3	399.99	0

CA14	Griddle	78	HW	3	39.99	0
CB03	Bike	44	SG	1	299.99	0
CX11	Blender	112	HW	3	22.95	0
CZ81	Treadmill	68	SG	2	349.95	0

9. ALTER TABLE PART
MODIFY PART_DESCRIPTION CHAR(30);
Table altered.

Henry Books

1. UPDATE INVENT
SET UNITS_ON_HAND = 5
WHERE BRANCH_NUMBER = '1';
10 rows updated.

SELECT *
FROM INVENT
WHERE BRANCH_NUMBER = '1';

0180	1	5
0200	1	5
1351	1	5
2226	1	5
2908	1	5
3350	1	5
5163	1	5
669X	1	5
8720	1	5
9611	1	5

3. INSERT INTO BOOK
VALUES
('9700','Using Microsoft Access 97','BF','CS',19.97,'Y');
1 row created.

INSERT INTO INVENT
VALUES
('9700','1',4);
1 row created.

INSERT INTO WROTE
VALUES
('9700','07',2);
1 row created.

5. CREATE TABLE FICTION
(BOOK_CODE CHAR(4),
BOOK_TITLE CHAR(30),
BOOK_PRICE NUMBER(4,2));
Table created.

INSERT INTO FICTION
SELECT BOOK_CODE, BOOK_TITLE, BOOK_PRICE
FROM BOOK
WHERE BOOK_TYPE = 'FIC';
5 rows created.

SELECT *
FROM FICTION;

0189	Kane and Abel	5.55
2766	Prodigal Daughter	5.45
3743	First Among Equals	3.95
8720	Castle	12.15
9611	Amerika	10.95

7. UPDATE FICTION
SET BOOK_PRICE = NULL
WHERE BOOK_TITLE = 'Amerika';
1 row updated.

SELECT *
FROM FICTION;

0189	Kane and Abel	6.22
2766	Prodigal Daughter	6.1
3743	First Among Equals	4.42
8720	Castle	13.61
9611	Amerika	

9. UPDATE FICTION
SET BEST_SELLER = 'Y'
WHERE BOOK_TITLE = 'Kane and Abel';
1 row updated.

SELECT *
FROM FICTION;

0189	Kane and Abel	6.22	Y
2766	Prodigal Daughter	6.1	N
3743	First Among Equals	4.42	N
8720	Castle	14.01	N
9611	Amerika		N

11. ALTER TABLE FICTION
    MODIFY BEST_SELLER NOT NULL;
    Table altered.

13. DROP TABLE FICTION;
    Table dropped.

CHAPTER 6 — Premiere Products

1. a.
    CREATE VIEW SMALLCST AS
    SELECT CUSTOMER_NUMBER, LAST, FIRST, STREET, BALANCE,
    CREDIT_LIMIT
    FROM CUSTOMER
    WHERE CREDIT_LIMIT <= 1000;
    View created.

    b.
    SELECT CUSTOMER_NUMBER, LAST, FIRST
    FROM SMALLCST
    WHERE BALANCE > CREDIT_LIMIT;
    315 Daniels Tom
    622 Martin Dan

    c.
    SELECT CUSTOMER_NUMBER, LAST, FIRST
    FROM CUSTOMER
    WHERE CREDIT_LIMIT <= 1000
    AND BALANCE > CREDIT_LIMIT;
    315 Daniels Tom
    622 Martin Dan

    d.   There are no problems updating the data in the SMALLCST view because the view
          includes the primary key of the CUSTOMER table as one of its fields. The only potential
          problem is that a customer can be added to the base table who has a credit limit of more
          than $1,000, in which case that customer's row disappears from the view.

3. a.
    CREATE VIEW ORDTOT (ORDER_NUMBER, ORDER_TOTAL) AS
    SELECT ORDER_NUMBER, SUM(NUMBER_ORDERED *
    QUOTED_PRICE)
    FROM ORDER_LINE
    GROUP BY ORDER_NUMBER;
    View created.

b.

SELECT ORDER_NUMBER, ORDER_TOTAL
FROM ORDTOT
WHERE ORDER_TOTAL > 500
ORDER BY ORDER. NUMBER;

12491	549.98
12494	1119.96
12504	651.98

c.

SELECT ORDER_NUMBER, SUM(NUMBER_ORDERED *
QUOTED_PRICE) AS ORDER_TOTAL
FROM ORDER_LINE
GROUP BY ORDER_NUMBER
HAVING SUM(NUMBER_ORDERED * QUOTED_PRICE) > 500;

12491	549.98
12494	1119.96
12504	651.98

d.   You cannot update data in the ORDER_LINE table using the ORDTOT
view because the view does not contain the primary key of the base
table, and the view consists of a computed column.

5.   REVOKE SELECT ON PART FROM STILLWELL;

7.   DROP INDEX PARTIND3;

9.   ALTER TABLE CUSTOMER
ADD CHECK (CREDIT_LIMIT IN (750, 1000, 1500, 2000))
PRIMARY KEY (CUSTOMER_NUMBER)
FOREIGN KEY (SLSREP_NUMBER) REFERENCES SALES_REP;

Henry Books

1.   a.
CREATE VIEW BANTAM AS
SELECT BOOK_CODE, BOOK_TITLE, BOOK_TYPE, BOOK_PRICE
FROM BOOK
WHERE PUBLISHER_CODE = 'BB';
View created.

b.
SELECT BOOK_CODE, BOOK_TITLE, BOOK_PRICE
FROM BANTAM
WHERE BOOK_PRICE < 10;

0180	Shyness	7.65
0200	Stranger	8.75

138X	Death on the Nile	3.95
2908	Hymns to the Night	6.75
3906	Vortex	5.45
6328	Vixen 07	5.55
7405	Night Probe	5.65

c.

```
SELECT BOOK_CODE, BOOK_TITLE, BOOK_PRICE
FROM BOOK
WHERE PUBLISHER_CODE = 'BB'
AND BOOK_PRICE < 10;
```

0180	Shyness	7.65
0200	Stranger	8.75
138X	Death on the Nile	3.95
2908	Hymns to the Night	6.75
3906	Vortex	5.45
6328	Vixen 07	5.55
7405	Night Probe	5.65

d.   You can use the BANTAM view to update data in the BOOK table because the view contains the primary key of the underlying base table.

3.   a.

```
CREATE VIEW VALUE (BRANCH_NUMBER, TOTAL_COUNT) AS
SELECT BRANCH_NUMBER, SUM(UNITS_ON_HAND)
FROM INVENT
GROUP BY BRANCH_NUMBER;
```
View created.

b.

```
SELECT *
FROM VALUE;
```

1	19
2	26
3	16
4	10

c.

```
SELECT BRANCH_NUMBER, SUM(UNITS_ON_HAND)
FROM INVENT
GROUP BY BRANCH_NUMBER;
```

1	19
2	26
3	16
4	10

   d. You cannot use the VALUE view to update data in the INVENT table because the view contains a computed column.

5. REVOKE INDEX ON BOOK FROM VERNER
REVOKE ALTER ON AUTHOR FROM VERNER

7. DROP INDEX BOOKIND3;

9. a.
ALTER TABLE BOOK
ADD CHECK (BOOK_TYPE IN
     ('SFI','PSY','FIC','HOR','MYS','ART','POE','SUS','MUS','CS'));

b.
ALTER TABLE BOOK
ADD CHECK (PAPERBACK IN ('Y','N'));

c.
ALTER TABLE BRANCH
ADD CHECK (BRANCH_NUMBER IN ('1','2','3','4'));

d.
ALTER TABLE WROTE
ADD CHECK (SEQUENCE_NUMBER IN ('1','2'));

CHAPTER 7 – Premiere Products

1. SELECT RTRIM(FIRST)||' '||RTRIM(LAST), STREET,
RTRIM(CITY)||', '||RTRIM(STATE)||' '||RTRIM(ZIP_CODE)
FROM CUSTOMER;

Sally Adams	481 Oak	Lansing, MI 49224
Ann Samuels	215 Pete	Grant, MI 49219
Don Charles	48 College	Ira, MI 49034
Tom Daniels	914 Cherry	Kent, MI 48391
Al Williams	519 Watson	Grant, MI 49219
Sally Adams	16 Elm	Lansing, MI 49224
Mary Nelson	108 Pine	Ada, MI 49441
Tran Dinh	808 Ridge	Harper, MI 48421
Mara Galvez	512 Pine	Ada, MI 49441
Dan Martin	419 Chip	Grant, MI 49219

3. COLUMN NAME HEADING 'CUSTOMER|NAME'
COLUMN ADDRESS HEADING 'CUSTOMER|ADDRESS'
COLUMN CITY HEADING 'CUSTOMER|CITY/STATE/ZIP'
SELECT *
FROM REPORT2;

CUSTOMER NAME	CUSTOMER ADDRESS	CUSTOMER CITY/STATE/ZIP
Sally Adams	481 Oak	Lansing, MI 49224
Ann Samuels	215 Pete	Grant, MI 49219
Don Charles	48 College	Ira, MI 49034
Tom Daniels	914 Cherry	Kent, MI 48391
Al Williams	519 Watson	Grant, MI 49219
Sally Adams	16 Elm	Lansing, MI 49224
Mary Nelson	108 Pine	Ada, MI 49441
Tran Dinh	808 Ridge	Harper, MI 48421
Mara Galvez	512 Pine	Ada, MI 49441
Dan Martin	419 Chip	Grant, MI 49219

5. CREATE VIEW REPORT3 (NAME, CREDIT_LIMIT, BALANCE) AS
    SELECT RTRIM(FIRST)||' '||RTRIM(LAST), CREDIT_LIMIT, BALANCE
    FROM CUSTOMER;
    View created.

    COLUMN NAME HEADING 'CUSTOMER|NAME'
    COLUMN CREDIT_LIMIT HEADING 'CUSTOMER|CREDIT LIMIT'
        FORMAT $9999.99
    COLUMN BALANCE HEADING 'CUSTOMER|BALANCE' FORMAT
        $9999.99

    SELECT *
    FROM REPORT3;

CUSTOMER NAME	CUSTOMER CREDIT LIMIT	CUSTOMER BALANCE
Sally Adams	$1000.00	$818.75
Ann Samuels	$1500.00	$21.50
Don Charles	$1000.00	$825.75
Tom Daniels	$750.00	$770.75
Al Williams	$1500.00	$402.75
Sally Adams	$2000.00	$1817.50
Mary Nelson	$1500.00	$98.75
Tran Dinh	$750.00	$402.40
Mara Galvez	$1000.00	$114.60
Dan Martin	$1000.00	$1045.75

10 rows selected.

7. SET FEEDBACK OFF
    SELECT *
    FROM REPORT3;

    Thu Jun 05
    CUSTOMER CREDIT LIMITS
    AND BALANCES

CUSTOMER NAME	CUSTOMER CREDIT LIMIT	CUSTOMER BALANCE
Sally Adams	$1000.00	$818.75
Ann Samuels	$1500.00	$21.50
Don Charles	$1000.00	$825.75
Tom Daniels	$750.00	$770.75
Al Williams	$1500.00	$402.75
Sally Adams	$2000.00	$1817.50
Mary Nelson	$1500.00	$98.75
Tran Dinh	$750.00	$402.40
Mara Galvez	$1000.00	$114.60
Dan Martin	$1000.00	$1045.75

Henry Books

1. The view to create the report is:
    CREATE VIEW BRANCH_REPORT (BRANCH_NUMBER, BOOK_TITLE,
    PUBLISHER_NAME, PUBLISHER_LOCATION, PRICE,
    UNITS_ON_HAND) AS
    SELECT BRANCH.BRANCH_NUMBER, BOOK_TITLE,
    PUBLISHER_NAME,
    RTRIM(PUBLISHER_CITY)||', '||RTRIM(PUBLISHER_STATE),
    BOOK_PRICE, UNITS_ON_HAND
    FROM BRANCH, INVENT, BOOK, PUBLISHER
    WHERE BRANCH.BRANCH_NUMBER = INVENT.BRANCH_NUMBER
    AND INVENT.BOOK_CODE = BOOK.BOOK_CODE
    AND BOOK.PUBLISHER_CODE =
    PUBLISHER.PUBLISHER_CODE;
    View created.

The script to format the report is:

```
CLEAR COLUMNS
CLEAR BREAK
CLEAR COMPUTE
TTITLE OFF

SELECT *
FROM BRANCH_REPORT
ORDER BY BRANCH_NUMBER

COLUMN BRANCH_NUMBER HEADING 'BRANCH|NUMBER'
FORMAT A6
COLUMN BOOK_TITLE HEADING 'BOOK TITLE' FORMAT A15
COLUMN PUBLISHER_NAME HEADING 'PUBLISHER NAME'
FORMAT A15
COLUMN PUBLISHER_LOCATION HEADING 'PUBLISHER|LOCATION'
FORMAT A12
COLUMN PRICE HEADING 'PRICE' FORMAT $990.99
COLUMN UNITS_ON_HAND HEADING 'UNITS|ON HAND' FORMAT 99

SET LINESIZE 70
SET PAGESIZE 66
SET PAUSE OFF
TTITLE 'INVENTORY LIST|HENRY BOOKS'

BREAK ON REPORT ON BRANCH_NUMBER SKIP 1

COMPUTE SUM OF UNITS_ON_HAND ON BRANCH_NUMBER
COMPUTE SUM OF UNITS_ON_HAND ON REPORT
```

CHAPTER 8 — Premiere Products

1. a.

```
EXEC SQL
    SELECT PART_DESCRIPTION, UNIT_PRICE
        INTO :W-PART-DESCRIPTION, :W-UNIT-PRICE
        FROM PART
        WHERE PART_NUMBER = :W-PART-NUMBER
END-EXEC
```

b.
```
EXEC SQL
SELECT ORDER_DATE, ORDERS.CUSTOMER_NUMBER, LAST,
        FIRST
    INTO :W-ORDER-DATE, W-CUSTOMER-NUMBER, W-LAST,
        W-FIRST
    FROM ORDERS, CUSTOMER
    WHERE ORDER_NUMBER = :W-ORDER-NUMBER
    AND ORDERS.CUSTOMER_NUMBER =
        CUSTOMER.CUSTOMER_NUMBER
END-EXEC
```

c.
```
EXEC SQL
    INSERT
    INTO PART
        VALUES (:W-PART-NUMBER, :W-PART-DESCRIPTION,
            :W-UNITS-ON-HAND, :W-ITEM-CLASS,
            :W-WAREHOUSE-NUMBER, :W-UNIT-PRICE)
END-EXEC
```

d.
```
EXEC SQL
    UPDATE PART
        SET PART_DESCRIPTION = :W-PART-DESCRIPTION
        WHERE PART_NUMBER = :W-PART-NUMBER
END-EXEC
```

e.
```
EXEC SQL
    UPDATE PART
        SET UNIT_PRICE = UNIT_PRICE * 1.05
        WHERE ITEM_CLASS = 'HW'
END-EXEC
```

f.
```
EXEC SQL
    DELETE
        FROM PART
        WHERE PART_NUMBER = :W-PART-NUMBER
END-EXEC
```

Henry Books

1. a.
```
EXEC SQL
    SELECT PUBLISHER_NAME, PUBLISHER_CITY
        INTO :W-PUBLISHER-NAME, :W-PUBLISHER-CITY
        FROM PUBLISHER
        WHERE PUBLISHER_CODE = :W-PUBLISHER-CODE
END-EXEC
```

b.
```
EXEC SQL
    SELECT BOOK_TITLE, BOOK.PUBLISHER_CODE, PUBLISHER_NAME
        INTO :W-BOOK-TITLE, W-PUBLISHER-CODE,
            W-PUBLISHER-NAME
        FROM BOOK, PUBLISHER
        WHERE BOOK_CODE = :W-BOOK-CODE
        AND BOOK.BOOK_CODE = PUBLISHER.BOOK_CODE
END-EXEC
```

c.
```
EXEC SQL
    INSERT
    INTO BRANCH
        VALUES (:W-BRANCH-NUMBER, :W-BRANCH-NAME,
            :W-BRANCH-LOCATION,
            :W-NUMBER-EMPLOYEES)
END-EXEC
```

d.
```
EXEC SQL
    UPDATE BOOK
        SET BOOK_TITLE = :W-BOOK-TITLE
        WHERE BOOK_CODE = :W-BOOK-CODE
END-EXEC
```

e.
```
EXEC SQL
    UPDATE BOOK
        SET BOOK_PRICE = BOOK_PRICE * 1.03
        WHERE PUBLISHER_CODE = 'BB'
END-EXEC
```

f.

```
EXEC SQL
      DELETE
            FROM BOOK
            WHERE BOOK_CODE = :W-BOOK-CODE
END-EXEC
```

APPENDIX

Premiere Products

Use the Oracle Forms Designer and Forms Runtime programs to create the form.

Henry Books

Use the Oracle Forms Designer and Forms Runtime programs to create the form.

Index

D

E

F

U

V

W